This book presents a comprehensive framework for critical approaches to translation. It discusses the many new developments in this lively new area of scholarship. This is the unavoidable reference for those who want to get a first idea as well as for those who are already established in the field.

Professor Johannes Angermuller, *The Open University, UK*

Critical Discourse Analysis in Translation Studies

Critical Discourse Analysis in Translation Studies is the first textbook to provide a systematic treatment of how CDA may be applied to the analysis of translated and interpreted texts.

Kyung Hye Kim provides in-depth explanations about how various strands of CDA, from the M.A.K. Hallidayan analytical framework to Norman Fairclough's dialectical relationship model and Teun van Dijk's ideological square, can be employed in translation studies to deliver rich analyses of translated text. She demonstrates the ability of CDA to address complex translation practices, in both traditional and digital media, using various examples in different languages. With numerous exercises using authentic texts, this textbook empowers readers to apply a CDA framework in their own work.

This accessible textbook is essential reading for all students of discourse and text analysis within translation and interpreting studies.

Kyung Hye Kim is Assistant Professor at Dongguk University, Seoul, South Korea.

Critical Discourse Analysis in Translation Studies

An Introductory Textbook

Kyung Hye Kim

LONDON AND NEW YORK

Designed cover image: Getty Images | Kateryna Kovarzh

First published 2025
by Routledge
4 Park Square, Milton Park, Abingdon, Oxon OX14 4RN

and by Routledge
605 Third Avenue, New York, NY 10158

Routledge is an imprint of the Taylor & Francis Group, an informa business

© 2025 Kyung Hye Kim

The right of Kyung Hye Kim to be identified as author of this work has been asserted in accordance with sections 77 and 78 of the Copyright, Designs and Patents Act 1988.

All rights reserved. No part of this book may be reprinted or reproduced or utilised in any form or by any electronic, mechanical, or other means, now known or hereafter invented, including photocopying and recording, or in any information storage or retrieval system, without permission in writing from the publishers.

Trademark notice: Product or corporate names may be trademarks or registered trademarks, and are used only for identification and explanation without intent to infringe.

British Library Cataloguing-in-Publication Data
A catalogue record for this book is available from the British Library

Library of Congress Cataloging-in-Publication Data
Names: Kim, Kyung Hye (Professor of translation studies), author.
Title: Critical discourse analysis in translation studies :
an introductory textbook / Kyung Hye Kim.
Description: Abingdon, Oxon ; New York, NY : Routledge, 2025. |
Includes bibliographical references and index.
Identifiers: LCCN 2024044076 (print) | LCCN 2024044077 (ebook) |
ISBN 9780367464950 (hardback) | ISBN 9780367464943 (paperback) |
ISBN 9781003029083 (ebook)
Subjects: LCSH: Critical discourse analysis. | Translating and interpreting. |
LCGFT: Introductory works. | Textbooks.
Classification: LCC P302 .K56 2025 (print) | LCC P302 (ebook) |
DDC 418/.02–dc23/eng/20241230
LC record available at https://lccn.loc.gov/2024044076
LC ebook record available at https://lccn.loc.gov/2024044077

ISBN: 978-0-367-46495-0 (hbk)
ISBN: 978-0-367-46494-3 (pbk)
ISBN: 978-1-003-02908-3 (ebk)

DOI: 10.4324/9781003029083

Typeset in Times New Roman
by Newgen Publishing UK

Contents

Author's note ix
Acknowledgements x

Introduction 1
Organisation of the book 3
How to use this book 4

1 What is critical discourse analysis? 7
   1.1 Discourse: a multiplicity of definitions 8
   1.2 Discourse: three main features 10
       1.2.1 Authentic, interactive, and naturally occurring language 11
       1.2.2 Both verbal and non-verbal material: context, context, and context! 11
       1.2.3 Text of any size 13
   1.3 Discourse studies = discourse theory + discourse analysis 15

2 Critical discourse analysis: three different approaches 23
   2.1 M.A.K. Halliday's SFL-informed discourse analysis: appraisal framework 24
   2.2 Norman Fairclough's three-dimensional model 30
       2.2.1 Criticisms 34
   2.3 Teun van Dijk's socio-cognitive approach 36

3 CDA in translation studies 48
   3.1 The three different approaches 49
       3.1.1 M.A.K. Halliday's SFL-informed discourse analysis and appraisal framework-informed discourse analysis in translation studies 49
       3.1.2 Norman Fairclough's three-dimensional model-informed research in translation studies 55

viii Contents

        3.1.3 Teun van Dijk's ideological square: structures and strategies of communicative events, ideology, and identity 58
   3.2 Text types 61
        3.2.1 Research on the political and diplomatic settings in translation studies 62
        3.2.2 Institutional discourses in translation studies 71
        3.2.3 Discourse studies in interpreting studies 74

4 Corpus-based critical discourse analysis in translation studies   85
   4.1 Corpus-based CDA: the benefits 88
   4.2 Analytical methodology for corpus-based CDA research: frequency lists, collocates, and concordances 90
        4.2.1 Analysing frequency lists 91
        4.2.2 Analysing a collocate list 94
        4.2.3 Some corpus techniques to consider 102
        4.2.4 Analysing concordance lines 108
   4.3 Linguistic analysis: semantic prosody and semantic preferences 111
   4.4 Analytical data: corpus-based CDA that reveals ideological orientations 115
   4.5 Corpus-based CDA approach to translation research 117

5 CDA-informed translation and interpreting research in a healthcare setting and the digital era   131
   5.1 Digital and new media era: discourse construction in social media 134
   5.2 CDA and health 141
        5.2.1 Corpus-based CDA analysis of health and the sustainability and health corpus 145

Index   155

Author's note

Part of this book, especially Chapter 4, is from the author's unpublished PhD thesis: Kim, Kyung Hye. 2013. "Mediating American and South Korean News Discourses about North Korea through Translation: A Corpus-Based Critical Discourse Analysis." Unpublished PhD thesis, The University of Manchester.

Every effort has been made to clear the copyright permission. Special thanks to Professor Juliane House and Professor Johanness Angermuller who granted me a permission to reuse the figures in Chapters 1 and 3.

Acknowledgements

The idea of writing a textbook covering CDA in translation studies was born out of my own need, and of conversations with colleagues in translation studies who also had a similar thirst for monographs and handbooks on the topic of CDA in translation studies. I am greatly indebted to those who inspired me and wish to express my gratitude to my dear colleagues and friends in Korea, China, Norway, and around the globe, who have been incredibly supportive and have given me both academic inspiration and emotional comfort.

However, I would have never been able to embark on this journey without the vision and encouragement of Professor Mona Baker who is my constant guiding light. Her advice and insights have been instrumental in my personal and career growth, going far beyond this work.

I would not have been able to get my work for this book completed without the continual support and immense patience of the Routledge editors, Louisa Semlyen, Ella McFarlane, and Elisha Daniels who constantly had to chase me up. All your infinite patience, professionalism, enormous skills, and precision have not gone unnoticed. Also huge thanks to Professor Christina Schaffner and Professor Johannes Angermuller for their constructive feedback, which helped immensely to enhance the argument in this book.

Sincere thanks to both K and F families, who used to call this book a "b-o-o-k" or "It-That-Must-Not-Be-Named" when they were forced not to use the word 'book'. Their unfailing love and unconditional support kept me going through both thick and think in this work. Special thanks go to M.S.C who has always been there to send his support and encouragement by dancing with his tails and forced me to have some time off for the regular walk.

And finally, my heartfelt thanks, love, and respect to *Chagi* who has been willing to read the chapters, giving constructive feedback, endlessly lending the shoulders to rest. You did a great job working 'behind the scenes' to constantly update family members on the right or wrong timing to ask about the 'book'.

I wish this book to be a solid block of cheddar cheese that has a long shelf-life, is rich in taste, and versatile. However, in case it turned out to be a slice of (holey) emmental cheese for some readers, the responsibility for the content and any remaining errors remains exclusively my own.

Introduction

In 1990, Hatim and Mason first published their work on discourse in translation studies, which has been widely accepted as the most extended application of discourse analysis. Since then, the (critical) discourse-informed approach has grown to include corpus-based CDA translation research, and corpus-based CDA interpretation of texts (Munday 2008; Kim 2013; Mouka, Saridakis, and Fotopoulou 2015; Gu 2018; 2023).

Although scholars have increasingly drawn on CDA as their main theoretical research framework as discussed in this book, they have made few attempts to review the extent of its development, its contributions, or review its position in the field of translation studies. Previous research has largely been restricted to general discourse analysis, whereas relatively few works have focused on CDA specifically. Moreover, despite the number of institutions that incorporate CDA in their curricula, to the best of my knowledge, no textbooks have been published on how CDA can be applied to translation studies. Consequently, owing to both CDA's abstract nature and the paucity of case studies demonstrating its application, students face challenges in applying and interpreting CDA.

Now is the time to reflect on CDA as it has been applied in the field of translation studies by reviewing various projects and examining numerous case studies, in several languages, which demonstrate the power of the CDA framework. Focusing exclusively on CDA's application in translation studies, this book will fill a neglected void, since it will focus on regions of the world, such as China and Korea, which have traditionally received little consideration by English and Anglophone European countries.

By engaging with the most current research and core works and offering various examples and exercises for students, *Critical Discourse Analysis in Translation Studies* aims to foster both individual and collaborative studies of international excellence, by explaining how to apply a CDA framework systematically to the analysis of translation and interpreting activities. Hence, this book is organised around the three main CDA models, the Hallidayan analytical framework-inspired appraisal theory-based approach, and two sociology-oriented models – Fairclough's dialectical relationship model (1992) and van Dijk's ideological square model (1993, 1998). Authentic examples are provided to support the unit of analysis in

DOI: 10.4324/9781003029083-1

each of these models and how they can be applied to analyse different types of translations.

Although all these models have been mentioned in various edited volumes, such as in Munday and Zhang (2017), and in short encyclopaedic entries, such as Hatim (2009), the individual models have rarely been systematically studied and applied. Therefore, this book offers a detailed methodological and analytical discussion of each model. Consequently, in most cases, only one model/approach is used merely as a tool for textual analysis. Hence, an exploration is needed in translation studies that provides a comprehensive picture of how CDA has been or can be employed.

Beyond the field of translation studies, the literature comprising handbooks (Widdowson 2007) and monographs and critical readings (Angermuller, Maingueneau, and Wodak 2014) is available, particularly in the social sciences. However, these works discuss discourse studies in general; CDA is mentioned only briefly. One of the few books highlighting CDA is *The Routledge Handbook of Critical Discourse Studies* (Flowerdew and Richardson 2018). Other few books that mention CDA from a translation studies perspective focus on a single specific topic or make a passing mention in relation to other specific text genres, such as discourse and the media (Bielsa and Bassnett 2009) and political discourse (Schäffner and Bassnett 2010).

Therefore, this book is intended to fill this void by showing how a CDA framework can be used subtly in various ways to analyse politics, media, and institutional discourse. Moreover, it demonstrates how CDA can help researchers in this 'post-truth' era to reveal the role of translation in articulating and challenging specific discourses. It will also explore how a CDA framework can enhance one's understanding of the role of translation in relation to translators and interpreters in civic engagements, or discourse construction in health behaviours and knowledge, or cyberspace (e.g. collective resistance), which have not been discussed in previous publications.

Unlike earlier publications that provided examples mostly from Indo-European languages, this book draws not only on English, but also on Chinese, Korean, Arabic, and Russian examples, thereby filling an important gap in the literature. By bringing attention to the non-European, English-language context, it also diversifies the research stream on CDA-inspired translation studies.

Furthermore, this book explains in depth the use of Martin and White's appraisal theory (Martin 2003; Martin and White 2005) combined with CDA when examining translations. Appraisal theory was developed in Australia but has been widely used by Chinese scholars as a main theoretical framework for analysing translations. Thus, the use of appraisal theory is more prevalent in China, where it often appears in academic articles (Zhang 2002, 2013; Li and Xu 2018; Li and Zhu 2020; Li and Pan 2020). Although several individual articles that examine translations within the framework of appraisal theory and CDA have been published, no in-depth discussion is currently available regarding where this approach is placed in the development of CDA or in terms of strands of CDA or how it can be applied to different text types.

This book features several exercises designed to motivate readers by encouraging them to review authentic texts and helping them apply CDA frameworks and tools in their own works. The aim of this book is to provide invaluable primary textbook for linguists, sociolinguists, sociologists and the media as well as translation students.

Organisation of the book

This book comprises five independent but interrelated chapters. Each chapter begins with a summary of the key points, provides in-depth discussions and several activities in the body, and ends with suggestions for further reading and references.

Chapter 1 introduces CDA and offers various definitions of 'discourse'. It provides a comprehensive history of CDA, including its birth and the development of discourse theory and analysis and the differences between them in language, context, and practice. Furthermore, it describes how CDA has been employed in both linguistics and translation studies. It also discusses the relationship among discourse theory, discourse analysis, and discourse studies, with an emphasis on key analytical elements of discourse studies, including power, subjectivity, knowledge, language, practice, and context.

Chapter 2 discusses several approaches, particularly the three major CDA models: the Hallidayan systemic functional linguistics approach (and Martin and White's appraisal theory-informed approach), Fairclough's dialectical-relational approach, and van Dijk's socio-cognitive model, tracing the development of CDA. The three models are discussed progressively, allowing readers to follow the movement and development of discourse analysis-informed studies from a purely linguistic understanding of discourse to its socio-political interpretation from a word to a sentence describing text as a combination of interaction and context. Through a discussion of various sociology-oriented frameworks that show language as a social practice, this chapter demonstrates how discourse is embedded in social conditions and the CDA framework helps reveal the ideologies underlying a text. Although other strands in discourse analysis of relevance to CDA are important, including interactionism, practice theory, poststructuralism and constructivism, this chapter focuses on the three approaches, due to space restrictions.

Chapter 3 focuses primarily on the use of CDA in translation studies, offering an in-depth discussion on how each model described in Chapter 2 can be applied when analysing translations. It presents several case studies that exemplify each model as applied in the CDA field to demonstrate how each model serves as a translation and analytical tool. These include Martin and White's Appraisal Theory-informed framework, Fairclough's dialectical-relational approach, as adopted in more recent works (Valdeón 2007; Kang 2008; Al-Hejin 2012; Pan 2015; Zhang and Pan 2015), and van Dijk's Ideological Square Model (van Dijk 1988b, 1988a). Hatim and Mason's (1990, 1997) contribution to translation studies, and Mason's work (1994) that widened the analytical perspective are also discussed.

4 *Critical Discourse Analysis in Translation Studies*

CDA has been used to examine a wide range of texts but is perhaps most frequently applied to analyses of translations of political, media, and institutional texts, such as in those related to courtrooms, the media, and asylums. Therefore, the first section of this chapter focuses on each approach – Martin and White's appraisal theory, Fairclough's approach, and van Dijk's ideological square – to show how the framework has been applied for each. Here, the chapter presents some case studies and other relevant examples that examine texts in terms of interaction and context. For instance, van Dijk's ideological square model discussed in Chapter 2 is mentioned again to explore how discourse is associated with identity construction and social structure in translation. The ideological square model is also mentioned when explaining the main discursive inclusionary and exclusionary discourse construction strategies in translation, used by polarised groups.

The second section discusses CDA in terms of the four most analysed types of text: political, institutional, media, and interpreting. It also presents Hatim and Mason's notion of how translation can be a communicative process within a social context, in that translators/interpreters negotiate meanings embedded in a source text and tailor them to a new environment, as well as how translators and interpreters intervene in the transfer process by placing "their own knowledge and beliefs into their processing of a text" (Hatim and Mason, 1997, 147) by featuring speeches of political figures as examples.

Chapter 4 provides an in-depth discussion of corpus-based CDA in translation studies. Although a corpus-based methodology is not new in linguistics, social sciences, or translation studies, the combined approach (i.e. corpus-based CDA) is relatively new in translation studies. Consequently, it has rarely been discussed, and methodological challenges are common. Therefore, this chapter discusses how these relatively new analytical approaches are used in translation research. The benefits and limitations of CDA, and its application in translation studies are discussed first, followed by a detailed account of analytical methodology, with various translations provided as examples, and some technical issues are explained for readers interested in adopting this approach.

Chapter 5 considers news directions, such as CDA-informed studies in the digital era, by discussing the application of CDA outside translation studies to analyse new types of data produced through social media. The works of Bouvier (2015, 2016) and McEnery, McGlashan, and Love (2015) are mentioned to demonstrate how discourse studies have engaged with theories and empirical work on social media to examine cross-cultural social relations in a rapidly evolving communicative environment. Attention is drawn to studies of digitally based translation activities to show that digital spaces are rich sources of data and CDA offers a robust framework for future research in translation studies, which is currently significantly under-explored.

How to use this book

This book is intended for use as a resource for postgraduate students and researchers in translation studies in particular, and linguistics in general, who conduct independent research, as it can help them comprehend the concepts and applications of CDA. A list of key points and research tips is provided at the beginning of each chapter together with discussion points throughout the text, which can also be used for group discussions in the classroom.

References

Al-Hejin, Bandar. 2012. "Linking Critical Discourse Analysis with Translation Studies: An Example from BBC News." *Journal of Language and Politics* 11 (3): 311–35. https://doi.org/10.1075/jlp.11.3.01alh.

Angermuller, Johannes, Dominique Maingueneau, and Ruth Wodak, eds. 2014. *The Discourse Studies Reader: Main Currents in Theory and Analysis*. Amsterdam & Philadelphia: John Benjamins.

Bielsa, Esperança, and Susan Bassnett. 2009. *Translation in Global News*. London and New York: Routledge.

Bouvier, Gwen. 2015. "What Is a Discourse Approach to Twitter, Facebook, YouTube and Other Social Media: Connecting with Other Academic Fields?" *Journal of Multicultural Discourses* 10 (2): 149–62.

Bouvier, Gwen, ed. 2016. *Discourse and Social Media*. London: Routledge.

Fairclough, Norman. 1992. *Discourse and Social Change*. Cambridge: Polity.

Flowerdew, John, and John E. Richardson, eds. 2018. *The Routledge Handbook of Critical Discourse Studies*. London and New York: Routledge.

Gu, Chonglong. 2018. "Forging a Glorious Past via the 'Present Perfect': A Corpus-Based CDA Analysis of China's Past Accomplishments Discourse Mediat(Is)Ed at China's Interpreted Political Press Conferences." *Discourse, Context & Media* 24: 137–49.

Gu, Chonglong. 2023. "Low-Hanging Fruits, Usual Suspects, and Pure Serendipity: Towards a Layered Methodological Framework on Translators and Interpreters' Ideological Language Use Drawing on the Synergy of CDA and Corpus Linguistics." *Perspectives* 31 (6): 1014–32.

Hatim, Basil. 2009. "Discourse Analysis." In *Routledge Encyclopedia of Translation Studies*, edited by Gabriela Saldanha and Mona Baker, second edition, 88–92. London and New York: Routledge.

Hatim, Basil, and Ian Mason. 1990. *Discourse and the Translator*. London: Longman.

Hatim, Basil, and Ian Mason. 1997. *The Translator as Communicator*. London and New York: Routledge.

Kang, Ji-Hae. 2008. "'Pŏnyŏgesŏ inyongŭi munje: CNN.com nyusŭt'eksŭt'ŭrŭl chungsimŭro' [Speech Representation in News Translation]." *The Journal of Translation Studies* 9 (4): 7–40.

Kim, Kyung Hye. 2013. "Mediating American and South Korean News Discourses about North Korea through Translation: A Corpus-Based Critical Discourse Analysis." Unpublished PhD Thesis. The University of Manchester.

Li, Tao, and Feng Pan. 2020. "Reshaping China's Image: A Corpus-Based Analysis of the English Translation of Chinese Political Discourse." *Perspectives* 29 (3): 354–370.

Li, Tao, and Fang Xu. 2018. "Re-Appraising Self and Other in the English Translation of Contemporary Chinese Political Discourse." *Discourse, Context & Media* 25: 106–13.

Li, Tao, and Yifan Zhu. 2020. "How Does China Appraise Self and Others? A Corpus-Based Analysis of Chinese Political Discourse." *Discourse & Society* 31 (2): 153–171.

Martin, James R., 2003. "Introduction." *Text* 2 (23): 171–181.

Martin, James R, and Peter R. R. White. 2005. *The Language of Evaluation: Appraisal in English*. New York: Palgrave Macmillan.

Mason, Ian. 1994. "Discourse, Ideology and Translation." In *Language, Discourse and Translation in the West and Middle East*, edited by Robert De Beaugrande, Abdulla Shunnaq and Mohamed Helmy Heliel, 23–34. Amsterdam: Benjamins.

McEnery, Tony, Mark McGlashan, and Robbie Love. 2015. "Press and Social Media Reaction to Ideologically Inspired Murder: The Case of Lee Rigby." *Discourse & Communication* 9 (2): 237–59. https://doi.org/10.1177/1750481314568545.

Mouka, Effie, Ioannis E. Saridakis, and Angeliki Fotopoulou. 2015. "Racism Goes to the Movies: A Corpus-Driven Study of Cross-Linguistic Racist Discourse Annotation and Translation Analysis." In *New Directions in Corpus-Based Translation Studies*, edited by Claudio Fantinuoli and Federico Zanettin, 35–70. Berlin: Language Science Press.

Munday, Jeremy. 2008. *Style and Ideology in Translation: Latin American Writing in English*. New York: Routledge.

Munday, Jeremy, and Meifang Zhang, eds. 2017. *Discourse Analysis in Translation Studies*. Amsterdam & Philadelphia: John Benjamins.

Pan, Li. 2015. "Ideological Positioning in News Translation: A Case Study of Evaluative Resources in Reports on China." *Target: International Journal on Translation Studies* 27 (2): 215–37.

Schäffner, Christina, and Susan Bassnett, eds. 2010. *Political Discourse, Media and Translation*. Newcastle upon Tyne: Cambridge Scholars Publishing.

Valdeón, Roberto A. 2007. "Ideological Independence or Negative Mediation: BBC Mundo and CNN En Español's (Translated) Reporting of Madrid's Terrorist Attacks." In *Translating and Interpreting Conflict*, edited by Myriam Salama-Carr, 99–118. Amsterdam and New York: Rodopi.

van Dijk, Teun A. 1988a. *News Analysis: Case Studies of International and National News in the Press*. Hillsdale, NJ: Erlbaum.

van Dijk, Teun A. 1988b. *News as Discourse*. Hillsdale, NJ: Erlbaum.

van Dijk, Teun A. 1993. "Principles of Critical Discourse Analysis." *Discourse & Society* 4 (2): 249–83.

van Dijk, Teun A. 1998. "Opinions and Ideologies in the Press." In *Approaches to Media Discourse*, edited by Allan Bell and Peter Garrett, 21–63. Oxford: Blackwell.

Widdowson, Henry G. 2007. *Discourse Analysis*. Oxford: Oxford University Press.

Zhang, Meifang. 2002. "Language Appraisal and the Translator's Attitudinal Positioning." *Foreign Languages and Their Teaching* 7: 15–18.

Zhang, Meifang. 2013. "Stance and Mediation in Transediting News Headlines as Paratexts." *Perspectives* 21 (3): 396–411.

Zhang, Meifang, and Hanting Pan. 2015. "Institutional Power in and behind Discourse: A Case Study of SARS Notices and Their Translations Used in Macao." *Target* 27 (3): 387–405. https://doi.org/10.1075/target.27.3.04zha.

1 What is critical discourse analysis?

Key points of learning

- Discourse consists of authentic, interactive, and naturally occurring language rather than invented examples.
- Discourse encompasses not only the verbal and non-verbal material used in interaction but also the context in which the interaction occurs.
- Discourse refers to texts of any size.
- Discourse studies = discourse theory + discourse analysis.
- CDA is an analytical methodology that considers language, practice, and context.
- CDA understands that discourse is constructed out of the interplay of language, practice, and context.

As discourse studies scholar van Dijk (2001, 352) defines it, CDA is "a type of discourse analytical research that primarily studies the way social power abuse, dominance, and inequality are enacted, reproduced, and resisted by text and talk in the social and political context". Thus, CDA aims to reveal how discourse structures are used to produce (or challenge) social dominance, discrimination, social order, and social inequality. CDA allows linguists to analyse specific features of language that have ideological implications and promises to offer a similarly productive framework for translation studies.

As indicated by the designation Critical Discourse Analysis, understanding the concept of discourse is fundamental to conducting any type of CDA research. Discourse has become a common currency across disciplines in many fields. Its use is not necessarily limited to the humanities or social sciences, since it has generated "many conflicting and overlapping definitions formulated from various theoretical and disciplinary standpoints" (Fairclough 1992; Baker 2018). Widdowson (2004) notes that various definitions of discourse are often contentious and highly abstract, with further confusion introduced by using the terms 'text' and 'discourse' interchangeably. Therefore, as a starting point for the journey to CDA in translation studies, the definitions and features of 'discourse' are crucial to discuss.

DOI: 10.4324/9781003029083-2

1.1 Discourse: a multiplicity of definitions

Discourse remains a relatively abstract term compared with other linguistic concepts. The term is unsurprisingly highly abstract, and conflicting interpretations and applications abound, thus leading to more confusion, to the extent that Stubbs (1983, 1) started his book with the statement, "[t]he term discourse analysis is very ambiguous". Used across a wide range of disciplines, discourse has become common currency to the extent that laypeople often use it in conversation, albeit without knowing its technical meaning. According to Widdowson (1995; 2004, 157–58), the concept is diffuse, admits diverse interpretations, and is intrinsically complex and quite abstract, unlike some other concepts in sociology.

As a result, several researchers suggest various definitions with diverse interpretations, to the extent that Fairclough (1992, 3) once said, "there are so many conflicting and overlapping definitions formulated from various theoretical and disciplinary standpoints". Therefore, the different interpretations proposed by a wide range of scholars need to be reviewed.

Definitions suggested by 'pure' linguistics restrict the definition of discourse to the text level, taking 'discourse' as a linguistic unit. For example, Brown and Yule (1983, 1) see it as 'language in use'; Sinclair and Coulthard (1978, 8) view spoken discourse as "the way in which units above the rank of clauses are related and patterned", whereas Georgakopoulou and Goutsos (1997a, viii), seeing it from a communicative sense, define it as "the study of the use of language for communication in context".

Sociolinguists are less concerned with linguistic features and phenomena, *per se,* instead defining discourse at a more macro- and pragmatic level in terms of context, identity, power, ideology, and institutions, thus viewing discourse from a wider perspective. Wodak (2002, 8) defines it as "[constituting] situations, objects of knowledge, and the social identities of and relationships between people and groups of people", whereas Mills (2003, 54–55) distinguishes between 'discourse' and 'language' by explaining that discourse is "not simply the imposition of a set of ideas on individuals", nor is it "the equivalent of 'language' [… as it] does not simply translate reality into language; rather, discourse should be seen as a system which structures the way that we perceive reality".

An early scholar who frequently used the term 'discourse' was Foucault (1972), a key thinker of the 20th century whose influence has been felt across a range of disciplines. As Mills (2003, 53) explained, Foucault (1982, 80) initially defined discourse as "the general domain of all statements, sometimes as an individualisable group of statements, and sometimes as a regulated practice that accounts for a number of statements". However, Fairclough (1989, 24) later saw it in a wider context to refer to the "whole process of social interaction of which a text is just a part", "a particular way of constructing a particular (domain of) social practice" (Fairclough 1995b, 76), and "a particular way of representing some part of the (physical, social, psychological) world" (Fairclough 2003, 17).

Mills (2002) stated that although Foucault provided several definitions that are sometimes contradictory, as a sociologist/sociolinguist, he was mostly interested in discourse as a vehicle of oppression and resistance. For Foucault (1981, 52), discourse is "at once controlled, selected, organised and redistributed by a certain number of procedures whose role is to ward off its powers and dangers, to gain mastery over its chance events, [and] to evade its ponderous, formidable materiality". Mills (2003, 62–65) concluded that discourse should be considered "groups of statements which are associated with institutions, which are authorised in some sense and which have some unity of function at a fundamental level" and an overarching term that encompasses all statements, together with the rules that govern how some statements are circulated and others are excluded.

In this context, the concept of power is important in understanding discourse, as seen in Foucault's work, for whom, discourse meant, "*both the means of oppressing and the means of resistance*" (Mills 2003, 55, emphasis added).

Discourses are not once and for all subservient to power or raised up against it, any more than silences are. We must make allowances for the complex and unstable process whereby *discourse can be both an instrument and an effect of power but also a hindrance, a stumbling block, a point of resistance and a starting point for an opposing strategy. Discourse transmits and produces power; it reinforces it but also undermines it and exposes it, renders it fragile and makes it possible to thwart it.*

(Foucault 1978, 100–101, emphasis added)

Later, scholars from various disciplines, perhaps noticing problems with Foucault's definition of discourse tied with the concept of power, attempted to delineate it by producing many more, subtly different definitions. For instance, Angermuller, Maingueneau, and Wodak (2014, 2) explain that discourse has been used principally in two different ways:

(a) in a *pragmatic understanding*, predominant among linguistic and microsociological discourse analysts, which considers discourse as a process or practice of contextualising text, language in use, the situated production of speech acts or a turn taking practice [...] (b) in a *socio-historical understanding*, preferred by more macrosociological discourse theorists interested in power, for whom 'discourse' refers to an ensemble of verbal and non-verbal practices of large social communities.

(Angermuller, Maingueneau, and Wodak 2014, 2, emphasis added)

To examine these two research strands in detail would require another full volume, which is not the purpose of this book. Therefore, this book focuses more on the term 'discourse' as used in sociolinguistics and pragmatics (i.e., '(a)' above) and translation studies. The CDA approach, as adopted by translation studies, has been largely inspired by sociolinguistics, pragmatics, and social sciences, although translation studies scholars, in their attempt to identify discourse as it features in the media, have also based their definition on its socio-historical context, in line with macrosociological theorists (to be discussed more fully in Chapter 3).

The analytical models used in translation studies, especially Fairclough's three-dimensional model and van Dijk's ideological square model, are based on the sociolinguistics and social sciences framework.

Reisigl and Wodak's (2009) suggested definition of discourse may be an optimal summary of how scholars in sociolinguistics/social sciences see it. They define it as

> "(1) a cluster of context-dependent semiotic practices that are situated within specific fields of social action; (2) socially constituted and socially constitutive; (3) related to a macro-topic; and (4) linked to the argumentation about validity claims such as truth and normative validity involving several social actors who have different points of view".
>
> (Reisigl and Wodak 2009, 89)

In summary, discourse analysts explain discourse as a language used in a particular social community at the macro level, in relation to contextual, social, and historical factors, wherein the roles of various social actors are examined in relation to the language used. Thus, the various ways in which language is used in social action are a central concern for discourse analysts. Considering discourse to be the relatively stable use of language serving to organise and structure social life (Wodak and Meyer 2009, 6), and as well as being socially constituted, most (critical) discourse analysts are interested in repeated linguistic behaviour and patterns that eventually lead to the formation and control of social and cultural structures. Therefore, it is not surprising that discourse scholars frequently visit the themes of ideology, political discourse, racism, institutional discourse, globalisation, capitalism, media language, gender, and immigration – topics that involve context-dependent practices and are socially constructed.

Then, how and to what extent is discourse different from text? When discourse is defined, the most recurrent theme is the difference between text and discourse. Some scholars do not distinguish between the two, whereas others place them in separate categories. This distinction is frequently made during discussions about the characteristics of discourse, which are discussed in the next section.

Practice essay question

Using your own examples, explain how linguists (most notably John Sinclair) and sociolinguists (most notably Ruth Wodak) have adopted and developed Michel Foucault's definition of 'discourse' in subtly different ways.

1.2 Discourse: three main features

Although discourse is understood both as an exercise of power and a site of social interaction, some of its definitions remain somewhat abstract; thus, what it signifies and how it differs from 'text' (Widdowson 2004) are not always clear.

Bax (2011) provided a more concrete and clear-cut definition, primarily based on the work of Michael Stubbs (1983), summarised in six main dimensions: (1) authentic, interactive, and naturally occurring language; (2) authentic texts of any size; (3) considered in context; (4) intertextuality; (5) ideology and viewpoints; and (6) socio-political implications and consequences. Each point merits further discussion, but I will focus on the following three dominant characteristics first, and will discuss (5) and (6) in the next chapter, which are more relevant to CDA-inspired translation studies.

1.2.1 Authentic, interactive, and naturally occurring language

Discourse consists of authentic, interactive, and naturally occurring language rather than invented examples, inspired by the recognition that "language, action and knowledge are inseparable" (Stubbs 1983, 1). Understanding discourse as a "complex of communicative purposes" (Widdowson 2007, 6) and "structured forms of knowledge" (Wodak and Meyer 2001, 6), discourse analysts are interested in the interactive nature of discourse, which is distinguished from texts, a "non-interactive monologue" (Stubbs 1984, 9).[1] Thus, everyday languages, such as those used in newspapers, rather than invented languages, are the main concern of analysis. For example, Minionese – or Minion Language, the fictional language created for the fictional characters Minions in *Despicable Me* movies cannot be subject to discourse analysis because they are 'invented' languages. However, if Minionese were to be regularly used in news articles to build a certain narrative or support a specific argument, a 'Minionese' may be constructed, which would then be subject to discourse analysis. Similarly, the Klingon language (created for the fictional alien characters in the Star Trek universe) found on a street wall cannot be a 'discourse'; however, it can be considered a text for discourse analysis if several continuous texts concerning the specific piece are produced and circulated within a community and have socio-political implications. Hansen's (2016) discourse analysis of the five hundred reader comments left for online newspaper articles about the removal of the street art Bansky's work *No Ball Games* is another example.

Furthermore, unlike text, 'discourse' materialises in variable stretches of language, irrespective of mode (i.e., written or spoken). Taking the example of a literary piece left on a street wall, different politicians' speeches regarding the literary piece could be subject to discourse analysis. For example, the bibliometric study of hate speech by Sirulhaq, Yuwono, and Muta'ali (2023) provides an example of CDA being employed to identify discourses in speech (a spoken mode). It may be equally argued that discourse can incorporate non-verbal material, such as images and signs, as long as they are used in real-life settings. However, some counterarguments have been made regarding this suggestion, as discussed below.

1.2.2 Both verbal and non-verbal material: context, context, and context!

Like discourse, context is another concept that is difficult to pin down but has been extensively studied. Blommaert defines it somewhat broadly as "the totality of conditions under which discourse is being produced, circulated and interpreted" (2005, 251). van Dijk's definition seems to be more concrete, and this is the definition I follow in this book: "the cognitive, social, political, cultural, and historical *environments* of discourse" (2005, 237, emphasis in original).

Discourse encompasses not only the verbal and non-verbal material used in interaction but also the context in which the interaction occurs; thus, discourse analysis investigates the "language in use in social contexts, and [...] interaction or dialogue between speakers" (Stubbs 1983, 1). With a discourse being a "complex of communicative purposes" (Widdowson 2007, 6), its recipient must make meaning out of it, which will largely depend on the context in which it has been produced, together with the social and ideological values to which the sender and receiver subscribe.

Therefore, context is "not an external set of circumstances but a selection of them internally represented in the mind" (Widdowson 2007, 20). Context is dynamic and is "negotiated between the participants in a discourse, depending upon their mental models" (Flowerdew 2017, 166). For example, *Analects*, a collection of sayings of the Chinese philosopher Confucius (551–479 BC) from conversations with his disciples and contemporaries, has long been regarded as a must-read classic containing the foundations of Confucian philosophy. However, his sayings have often been considered to be from a male-dominated perspective and therefore declared anti-feminist discourse. Conversely, more recent interpretations/discourses argue that *Analects* is not anti-feminist but merely adopts an egalitarian educational approach in which men and women play different roles within families (e.g., Kim 2013). This suggests that the same text can be interpreted differently at different times in history (i.e., different historical contexts).

Context is indeed an integral factor in understanding and analysing discourse. Discourse is heavily influenced by the contexts in which it is produced; conversely, it contributes to transforming context. Therefore, CDA scholars, such as Foucault, have argued that discourse often leads to the reproduction of other discourses with which it is compatible. Fairclough (1995a, 258) thus defined discourse as "a form of social practice" born out of "a dialectical relationship between a particular discursive event and the situation(s), institution(s) and social structure(s) which frame it". He added that:

> The discursive event is shaped by [the situation(s), institution(s) and social structure(s)], but it also shapes them. That is, discourse is socially constitutive as well as socially conditioned – it constitutes situations, objects of knowledge, and the social identities of and relationships between people and groups of people. It is constitutive both in the sense that it helps to sustain and reproduce the social status quo and in the sense that it contributes to transforming it.
> (Fairclough 1995a, 258)

For example, the dominant patriarchal discourse in the 1910s in the UK, and the same discourse in the US in the 1960s, marginalised women in society, contributed to their subordination, and limited their human rights and equality. In the UK,

What is critical discourse analysis? 13

Oxford University only finally granted women full membership and the right to take degrees in October 1920, whereas at Girton College, Cambridge, it was not until 1948 that women were awarded degrees, although they were first admitted in 1869 (BBC 2019; Sultan 2019). Similarly, although it varied by state, women in the US in the 1960s were not allowed to have credit cards in their name, serve on juries, use birth control pills, receive Ivy League educations, or receive equal treatment in the workplace (McLaughlin 2014). However, feminist discourses and gender equality and equity (known as second-wave feminism) in the US challenged patriarchal discourse and led gay and lesbian liberation movements (Podmore and Tremblay 2015). These examples clearly show how discourse is used to "sustain and reproduce the social status quo" and how it "contributes to transforming it" (Fairclough 1995a, 258). Other scholars, including van Leeuwen (1993) and van Dijk (1993), developed this argument by stressing the role of discourse in constructing dominant–dominated relationships in relation to social conflict, a point that is discussed in more detail in Chapters 2 and 3.

1.2.3 Text of any size

The final predominant feature of discourse is that, as Bax (2011, 24–25, emphasis added) stated, discourse refers to "texts of any size, written or spoken, *so long as they are authentic and considered in context*". Acknowledging the abstract nature of discourse, scholars have attempted to clarify the term by questioning the nature, quality, or textuality that dictates discourse, such as by explaining it in relation to 'text', which is a relatively concrete concept when used in linguistics.[2] For example, van Dijk (1977, 3) described it as an "abstract theoretical construct" underlying a discourse, whereas Chafe (2003, 439–40) says:

> The term discourse is used in somewhat different ways by different scholars, but underlying the differences is a common concern for language beyond the boundaries of isolated sentences. The term text is used in similar ways. Both terms may refer to a unit of language larger than the sentence: one may speak of a "discourse" or a "text".

Similarly, Salkie (1995, ix) states that a text, or a discourse, is "a stretch of language that may be longer than one sentence". Stubbs, in his early definition of the characteristics of discourse proposed in 1983, limited the size of discourse to a larger linguistic unit beyond the sentential level. Thus, discourse refers to larger linguistic units, "the organization of language above the sentence or above the clause", whereas a text can be very short (Stubbs 1983, 1–9). For example, signs such as 'Exit' or 'No Smoking' cannot be described as discourse because of their brevity. According to Widdowson (1995, 160), Zellig Harris, a linguist, understood discourses as "the manifestation of formal regularities across sentences in combination"; hence, a discourse can be longer than a sentence.

However, some scholars, including Widdowson (1995, 2004) and Bax (2011), disagree with such a view that handles units of language smaller than a sentence

14 *Critical Discourse Analysis in Translation Studies*

in scope. They have provided numerous counterexamples, such as a typically brown or white 'i' referring to a tourist information centre. A 'WC' sign stands for 'water closet' and refers to a toilet, whereas a figure of an aeroplane on a motorway sign usually indicates either a high risk of low-flying aircraft or a road to an airport. These examples of tourist information, WC, and an aeroplane image on a motorway sign constitute meanings and are intuitively textual. The signs are written in authentic languages and understood in a specific context. Using other examples, such as 'BC' (Before Christ), 'PC' (personal computer), 'P' (parking), and 'BBC' (British Broadcasting Corporation), Widdowson (1995, 164) has explained that our interpretation of such short text depends on the context and our engagement with extra-linguistic reality, arguing that a text is inert unless activated by contextual connection.

As early as 1995, Widdowson raised questions regarding the extent to which 'discourse' can be differentiated from 'text'. In this 1995 work, Widdowson criticised Harris' (1952) discourse analysis work for causing much confusion and contradiction and explained them in detail. One criticism concerned Harris' unnuanced use of the terms discourse and text. He added that Harris' view of discourse was limited to the study of language patterns above the sentence level because Harris' focus was only on the language and not its *use* (Widdowson 1995, 160, emphasis added).

In his later work, Widdowson (2004, 8) makes a clear distinction that discourse is "the pragmatic process of meaning negotiation" and text is "its product" that does not contain meaning but is used to "mediate it across discourses" (Widdowson 2007, 6). In agreement with this view proposed by Widdowson, while acknowledging some limitations of the view on the length of discourse, Bax (2011, 23) argued that excluding such short texts from discourse analysis merely because they are not above the sentence level is unhelpful because these short texts, such as the examples above, are "perfectly comprehensible discourse, no matter how brief". Particularly in a digital world where other modes are used to deliver meanings, such as visual images, signs, and emojis, adopting a broader definition of discourse is logical. Consequently, this view and definition are adopted in this book. Throughout this book, therefore, 'discourse' refers to texts of "any size, written or spoken, so long as they are authentic and considered in context" (Bax 2011, 24–25), and 'text' is as defined by Halliday and Hasan (1985, 10) "language that is functional".

☞ **Tip!**

As discussed in this section, different scholars have defined 'discourse' and 'text' in various ways. Therefore, in your own writing, it is important to make it clear which definition you follow and at least briefly explain your rationale for the choice of that definition or provide your own definition.

What is critical discourse analysis? 15

Practice essay questions

1 Using authentic examples, discuss the three distinctive features of 'discourse'.
2 Using your own examples, discuss how 'discourse' differs from 'text'.
3 Figure 1.1 shows a poem written by Lemn Sissay on a wall in Manchester, UK, which creates the image of raindrops. Discuss whether this can be subject to discourse analysis and why.

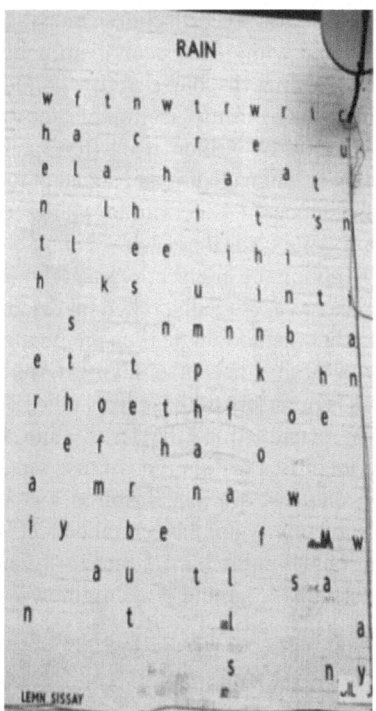

Figure 1.1 A poem written on a wall in Manchester, UK.

1.3 Discourse studies = discourse theory + discourse analysis

We have thus far discussed the definition and characteristics of discourse. Before moving to discuss CDA's different strands and development in more detail in the next chapter, we need to discuss its contribution within the larger area of discourse studies. Discourse studies, discourse theory, and discourse analysis are often mentioned without being accompanied by specific definitions. Although an in-depth examination of the genealogy of discourse studies is not the focus of this book, examining the place and the root of CDA within discourse studies will help provide a better understanding of the primary focus.

This section explains that discourse studies include both discourse theory (theory) and discourse analysis (methodology), with the difference between the two discussed in depth in terms of where the focus lies. Angermuller, Maingueneau, and Wodak (2014), among others, explained the differences among discourse studies, discourse theory and discourse analysis in depth. They have not only discussed the development of discourse studies and subtle differences in their growth in the US, France, the UK, and Germany, but also succinctly summarised the differences between the focus of discourse analysis and that of discourse theory.

According to the definition of Angermuller, Maingueneau, and Wodak (2014, 5), **discourse studies = discourse theory + discourse analysis**. They explain that discourse theory is often equated with poststructuralism, whereas discourse analysis is associated with pragmatics; thus, discourse studies include both discourse theory and discourse analysis. While the former examines "the symbolic constitution of society through the circulation of written texts from a more macrosociological viewpoint", the latter looks at language use and social practices and "analyses oral conversations as situated practices" (Angermuller, Maingueneau, and Wodak 2014, 5). However, they make it quite clear that each is *complementary* and simply dividing the two is unhelpful, noting the intersections and dynamic exchanges between them: "[d]iscourse theorists have, crucially, relied on discourse analysis" and "discourse analysts with an ethnomethodological or pragmatic background [...] have built bridges with poststructuralist discourse theory" (Angermuller, Maingueneau, and Wodak 2014, 5). This is precisely the case for studies of CDA-informed examination of translations. As discussed in Chapter 3, studies examining translation patterns, for example, to identify a certain type of discourse constructed as a result of consistent translation choices, are also inspired by poststructuralism, where power, knowledge, and subjectivity are the central concerns.

The following illustrations (Figures 1.2, 1.3, and 1.4), adapted from Angermuller, Maingueneau, and Wodak (2014, 6) and Angermuller (2015, 513), amply summarise this point.

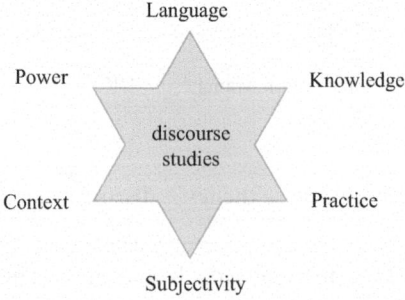

Figure 1.2 Discourse Studies as discourse analysis and discourse theory adapted from Angermuller, Maingueneau, and Wodak (2014, 6) and Angermuller (2015, 513).

Angermuller, Maingueneau, and Wodak (2014, 6) describe the main features and focus of 'Discourse Theory' as follows:

> Discourse theory often revolves around the nexus of power, knowledge and subjectivity [...] indeed, society and its actors, social inequality and its agents, symbolic and cultural orders and their subjects are no givens; they are made and unmade in discursive practices. in this sense, discourse does not only represent what people do, think and are in the social world; representing the world can also mean constituting it in a certain way. At the same time, discursive practices testify to the intricate relationship of power and subjectivity. Who is entitled to say what from what position with what effect is discursively regulated: not everybody has the same chance to become visible and exist as a subject, to participate in exchanges with others and thus to shape what counts as reality in a community.

The dialectical relationship between discourse and society, that is, the discourse contributing to *construct* society and *being constructed by* discursive practices as discussed above, is worth highlighting here. This is because CDA research in both discourse studies and translation studies predominantly seeks to reveal certain discursive practices constructed by society through identifying and investigating certain discourses or the way and extent to which certain discourses circulated in society contribute to the change in discursive practices of the society. For example, Kim (2012) investigated Korean media discourse on migrants from 1990 to 2009 to identify the dominant attitude in the Korean media towards migrants (i.e., "identify the discourse that represent what people do"), whereas Kim (2014) examined mainstream news media reports in the US about North Korea to show how American media divides the world into pro-US and anti-US groups (i.e., revealing how the discourse contributes to constituting the world in such a way). As discussed in greater depth later, CDA-informed interpretations also recognise these two divisions. For example, Gu (2018, 148) showed the extent to which the Chinese government interpreters strengthen the "already ideological discourse" of China's past actions and achievements by identifying the discourses, as constructed by interpreters, from its Premier's press conferences.[3]

As the studies mentioned above show (e.g., Kim 2014; Gu 2018), 'power' is another crucial element that motivates discourse theory. CDA can determine who has the power to indicate the type of discourse that is disseminated more widely and ultimately (re)shapes reality in society. For example, just as politicians' public speeches carry more authority than those of private individuals, media institutions have more influence and power when they circulate information. These powerful institutions have more control over the information they disseminate, as seen from gatekeeping in the media, in which information is filtered and censored. In summary, discourse studies analyse discourse, considering the role that power has in constructing and disseminating discourses.

18 *Critical Discourse Analysis in Translation Studies*

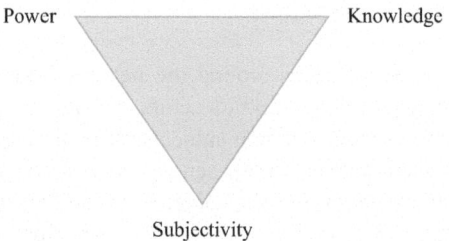

Figure 1.3 The triangle of discourse theory: power, knowledge, subjectivity.
Source: Angermuller, Maingueneau, and Wodak (2014, 6).

Such perceptions of power are also recognised in some CDA-informed examinations of translations, which led Angermuller, Maingueneau, and Wodak (2014, 6) to identify power, knowledge, and subjectivity as the three main components of discourse theory. As discussed in Chapter 3, this is one reason why some translation studies scholars inspired by the CDA approach focus greater attention on how large institutions such as news media organisations exercise power by constructing and disseminating discourses, e.g., Kang (2008) (see Chapter 3 for more details).

As a framework, discourse analysis considers language, practice, and context, understanding that discourse is constructed from the interplay among these three components. Thus, a single component cannot be the sole focus. As Angermuller, Maingueneau, and Wodak (2014, 6–7) explain, "discourse analytical approaches focus on one point empirically while accounting for the other two theoretically"; thus, "all three components must be acknowledged and integrated", which makes discourse studies distinctively different from other approaches. The authors offer a more detailed explanation for each component of the triangle, as follows:

> 'Language' designates the semiotic material (formal patterns, conventions, resources) in the broadest sense. It can consist of written and oral texts, but as easily of audio-visual materials (images, film…) […] 'Practice' refers to specific ways of appropriating and processing language and extends to everything that may take place between the participants in interaction. […] 'Context' refers to the setting, situation or knowledge available to the discourse participants contextualizing texts. Such knowledge can be situation-dependent or situation-transcendent, individual or shared by large collectives.
> (Angermuller, Maingueneau, and Wodak 2014, 7)

Therefore, CDA-informed examinations of translations should also consider context when examining language use (translation and interpreting) in practice. For example, Kim (2018) examined three (re)translations of the same text published in different periods (1999, 2006, and 2014) and explained the shifts in translations, editorial decisions, and contextual voices in terms of the ideological, sociological,

What is critical discourse analysis? 19

and political contexts. Her study revealed that (re)translations ("language") are (re)framed ("practice") and temporally repositioned ("contexts") to reflect the then-dominant values and ideas of the target culture and relate information of immediate interest to the target audience at the time of publication, resulting in some changes to the discourse presented in the text.

Such attempts made by agents during the transaltion process and shifts in discourse cannot be fully explained when texts are examined in isolation. Given that translation is a highly socially and temporally engaged activity, context plays a crucial role in identifying discourse. Thus, many discourse analysis-informed case studies in translation studies are unsurprisingly CDA-informed *discourse analysis* (i.e., not discourse studies) in translation, in the sense that they examine translation (semiotic material, i.e., language) shifts (e.g., reapproapriation, reframing, i.e., practice) and explain them in terms of the historical, socio-political, and linguistic contexts (context).

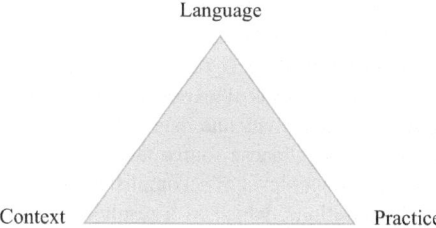

Figure 1.4 The triangle of discourse analysis: language, practice, context.
Sources: Angermuller, Maingueneau, and Wodak (2014, 7); Angermuller (2015, 513).

Practice essay questions

1 Compare discourse theory and discourse analysis based on the main foci.
2 Explain the three main foci of discourse analysis, using some of the literature.
3 Carol O'Sullivan, a translation studies scholar, in her work on multimodality, explains the following as a resource for translation:

> Georg Rörer, who supervised the printing of the Wittenberg editions of Martin Luther's translation of the Bible, developed typographical 'aids' for the reader in the form of roman typeface in certain words. The idea (and we must remember the Reformation context in which this was taking place) was that roman typeface was used for negatively connoted words, while positively connoted words were presented exclusively in gothic (Flood 1993: 133–135). George Flood hypothesises (ibid.) that this typographical device was part of Protestant anti-papal

> propaganda which sought to link certain Biblical elements with the Church of Rome; so for instance in Revelations 17, the 'Whore of Babylon' is presented in the text using roman type. Here typography is an important meaning-making resource for ideological shifts in translation
>
> (O'Sullivan 2013, 4–5)
>
> Compare the definitions of discourse proposed by Norman Fairclough and Stephen Bax, considering the example from O'Sullivan discussed above.

Notes

1 Several scholars have attempted to delineate the differences between text and discourse, which is well summarised in Stubbs (1983; 1984).
2 However, it should be acknowledged that extensive work has been carried out on 'textuality'. Beaugrande and Dressler (1981, 3), for example, defined it as a "communicative occurrence which meets seven standards of textuality: cohesion, coherence, intentionality, acceptability, situationality, informativity and intertextuality".
3 In this work, Gu argued that the Chinese source texts, as mediated by the interpreters, led to the appearance of a "stronger level of accomplishment, positive self-portrayal and, resultantly, political legitimisation", which as a result contributes to "(re)constructing China's image as important (re)tellers of "China's story" beyond national borders" (2018, 137).

Suggestions for further reading

Angermuller, Johannes, Dominique Maingueneau, and Ruth Wodak, eds. 2014. *The Discourse Studies Reader: Main Currents in Theory and Analysis*. Amsterdam & Philadelphia: John Benjamins.
Mills, Sara. 2002. "Discourse." In *Michel Foucault*, edited by Sara Mills, 53–66. London: Routledge.
Stubbs, Michael. 1983. *Discourse Analysis: The Sociolinguistic Analysis of Natural Language*. Chicago: The University of Chicago Press.
Widdowson, Henry G. 1995. "Discourse Analysis: A Critical View." *Language and Literature* 4 (3): 157–72.

References

Angermuller, Johannes. 2015. "Discourse Studies" In *International Encyclopedia of the Social & Behavioral Sciences*, 2nd edition, vol 6, 510–515. Oxford: Elsevier.
Angermuller, Johannes, Dominique Maingueneau, and Ruth Wodak, eds. 2014. *The Discourse Studies Reader: Main Currents in Theory and Analysis*. Amsterdam & Philadelphia: John Benjamins.
Baker, Mona. 2018. "Narrative Analysis and Translation." In *Routledge Handbook of Translation Studies and Linguistics*, edited by Kirsten Malmkjaer, 179–93. London & New York: Routledge.

Bax, Stephen. 2011. *Discourse and Genre: Analysing Language in Context.* London: Palgrave Macmillan.
BBC. 2019. "Cambridge University Marks 150 Years of Female Students." BBC. 2019. www.bbc.com/news/uk-england-cambridgeshire-49595057.
Beaugrande, Robert de, and Wolfgang Dressler. 1981. *Introduction to Text Linguistics.* London & New York: Longman.
Blommaert, Jan. 2005. *Discourse.* Cambridge: Cambridge University Press.
Brown, Gillian, and George Yule. 1983. *Discourse Analysis.* Cambridge: Cambridge University Press.
Chafe, Wallace L. 2003. "Discourse: Overview." In *International Encyclopedia of Linguistics,* edited by William Frawley, 2nd edition, 439–42. New York: Oxford University Press.
Fairclough, Norman. 1989. *Language and Power.* London: Longman.
Fairclough, Norman. 1992. *Discourse and Social Change.* Cambridge: Polity.
Fairclough, Norman. 1995a. *Critical Discourse Analysis.* London: Sage.
Fairclough, Norman. 1995b. *Media Discourse.* London: Arnold.
Fairclough, Norman. 2003. *Analysing Discourse: Textual Analysis for Social Research.* London: Routledge.
Flowerdew, John. 2017. "Critical Discourse Studies and Context". In *Routledge Handbook of Critical Discourse Studies,* edited by John Flowerdew and John E. Richardson, 165–78. Oxon and New York: Routledge.
Foucault, Michel. 1972. *The Archaeology of Knowledge.* London: Routledge.
Foucault, Michel. 1978. *The History of Sexuality, Volume 1, Translated from the French by Robert Hurley.* New York: Pantheon Books.
Foucault, Michel. 1981. "The Order of Discourse", translated by Ian McLeod. In *Untying the Text: A Post-Structuralist Reader,* edited by Robert Young, 48–78. London: Routledge and Kegan Paul.
Georgakopoulou, Alexandra, and Dionysis Goutsos. 1997. *Discourse Analysis: An Introduction.* Edinburgh: Edinburgh University Press.
Gu, Chonglong. 2018. "Forging a Glorious Past via the 'Present Perfect': A Corpus-Based CDA Analysis of China's Past Accomplishments Discourse Mediat(Is)Ed at China's Interpreted Political Press Conferences." *Discourse, Context & Media* 24: 137–49.
Halliday, Michael Alexander Kirkwood, and Ruqaiya Hasan. 1985. *Language, Context and Text: Aspects of Language in a Social Semiotic Perspective.* Oxford: Oxford University Press.
Hansen, Susan. 2016. "'Pleasure Stolen from the Poor': Community Discourse on the 'Theft' of a Banksy." *Crime Media Culture* 12 (3): 289–307.
Harris, Zellig S. 1952. "Discourse Analysis." *Language* 28 (1): 1–30.
Kang, Ji-Hae. 2008. "Pŏnyŏkkisaŭi chemoge kwanhan yŏn'gu [An Analysis of Headlines of Translated News Magazine Articles]." *Pŏnyŏkhagyŏn'gu [The Journal of Translation Studies]* 9 (2): 7–43.
Kim, Deuk-soo. 2013. "Kongjaŭi yŏsŏnggwan – nonŏrŭl chungsimŭro" [Confucius' perspectives on women –focusing on The Analects]. *Yŏsŏngyŏn'gunonch'ong [The Journal of Women's Studies]* 12: 59–88.
Kim, Kyung Hye. 2014. "Examining US News Media Discourses about North Korea." *Discourse and Society* 25 (2): 221–44.
Kim, Kyung Hye. 2018. "Retranslation as a Socially Engaged Activity: The Case of The Rape of Nanking." *Perspectives: Studies in Translatology* 26 (3): 391–404. https://doi.org/10.1080/0907676X.2017.1388413.
Kim, Sookyung. 2012. "Racism in the Global Era: Analysis of Korean Media Discourse around Migrants, 1990–2009." *Discourse & Society* 23 (6): 657–78.

McLaughlin, Katie. 2014. "5 Things Women Couldn't Do in the 1960s." CNN. 2014. https://edition.cnn.com/2014/08/07/living/sixties-women-5-things/index.html.
Mills, Sara. 2002. "Discourse." In *Michel Foucault*, edited by Sara Mills, 53–66. London: Routledge.
Mills, Sara. 2003. *Michel Foucault*. London & New York: Routledge.
O'Sullivan, Carol. 2013. "Introduction: Multimodality as Challenge and Resource for Translation." *Journal of Specialised Translation* 20: 2–14.
Podmore, Julie, and Manon Tremblay. 2015. "Lesbians, Second-Wave Feminism and Gay Liberation." In *The Ashgate Research Companion to Lesbian and Gay Activism*, edited by David Paternotte and Manon Tremblay, 121–34. London and New York: Routledge.
Reisigl, Martin, and Ruth Wodak. 2009. "The Discourse-Historical Approach (DHA)." In *Methods of Critical Discourse Analysis*, edited by Ruth Wodak and Michael Meyer, 2nd edition, 87–121. London: Sage.
Salkie, Raphael. 1995. *Text and Discourse Analysis*. London and New York: Routledge.
Sinclair, John McHardy, and Malcolm Coulthard. 1978. *Towards an Analysis of Discourse: The English Used by Teachers and Pupils*. Oxford: Oxford University Press.
Sirulhaq, Ahmad, Untung Yuwono, and Abdul Muta'ali. 2023. "Why Do We Need a Sociocognitive-CDA in Hate Speech Studies? A Corpus-Based Systematic Review." *Discourse & Society* 34 (4): 462–84.
Stubbs, Michael. 1983. *Discourse Analysis: The Sociolinguistic Analysis of Natural Language*. Chicago: The University of Chicago Press.
Stubbs, Michael. 1984. "Applied Discourse Analysis and Educational Linguistics." In *Applied Sociolinguistics*, edited by Peter Trudgill, 203–44. London: Academic Press.
Sultan, Mena. 2019. "October 1920: Women Granted Full Membership of Oxford University." The Guardian. 2019. www.theguardian.com/gnmeducationcentre/2019/oct/08/october-1920-women-granted-full-membership-of-oxford-university.
van Dijk, Teun A. 1977. *Text and Context: Explorations in the Semantics and Pragmatics of Discourse*. London and New York: Longman.
van Dijk, Teun A. (1993) 'Principles of Critical Discourse Analysis.' *Discourse & Society* 4: 249–283.
van Dijk, Teun A. 2001. "Critical Discourse Analysis." In *The Handbook of Discourse Analysis*, edited by Deborah Schiffrin, Deborah Tannen and Heidi E. Hamilton, 1st edition, 352–71. Blackwell Publishers.
van Dijk, Teun A. 2005. "Contextual knowledge management in discourse production: A CDA perspective". In *A New Agenda in (Critical) Discourse Analysis*, edited by Ruth Wodak and Paul Chilton, 71–100. Amsterdam: Benjamins.
van Leeuwen, Theo. 1993. "Genre and Field in Critical Discourse Analysis: A Synopsis." *Discourse & Society* 4 (2): 193–223.
Widdowson, Henry G. 1995. "Discourse Analysis: A Critical View." *Language and Literature* 4 (3): 157–72.
Widdowson, Henry G. 2004. *Text, Context, Pretext: Critical Issues in Discourse Analysis*. Edited by Kirsten Malmkjaer. Oxford: Blackwell.
Widdowson, Henry G. 2007. *Discourse Analysis*. Oxford: Oxford University Press.
Wodak, Ruth. 2002. "Aspects of Critical Discourse Analysis." *Zeitschrift Für Angewandte Linguistik* 36: 5–31.
Wodak, Ruth, and Michael Meyer. 2001. *Methods of Critical Discourse Analysis*. Edited by Ruth Wodak and Michael Meyer. First edition. London: Sage.
Wodak, Ruth, and Michael Meyer. 2009. "Critical Discourse Analysis: History, Agenda, Theory, and Methodology." In *Methods for Critical Discourse Analysis*, edited by Michael Meyer and Ruth Wodak, second rev, 1–33. London: Sage.

2 Critical discourse analysis
Three different approaches

Key points of learning

- Appraisal theory concerns how relationships are enacted through sharing stance/evaluation/emotion/judgement represented in discourse, focusing on the evaluative positioning of the speaker/writer in a communicative context.
- While adopting M.A.K. Halliday's work on SFL theory, Norman Fairclough focused more on the role of language as communicative and interactional reciprocal processes, as it shuttles between language use and society.
- Fairclough's three-dimensional framework acknowledges the inextricable connection between language and society and shows that discourse is both socially constitutive and socially conditioned.
- CDA pays relatively little attention to the bottom-up resistance movement (c.f. socio-narrative theory) but focuses more on revealing how powerful elites and institutions exercise their power using language, control society, and reproduce dominance, inequality, and racism.
- Teun A. van Dijk focuses more on the minds of language users (the *cognitive* aspect of interpretation), examining the mediation between textual and social structures through social cognition.
- van Dijk's ideological square model explains the discursive group polarisation and ideological construction strategy that justifies inequality.

This chapter describes three major CDA models developed within CDA that have been widely adopted in translation studies: (1) the M.A.K. Hallidayan SFL-informed appraisal theory-informed model, (2) Norman Fairclough's dialectical-relational approach (1992), and (3) Teun A. van Dijk's socio-cognitive model (1993; 1998).[1]

Subtle differences in understanding discourse, together with differences in focus, have resulted in the development of CDA, which, in turn, has led to the emergence of various strands, or sub-branches. Some of the different approaches

DOI: 10.4324/9781003029083-3

to discourse analysis suggested by Wodak and Meyer (2009, 20) include the corpus-based approach (e.g., Gerlinde Mautner's work), the discourse-historical approach (e.g., Ruth Wodak and Martin Reisigl's work), the social actors approach (e.g., Theo van Leeuwen's work), the socio-cognitive approach (e.g., Teun van Dijk's work), and the dialectical-relational approach (e.g., Norman Fairclough's work). The UK-based scholars, particularly Fairclough and Wodak (1997) and Wodak (2011), identified the following sub-branches of CDA, which include Foucauldian poststructuralism; the socio-cognitive model proposed by van Dijk; the Fairclough's dialectical-relational approach; the discourse-historical approach associated with Wodak; and van Leeuwen's socio-semantic network of social actors model. Among these sub-branches, the models of Fairclough and van Dijk are most frequently applied in translation studies to date. Therefore, this chapter will comprehensively discuss the Fairclough's dialectical-relational approach, which offers an understanding of discourse as a socio-cultural discursive practice, and van Dijk's socio-cognitive model.

This section starts with Halliday's SFL-informed discourse analysis. The Hallidayan model, as discussed below, is more of a 'discourse analysis' than a 'critical discourse analysis' in the strictest sense because it does not focus on abuses of power. However, his work greatly influenced and inspired many scholars, becoming the starting point of discourse analysis, paving the way for the development of Fairclough's analytical model and Martin and White's (2005) work, which has been adopted by translation studies scholars in their various CDA-informed works. Therefore, Halliday's model is discussed in this chapter alongside other CDA models.

2.1 M.A.K. Halliday's SFL-informed discourse analysis: appraisal framework

As Munday (2001) rightly notes, Halliday's SFL theory has greatly influenced discourse analysis in translation studies. A prominent CDA scholar, Norman Fairclough, pinpoints what the SFL offers to CDA by explaining that "SFL is profoundly concerned with the relationship between language and other elements and aspects of social life, and its approach to the linguistic analysis of text is always oriented to the social character of texts" (Fairclough 2003, 5). Although Halliday's model is not a direct precursor of CDA, it arguably sets the foundation and has been applied by many linguists and sociolinguists. Moreover, his SFL model was further developed by Martin and White (2005) into 'appraisal theory', which has been widely adopted by many scholars in translation studies (e.g., Zhang 2002; Munday 2015; Li and Xu 2018).[2] However, SFL theory goes beyond the remit of this book, and owing to both space restrictions and the book's aim, Halliday's model will be discussed only briefly.

The origin of Halliday's SFL model can be traced back to the Polish-British anthropologist Malinowski's (1994) discussion of *context* (see the significance of 'context' in discourse analysis research). Emphasising the role of context in the meaning-making process, Malinowski coined the phrase 'context of situation' in

1923, defining it as "the cultural context of use in which an utterance was located; furthermore, 'the whole way of life' (cultural context) had to be borne in mind in interpreting an utterance" (Oxford Reference 2021). His pragmatic approach to language and his emphasis on context can be found in the following:

> Each utterance is essentially bound up with the context of situation and with the aim of the pursuit, whether it be the short indications about the movements of the quarry, or references to statements about the surroundings, or the expression of feeling and passion inexorably bound up with behaviour, or words of command, or correlation of action. *The structure of all this linguistic material is inextricably mixed up with, and dependent upon, the course of the activity in which the utterances are embedded.* The vocabulary, the meaning of the particular words used in their characteristic technicality is no less subordinate to action.
>
> (Malinowski 1994, 8, emphasis added)

Therefore, interpretations of utterances, actions, communications, and vocabularies are subject to the context of the situation, the understanding of which is also conditional on the context of culture. Thus, Malinowski's understanding of the relationship between text and context can be summarised as shown in the following figure:

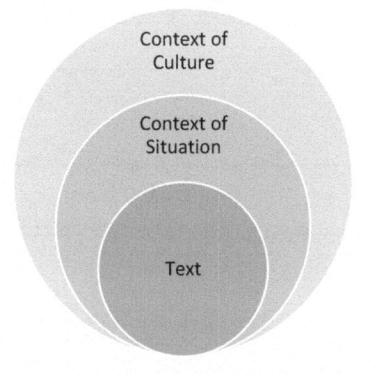

Figure 2.1 The relationship between text, situation, and culture.

This view of context inspired English linguist John Rupert Firth, who took the social and functional approach to language, emphasised that meaning is context-dependent, and understood the meaning as "function in context" (Firth 1957). According to Hasan (2014, 2), Halliday followed Firth's understanding of context as "a viable schematic construct" that can be used to analyse language events and "positioned 'text' as language event, relating the variations of text in context to inherent linguistic phenomenon". Thus, for Halliday, the 'context of situation' refers to the "extralinguistic circumstances of use that influence the linguistic form of an utterance: not only the social and physical setting but also such factors as social relationships, the nature of the medium, the task, and the topic" (Oxford Reference 2021). With this view, alongside his goal of providing a theory of how language works, Halliday attempted to explain more systematically language use that varies greatly depending on the situation. Therefore, he further developed Firth's 'system' and expanded the concept to a network of situations, which is now called 'systemic functional linguistic theory (SFL)'.[3] SFL considers language to function as a tool to create the meanings necessary for communication within given social and cultural contexts, as well as how language functions and is influenced by its social context. Hence, SFL theory considers communication to be the primary function of language and therefore considers language contextually.

In Halliday's view, 'text', 'context of situation', and 'context of culture' are interdependent, and the context of a situation has three key variables/dimensions that influence language use: 'field', 'tenor', and 'mode' of discourse. 'Field' refers to "what is happening to the nature of social action that is taking place: what is it that the participants are engaged in" (Halliday and Hasan 1985, 12) (i.e., 'content'). 'Tenor' refers to 'who is taking part' in it and their relationships, attitudes, and emotions. 'Mode' refers to 'what part the language is playing' (i.e., the logical structure of a text) (Halliday and Hasan 1985, 12).[4] Halliday has argued that language has three main functions: ideational, interpersonal, and textual, and these three components (field, tenor, and mode) are associated with the metafunctions – ideational, interpersonal, and textual, as shown in Figure 2.2.

Situation: *Feature of the context*		*Text:* *Functional component of semantic system*
Field of discourse (what is going on)	(realised by)	Ideational meanings (transitivity, naming, etc)
Tenor of discourse (who are taking part)		Interpersonal meanings (mood, modality, person, etc)
Mode of discourse (role assigned to language)		Textual meanings (theme, information, cohesive relations)

Figure 2.2 Relation of the text to the context of situation.
Source: Adapted from Halliday and Hasan (1985, 26).

Some scholars have adopted Halliday's metafunctions of language in news analysis to identify the types of grammatical and lexical items chosen and their functions. For example, González Rodríguez (2006) examined news articles published in *The Times* and *The Sun* in the UK in terms of three metafunctions (i.e., field and experiential meanings, tenor and interpersonal meanings, and mode and textual meanings) to show how news writing is systematically structured to achieve a particular goal in media discourse.

The interpersonal element, which had previously received relatively little attention within the three metafunctions, attracted SFL scholars in Australia. A research group now called the 'Sydney School' and led by James R. Martin and Peter R. R. White developed the concept further into a system of analysis, which is now called *appraisal theory*. The term appraisal here refers to "the semantic resources used to negotiate emotions, judgements, and valuations, alongside resources for amplifying and engaging with these evaluations" (Martin 2000, 145).

Located within the SFL and based on the 'interpersonal' variable, appraisal theory is concerned with how relationships are enacted through sharing stance/evaluation/emotion/judgement represented in discourse, focusing on the evaluative positioning of the speaker/writer in a communicative context, i.e., the "language of evaluation" (White 2015, 1), aiming at "exploring, describing and explaining the way language is used to evaluate, to adopt stances, to construct textual personas and to manage interpersonal positionings and relationships" (White 2001, 1).

Here is an example from Mayo and Taboada's study that examined *Cosmopolitan*'s online coverage to identify how political discourse addressing women is evaluated.[5] Shown below is a comment left with regard to the abortion topic.

> **Example 1 from Cosmovotes, November 2014 (Mayo and Taboada 2017, 42)**
>
> You are a sexist asshole. And what are you? A feminist, lonely murderer? I'd rather be a sexist asshole that supports human life and not murder. Thank you. That was quite a compliment, compared to the latter.

In this example, expressions of appraisal can be easily found, although this is not always as evident as it is here. 'Sexist asshole', 'lonely murderer', 'quite a compliment', and 'feminist' are all negative judgements. Notably, while 'quite a compliment' in isolation may read as positive, here, it is used sarcastically and presents a negative load (Mayo and Taboada 2017, 42), demonstrating the importance of context.

Martin explained that appraisal theory was started by a group of linguists in Sydney who were developing a comprehensive and systematic analytical framework within the general framework of the SFL to analyse evaluation in discourse, since they were "concerned with the *social function* of these resources [interpersonal resources], not simply as expressions of feeling but in terms of *their ability to construct community*" (Martin 2003, 171, emphasis added). Therefore, the Sydney linguists' primary concern was identifying how the evaluations or textual voices of speakers/writers are codified through language to construct a relationship or "solidarity" (Oteíza 2017) with the interlocutor/reader. By doing so, appraisal theory distances itself from grammar-based tradition that, as Martin (2000, 143) stated, "focused on dialogue as an exchange of goods and services […] or information". Martin (2000, 143, emphasis added) explains that

28 *Critical Discourse Analysis in Translation Studies*

[t]he expression of attitude is not, as is often claimed, simply a personal matter – the speaker "commenting" on the world – but a truly interpersonal matter, in that the basic reason for *advancing an opinion is to elicit a response of solidarity from the addressee.*

As it initially unfolded, this theory was based on the English language; however, it has been continually revisited by many scholars worldwide, who tested, contested, and revised it in other languages. The website of Martin and White and their associates,[6] which is specifically dedicated to the model, has enabled extensive discussions among scholars worldwide, thereby resulting in further refinement and making the theory more comprehensive and extensive. However, this has also resulted in the theory having too many sub-systems, as shown in Figure 2.3, which is not an exhaustive list but a mere snapshot of the whole, still expanding, system.

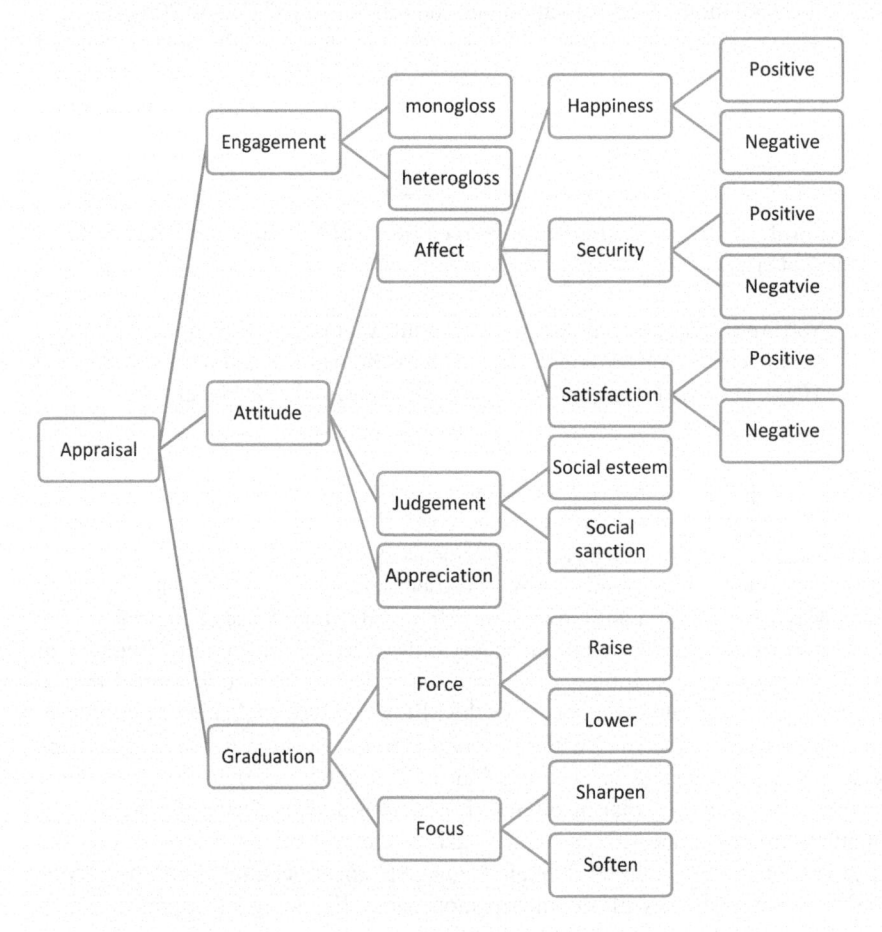

Figure 2.3 A snapshot of sub-systems of appraisal theory model of evaluation.
Source: Adapted from Martin (2003); Martin and White (2005).

As seen from Figure 2.3, the appraisal framework thus offers a systemic account of appraisal resources that place values or engage with feelings and evaluation and proposes three domains of semantic resources: *engagement* ("the play of voices around opinions in discourse"), *graduation* (how "feelings are amplified and categories blurred"), and *attitude* ("our feelings, including emotional reactions, judgement of behavior and evaluation of thing") (Martin and White 2005, 35).

Concerned with a social dialogic perspective, the semantic system of *engagement* enables researchers to see how speakers and writers project themselves onto the text or the audience. Specifically, either their utterances or writings are aligned with the audience ('monoglossic') or they adopt alternative positions in the discourse and acknowledge diversity across voices ('heteroglossic'). Thus, engagement is often used to analyse how journalists attend to other voices (i.e., the use of 'the report shows that...' or 'X claims that...'), or to compare the different ways in which journalists in different cultures engage with hard news (e.g. Huan, 2016).

Graduation explains how an author or speaker scales the strength of a text or utterance up or down. Inscribed intensified/scaled-up evaluation examples include phrases such as 'it *must* be taken into account'. Li and Zhu (2020) used the semantic system of graduation to identify and explain the positive self-presentation and negative other-presentation inscribed in Chinese political texts. Their study shows China to be largely upscaled, while negative descriptions of other countries are also upgraded (which is in line with van Dijk's ideological square model; see Section 2.3 in this chapter). However, some contradictory results have also been reported, where "downscaling of positive description of self (China) is significantly more than the downscaling of positive description of others, and the frequency of downscaling the negative description of others is significantly higher than that of downgrading the negative description of self" (Li and Zhu 2019, 161–62). See the following examples of graduation from their work.

Example 2 Li and Zhu (2019, 162)

中国 中 东部 地区 **多次** 出现 大 范围 雾 霾 天气 [force up graduation]

Translation: Large-scale smog has appeared **many times** in China's central and eastern areas.

中国 石油 资源 **比较** 丰富 。

Translation: China boasts **fairly** rich oil resources.

Attitude is an assessment, either positive or negative, that can further be divided into (1) *affect*, which, as either positive or negative positioning, "presented as *emotional* reactions"; (2) *judgement*, which is either "positive or negative *assessment*s of human behavior and character by reference to ethics/morality and other systems of conventionalized or institutionalized norms" (White 2015,

2, emphasis added); and (3) *appreciation*, which "construes attitude about texts, performances and natural phenomena, and fits into frames such as *I consider it 'x'*" (Martin 2003, 173). Since this form clearly shows the reactions, feelings, and evaluations of the writer/speaker, the concept of graduation has been widely employed in discourse analysis and is often seen as "the central system" within Appraisal (Mayo and Taboada 2017, 42). This is demonstrated in the following example, in which the author uses the word 'stupid' to intensify his/her negative attitude.

Example 3 From Mayo and Taboada (2017, 22)

One doesn't have to be stupid to be a conservative, but it sure seems that way.

Concerning how the issue of power is considered in the appraisal framework, Oteíza (2017, 458) summarises the essence and power of the appraisal framework as follows:

> This model maintains that intersubjectivity is built by writers and readers who have certain social roles and who act in determinate social and cultural realms that shape and institutionalise the way in which emotions and opinions are codified through language.

Thus, as discussed above, the appraisal framework provides more descriptive and systematic comprehensive linguistic resources that can be considered when examining interpersonal meaning across discourses. The appraisal system can prove useful in identifying the interpersonal relationships between the speaker and writer and their audiences and allows researchers to identify and investigate the distribution of appraisal resources.

2.2 Norman Fairclough's three-dimensional model

Norman Fairclough is one of the founders of CDA, and the term 'critical discourse analysis' stems from his early work on critical language study; however, as van Dijk (2001, 352) explains, some tenets of CDA were already discussed in the critical theory of the Frankfurt School, and its focus on language and discourse began with the critical linguistics that emerged in the UK and Australia. Fairclough distinguished between 'critical' (e.g., critical linguists' approaches) and 'non-critical' (e.g., Sinclair and Coulthard's approaches) approaches in greater detail in his work *Discourse and Social Change*, although he acknowledges that the division is not absolute:

> Critical approaches differ from non-critical approaches in not just describing discursive practices, but also showing how discourse is shaped by relations of

power and ideologies, and the constructive effects discourse has upon social identities, social relations and systems of knowledge and belief, neither of which is normally apparent to discourse participants.

(Fairclough 1992, 12)

Unlike the other strands of discourse analysis involving philosophical enquiries, Fairclough's work – both text and talk – is textually oriented. However, this does not mean that his research was focused primarily on texts. Rather, he attempted to transcend the divide between pure textual analysis and the Foucauldian approach, in which text is largely disregarded, arguing that

any analysis of texts which aims to be significant in social scientific terms has to connect with theoretical questions about discourse [...but] no real understanding of the social effects of discourse is possible without looking closely at what happens when people talk or write. So, *text analysis is an essential part of discourse analysis, but discourse analysis is not merely the linguistic analysis of texts.*

(Fairclough 2003, 2–3, emphasis added)

Here, his view on the relationship between language use and society/social change is clear: interconnection and mutual influence exist between them. While adopting Halliday's work on SFL, Fairclough focused more on the role of language as a communicative and interactional reciprocal process, as it shuttles between language use and society, thus enabling scholars to reveal "how language can be exploited in the manipulation of opinion and the abuse of power" (Widdowson 1996, 57). His understanding of language use and society and views on language as discourse and social practice are well summarised in his three-dimensional CDA framework/model (Fairclough 2013, 133), which he first developed in 1989 in his early work and was modified and updated later in 1992 and 2013 (see Figure 2.4). This three-dimensional framework is explained here at greater length, as it has been immensely influential and adopted in many works, including those published in translation studies (see Chapter 3).

This model explains that analysis has three dimensions: (1) text, (2) discourse/discursive practice, and (3) socio-cultural/social practice. The first dimension, which is carried out at the word level, concerns the analysis of a text in any communicative form, spoken or written language, from a word to an image. The agent who has the power to set the agenda, quotations, titles, grammar, transitivity, vocabularies, and metaphors can be analysed in this phase of the investigation. The second dimension relates to where a text is produced, with the unit of analysis being the whole text. The research focus in this step is identifying how the text is produced and consumed. The distribution of a discourse, discourse/rhetorical representation, and presuppositions are examined. Conversely, Fairclough views this as a collection of words speakers choose, which can change social structures. In the third dimension, the unit of analysis is the social structures that govern social norms (i.e., what is, or is not, accepted). The networks of discourses and the effects of discourse practices on social practice need to be examined (Fairclough 1992, 237).

Sociocultural practice (situational, institutional, and societal)	• explanation (social analysis)
Discourse practice (proccess of production, process of interpretation)	• interpretation (processing analysis)
text	• description (text analysis)

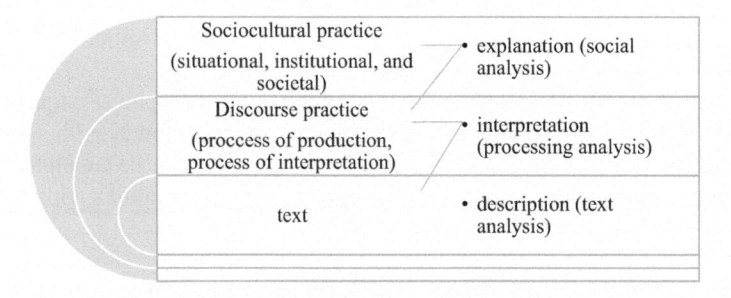

Figure 2.4 Fairclough's three-dimensional CDA framework.
Source: Adapted from Fairclough (2013, 133).

In terms of each dimension, Fairclough further elaborates, as follows.

- Description is the stage that is concerned with the formal properties of the text
- Interpretation is concerned with the relationship between text and interaction; it sees the text as the product of a process of production and as a resource in the process of interpretation
- Explanation is concerned with the relationship between interaction and social context, with the social determination of the processes of production and interpretation and their social effects.

(Fairclough 1989, 26)

This three-dimensional framework shows the inextricable connection between language and society. For example, a word (the first dimension) is influenced by discourse/discursive practice (the second dimension), and discourse is shaped by social structures (i.e., what society does or does not accept) (the third dimension). Conversely, a discourse, which Fairclough sees as the collection of words speakers choose (the second dimension), can change social structures (the third dimension), and a word (language, the first dimension) can change a discourse (the second dimension). Thus, language use is governed by social structures, which in turn are often changed by language. Fairclough and Wodak develop this further to argue:

> the discursive event is shaped by [the situation(s), institution(s) and social structure(s)], but it also shapes them. That is, discourse is socially constitutive as well as socially conditioned – it constitutes situations, objects of knowledge, and the social identities of and relationships between people and groups of people. It is constitutive both in the sense that it helps to sustain and reproduce the social status quo and in the sense that it contributes to transforming it.
>
> (Fairclough and Wodak 1997, 258)

For example, the global challenges we face, especially in relation to environmental sustainability, have created new social norms, such as in the exhortation, 'bring your own travel mug', 'use a reusable bag', and 'reduce plastic waste'. This change in society has led to the addition of another layer of meaning to the word 'sustainability', as seen from the United Nations' 'Sustainable Development Goals'. Similarly, because of the constant challenges faced by feminist writers, it became common practice to use 's/he' in writing, as a representation of 'he or she' to indicate someone of either sex, as opposed to using 'he'. A similar shift can be found in Piser's (2021) report about feminist activists' movements to make the gendered French language more gender inclusive, as they argued that linguistic bias has real-life consequences. Similar efforts are being made in Germany and Brazil.

Conversely, examples can be found of how the words we choose ultimately shape our view of society and the norms and stands of society in which language is used. For example, World Bank economist Owen Ozier has reportedly further supported the argument that gendered language may play a role in limiting women's opportunities. Ozier (2019, para 7) studied grammatical gender structures in 4,334 languages and revealed the striking result that "gendered languages could translate into outcomes like lower female labour force participation".

Thus, words have the power to change people's behaviour and ultimately change the norms and standards of society. In his work *Language and Power*, which led to the development and further refinement of the CDA framework, Fairclough (1989) pronounced all its key concepts, including discourse, power, and ideology, and proposed his main argument that language is a social practice. Fairclough's (1989) CDA focuses on how discourse is constructed and influenced by power, ideology, and social relations and, equally, how power, social relations, beliefs, norms, and knowledge influence discourses and how these relations are practised and realised in language use. In this sense, Fairclough's view is that language carries value, expresses the attitudes of a speaker/writer, and is a social practice and powerful tool that can influence society and reveal the power relations among individual social agents, whereas the Hallidayan approach towards language viewed it more as only a communicative tool.

Fairclough's CDA understands discourse as a phenomenon that plays a crucial role in socio-cultural reproduction and texts as "sensitive indicators of sociocultural processes and change" (Fairclough 1995, 2–8). His model is novel in the sense that it expresses the relationship between language and society more explicitly and expands the discussion of language beyond a purely communicative event. This is perhaps why some CDA scholars are politically committed and are therefore often criticised for adopting such positions or for giving more priority to politically espoused views, with the most notable critic being Henry Widdowson, as discussed below.[7] Fairclough (1996, 52), however, emphasised that "CDA is emphatically not a political party, and the particular nature of political commitments and strategies of intervention differ widely":

> Practitioners of CDA are indeed generally characterised by explicit political commitments. They are people who see things wrong with their societies, see

language as involved in what is wrong, and are committed to making changes through forms of intervention involving language.

(Fairclough 1996, 52)

Fairclough's framework explains that social conditions and context control how a text is produced and interpreted. Thus, the process in which a text is interpreted needs to be considered within the wider context of the social conditions in which it was produced or interpreted.

However, what happens when the discourse or context (i.e., the second and third dimensions in Fairclough's three-dimensional model) changes? What process of interpretation should be applied to make sense of the word (i.e., text, the first dimension)? This may be one reason why Fairclough's approach has inspired many translation studies scholars: it allows them to interpret translations against the socio-political context in which a text is produced and embedded (this is discussed in the next chapter).

The main tenets of CDA, as explained by Fairclough and Wodak (1997), are summarised by van Dijk (2015b, 467) as follows:

- CDA addresses social problems.
- Power relations are discursive.
- Discourse constitutes society and culture.
- Discourse does ideological work.
- Discourse is historical.
- The link between text and society is mediated.
- Discourse analysis is interpretative and explanatory.
- Discourse is a form of social action.

These tenets were later further developed into specific strands of CDA. For instance, van Dijk focused on what mediates text and society ('the link between text and society is mediated'), whereas Wodak paid more attention to the historical aspect of discourse (i.e., 'discourse is historical'), consequently developing what is called 'historical discourse analysis'.

2.2.1 Criticisms

Although this three-dimensional framework describes the link between language and society and the power of language, it is not immune to criticisms. To date, several scholars have critically reviewed CDA. Breeze (2011), for example, has provided an in-depth discussion of the criticisms of CDA, from the underlying premises of CDA to its method. One of them concerns context. Breeze explains that Schegloff considers context should be considered only when it features in the interaction as a "concern for the participants", but it is impossible to determine just one that is analytically relevant because there can be "an almost infinite number of contextual factors that might influence a given interaction" (Breeze 2011, 513). Other criticisms that have levelled at CDA include that the focus of CDA work has been "overwhelmingly negative and seems to propagate a deterministic vision of society" (Breeze 2011, 521).[8]

Some other criticisms concern how data are collected. For example, Stubbs (1997) levelled some criticisms against CDA, noting that CDA scholars' textual interpretations are politically motivated in textual analysis and are often too fragmented and that their text selection criteria are implicit. Stubbs (1997, 4) also criticised Fairclough's CDA, arguing that it fails to provide quantitative diachronic findings for different types of texts. Later, scholars, acknowledging such criticisms about fragmented analysis, particularly those addressing the issue of the representation of data, adopted a typically quantitative analytical methodology called the corpus-based approach (this will be discussed in Chapter 4).

Another point related to the limitations of CDA, although not necessarily criticism, is that it focuses mostly on the "top-down relations of dominance than to bottom-up relations of resistance, compliance and acceptance" (van Dijk 1993, 250). In taking Fairclough's approach, CDA scholars acknowledge the joint production of a power and dominance relationship but focus more on how powerful players in society, such as the media and politicians, use language and discourse for dominance. van Dijk explains as follows:

> although an analysis of strategies of resistance and challenge is crucial for our understanding of actual power and dominance relations in society, and although such an analysis needs to be included in a broader theory of power, counter-power and discourse, our critical approach prefers to focus on the *elites and their discursive strategies for the maintenance of inequality*.
>
> (van Dijk 1993, 250, emphasis added)

This shows a preference for revealing how powerful elites and institutions exercise their power using language and control over society and reproducing issues such as dominance, inequality, and racism through discourse analysis. A bibliometric analysis of CDA studies conducted by Xiao and Li (2021) revealed this point, where the top ten keywords of CDA research identified on the basis of frequency include politics, identity, gender, policy, media, power, and race. This means that CDA scholars are most interested in the language and texts produced by powerful institutions, elites, decision-makers, and policymakers, particularly in revealing the institutional voices/discourses constructed and circulated in society while paying little attention to the bottom-up resistant movement. Therefore, CDA may not be very helpful for revealing how individual voices could contribute to subverting social norms or analysing how one translation, or an act of one translator, could challenge and subvert the global voice, even when, often, a short text or saying produces a spark that could grow into a larger discourse.

Some scholars, and most notably Widdowson (1995a, 1995b, 1996), criticised CDA for not being very systematic. Widdowson (1995b, 159) noted the potential pitfalls, wherein a direction of enquiry "inevitably privilege one perspective over the other" and the analysis can be too politically oriented, to the extent that he somewhat harshly claims that CDA is "an exercise in interpretation" and "invalid as analysis" (Widdowson 1995b, 159). Furthermore, he argues that Fairclough is more interested in "socio-political theory, and linguistic ideas are adduced as necessary" (Widdowson 1995a, 515). He further explains that:

> It is possible to accept the need to extend the scope of discourse description by taking social factors into account without commitment to the kind of socio-political interpretation that is implied by a critical approach. Political commitment is not the same thing as social theory, although the two are easy to confuse. [...] *It presents a partial interpretation of text from a particular point of view. It is partial in two senses: first, it is not impartial in that it is ideologically committed, and so prejudiced; and it is partial in that it selects those features of the text which support its preferred interpretation.*
> (Widdowson 1995b, 159, emphasis added)

While admitting that CDA has given particular focus to questions of ideology in that it reflects some of its practitioners' political commitments, Fairclough (1996) refuted Widdowson's criticism of his framework by articulating the two senses of interpretation, which he labelled, 'interpretation' and 'explanation'. The former is an "inherent part of ordinary language use [...]: make meaning from/with spoken or written texts" and the latter is "a matter of analysis seeking to show connections between both properties of texts and practices of [explanation] in a particular social space, and wider social and cultural properties of that particular social space" (Fairclough 1996, 49–50). In response to Widdowson's criticism of CDA's partial interpretation, Fairclough acknowledges that CDA allows for diversity in the interpretation of texts and that everyone writes from "within particular discursive practices, entailing particular interests, commitments, inclusions, exclusions, and so forth" (Fairclough 1996, 52).

These academic criticisms and rebuttals enrich discussions on CDA, providing opportunities for this approach to be further refined. In their attempts to address Widdowson's criticisms, particularly in terms of them being 'partial' where texts are selected to support the 'biased' argument, some scholars have adopted a quantitative approach: the corpus-based method (this is discussed in Chapter 4). However, it should be mentioned here that both Widdowson and Fairclough agree on the dialectical relationship between language and society even when their views on discourse may differ, and Widdowson acknowledges that CDA has significance as a line of enquiry and is influential.

2.3 Teun van Dijk's socio-cognitive approach

Teun A. van Dijk is a key figure in discourse studies. He has worked extensively on discourse, racism, and the media since the 1980s and has investigated social cognition, group identity, and prejudice, and more specifically, racism discourse in both text and talk. As in Fairclough's CDA, van Dijk's socio-cognitive approach to CDA examines the link between language and society. For him, too, discourse is "a specific form of language use, and as a specific form of social interaction, interpreted as a complete communicative event in a social situation" (van Dijk 1990, 164). He considers discourse to be beyond a sentence in length and not only through text but also in the form of both text and talk. Like Fairclough and other CDA scholars, he acknowledges the important role of context in constructing discourses and discusses it in more depth. For example, in his work on context, van Dijk (2015a) postulated that (racist) discourse depends on "Setting (Place, Time), Participants (and their identities, roles and relationships), Goals, current Social Acts as well as Knowledge" (van Dijk 2011, 8) and that discourse analysis needs to include a detailed analysis of text or talk, as well as of communicative situations.

However, the fundamental difference between van Dijk and Fairclough is that van Dijk focuses on the minds of language users by emphasising the cognitive aspect of interpretation (i.e., the thinking process – the space in between), which is now called the 'socio-cognitive model'. This is based on the understanding that it is through discourse – in the form of text and talk – in society that social representations and socially shared knowledge are acquired, used, changed, and reproduced (van Dijk 1990, 165).

The socio-cognitive model explains that the mediation between language (i.e., textual structures) and society (social structures) occurs through social cognition. van Dijk categorises 'cognition' at two different levels, i.e., personal and social cognition, and argues that the real interface between society and discourse is socio-cognitive because "language users as social actors *mentally represent and connect both levels*" (van Dijk 2015b, 469, emphasis added). Thus, although it may seem as if Fairclough and van Dijk share a common understanding of the role of languages, van Dijk focuses more on the *actors* whereas Fairclough places greater emphasis on *social practices and structures*. Wodak and Meyer (2009, 22) have provided a clear picture of the differences and categorisation of these approaches, identifying van Dijk's socio-cognitive approach as focusing more on agency than the greater focus on structure found in Fairclough's dialectical-relational approach.

With such an understanding of language users and context, van Dijk acknowledges that the same discourse may be accepted differently depending on the social actors and context because social actors share "socio-cultural knowledge of the world with other members of various epistemic communities, as well as attitudes, ideologies, norms and values with other members of various kinds of social groups" (van Dijk 2017, 31). The fact that a certain discourse may be racist in one context but not in another context has significant implications for scholars not only in discourse studies but also in translation studies. This awareness of the function of context in making certain discourses (un)acceptable also acknowledges that translators must negotiate the meanings of a source text to make it accessible to the audience in a target culture. This may be one reason why this model, in addition to that of Fairclough, has inspired scholars in translation studies who adopted van Dijk's approach to explaining a translator's role in communicating and negotiating the source text for a new environment/receiving culture.

Unlike Widdowson, who critiqued CDA scholars for being socio-politically oriented, van Dijk (1993, 252) admits and highlights that CDA takes an explicit socio-political stance but is more concerned with pressing social issues, noting that

CDA scholars "should also be social and political scientists, as well as social critics and activists" (van Dijk 1993, 253). However, this does not mean that he dismissed the criticisms. He also warns analysts that they should not over-interpret discourse data (van Dijk 2006b, 129).

The social and critical dimensions of discourse were of particular interest to van Dijk, especially in relation to the historical and social context, in which different immigrants shape society. Thus, much of his research focused on racism, media, and ideology. His initial research interest in racism expressed in text and talk resulted in several subsequent studies on how ideology features discourse. As much as CDA, or in his terminology, critical discourse studies, emphasises how powerful institutions legitimise existing systems and values, rather than on individuals' exercise of power (as discussed earlier), he has critically examined how institutions, groups, and elites exercise social power to (re)create and (re)produce inequality in society. To this extent, he has argued that CDA focuses on the role of discourse in the (re)production and challenge of dominance, which he saw as "a form of social power *abuse*" (van Dijk 1996, 84, emphasis in original). Whilst accepting that CDA pays more attention to "'top-down' relations of dominance than to 'bottom-up' relations of resistance, compliance and acceptance", van Dijk also highlights that CDA scholars do not "see power and dominance merely as unilaterally 'imposed' on others" and that they focus on elites and their discursive strategies because power is jointly produced, legitimately executed, and considered natural, which in turn contributes to the maintenance of social inequality (van Dijk 1993, 250).

Because social power and dominance are often "*organised* and *institutionalised* so as to allow more effective control, and to enable routine forms of power reproduction", van Dijk stated that CDA aims to study and reveal "the precise cognitive structures and strategies involved in these processes affecting the *social cognitions* of groups" (van Dijk 1996, 85, emphasis in original). This is in line with Mills' (2003, 54) idea that a discourse should be thought of as "existing because of a complex set of practices which try to keep them in circulation and other practices which try to fence them off from others and keep those other statements out of circulation".

This is one reason why van Dijk's work has focused mostly on media discourse and minorities in society, particularly refugees and immigrants, as portrayed in the media. His consistent revelations of how underlying racist ideologies manifest in media across different cultures should be viewed in this context and have shown somewhat universal argumentation styles, semantic patterns, and storytelling strategies against immigration, as manifested in the media. By examining several empirical studies conducted in different cultures and languages, van Dijk revealed recurrent patterns in media practices and attitudes towards immigrants and ethnic minorities. For instance, his findings on conversations about immigrants in California and the Netherlands show similar patterns in terms of semantic strategies, storytelling, and argumentation against immigration and both exhibit "general patterns of Northern/Western prejudice against people in and from the South" (van Dijk 2011, 3). In addition, his later work has shown the significant and powerful role of the media in the discursive reproduction of racism by conforming to, constructing, and controlling group identity. He found that people who have no personal experience with immigrants or minorities tend to talk about them in a very similar way, on the basis of which he expanded existing studies of racism in the news to everyday talk and attributed the causal role to the mass media (van Dijk 2011, 3–4).

With such views regarding language and the media based firmly on his findings on the powerful role that the news media plays in influencing readers' mindsets, particularly in terms of racism, van Dijk has also analysed public discourse through textbooks, but his particular interest has been in ethnic (or racial) ideology.

Ideology, which is a system of beliefs, needs "a cognitive component that is able to properly account for the notions of 'belief' and 'belief system'" (van Dijk 2006b, 116). To a great extent, van Dijk has contributed to research on the relationship between ideology and discourse, particularly in terms of how people establish individual and group identities. Given that this process usually occurs through text and talk, van Dijk has extensively discussed ideology within his presentation of discourse analysis (e.g., van Dijk 1998; 2006b). Defining identity as "the fundamental beliefs of a group and its members" (van Dijk 2012, 5), van Dijk explained that it is shared by a collective of social actors but is also more fundamental than that in that it controls and organises other socially shared beliefs than types of shared knowledge that people have gradually acquired. Consequently, ideology is not necessarily negative. In addition, he argues that:

> if ideologies can be gradually developed by (members of) a group, they also gradually disintegrate [...] as, e.g. was the case for the pacifist and anti-nuclear movements of the 1970s [...] they are not some kind of 'false consciousness'[...] they are not necessarily dominant, but may also define resistance and opposition; they are not the same as discourses or other social practices that express, reproduce or enact them; and they are not the same as any other socially shared beliefs or belief systems [...] Some ideologies may thus *function to legitimate domination, but also to articulate resistance in relationships of power*, as is the case for feminist or pacifist ideologies. Other ideologies function as the basis of the 'guidelines' of professional behaviour—for instance for journalists or scientists.
>
> (van Dijk 2006b, 117, emphasis added)

As discussed in the next chapter, this view of ideology has inspired translation studies, not only because such a system of shared beliefs is the "basis of social practices" (van Dijk 2012, 8) but also because shared beliefs are inevitably different from one culture to another, as the members of each society must agree to and share them. Because the shared knowledge and beliefs of the source culture do not necessarily correspond with those of the target culture, a text produced in the source culture will not necessarily be acceptable to a target audience that has a different set of values; therefore, it would require various translation shifts, such as choosing different lexical items over others or censoring part of a text.

For van Dijk, ideology makes beliefs and shared knowledge more coherent; therefore, because ideology is represented through text and talk, it governs everyday situations. As a discourse studies scholar, his attention was drawn to how ideology has been appropriated by powerful institutions, primarily the news media, to control and legitimise certain discourses. With respect to the relationship between media discourses and readers, his interest lies in how media discourses form and alter the social presentations of readers about themselves as a group and about other groups, such as ethnic minority groups.

This explains why van Dijk has focused mostly on various media case studies concerning racist discourse, although he has examined various discourse genres, from business, academia, and politics to the media. His work was to investigate how "social representations about ethnic groups monitor the actions of the media users" (1991, 226–27) because he views racism as a system of domination (e.g., van Dijk 1987, 1991, 2000, 2011, 2016), arguing that many media end-users do not fully understand what they read, see, or hear; rather, they use information they can remember later and interpret it in their own way to suit their understanding of the world (van Dijk 1991, 228). Moreover, these processes are embedded in social, cultural, and political contexts, which means that the "socio-cultural action of newspaper reading, media use, or the socio-political position of the readers affect the process of understanding and belief formation" (van Dijk 1991, 228). His analysis of the properties of dominant discourses, such as the use of metaphor, storytelling, pronouns, and lexicon, as summarised in van Dijk (2015b, 475), reveals some common linguistic strategies that form the discourse of an 'imagined community'.[9]

Among many interesting models and concepts van Dijk developed in a series of discourse analytical studies is the Us–Them binary. The Us–Them binary, as a strategy that justifies inequality, may be among the most widely used models in media analysis and has been adopted by translation studies scholars (discussed in the following chapter). One pattern he identified in his continuous research on racism discourse is that racist ideologies typically organise people and society in polarized terms, which define who belongs to the in-group or out-group and is in the dominant or dominated position (van Dijk 2012, 33). Typically, the positive characteristics of an in-group (Us) are highlighted, and ideological beliefs may be presupposed, whereas the negative characteristics of an out-group (Them) are highlighted, and their ideological beliefs may be censored or modified. Negative in-group characteristics and positive out-group characteristics are mitigated (van Dijk 2006b, 2011). van Dijk (1998, 267) calls this the 'ideological square model'. van Dijk (2006a, 374) offers a good example that clearly shows discursive group polarisation and ideological constructions of the US and Them:

In the manipulative discourses that followed the September 11 and March 11 terrorist attacks in New York and Madrid, nationalist, anti-terrorist, anti-Islam, anti-Arab and racist ideologies were rife, emphasizing the evil nature of terrorists, and the freedom and democratic principles of the 'civilized' nations.

Thus, if Bush & Co. want to manipulate the politicians and/or the citizens in the USA into accepting going to war in Iraq, engaging in worldwide actions against terrorists and their protectors (beginning with Afghanistan), and adopting a bill that severely limits the civil rights of the citizens, such discourse would be massively ideological. That is, they do this by emphasizing 'Our' fundamental values (freedom, democracy, etc.) and contrast these with the 'evil' ones attributed to Others. They thus make the citizens, traumatized by the attack on the Twin Towers, believe that the country is under attack, and that only a "war on terrorism" can avert a catastrophe. And those who do not accept such an argument may thus be accused of being unpatriotic.

Discussion

The following examples, taken from an examination conducted by Gales (2009, 34) on discourses in threatening letters, show a clearer divide. These two excerpts are from threats sent to Senator Tom Daschle and Goldman Sachs following the catastrophic events of 9/11.

YOU CAN NOT STOP US.
WE HAVE THIS ANTHRAX.
YOU DIE NOW.
ARE YOU AFRAID?
DEATH TO AMERICA.
DEATH TO ISRAEL.
ALLAH IS GREAT.

GOLDMAN SACHS.
HUNDREDS WILL DIE.
WE ARE INSIDE.
YOU CANNOT STOP US.
A.Q.U.S.A.

How can you group the actors mentioned in the texts above? What about the power balance between/among the groups? Who has control over the situation? Who is powerless?

Here is an example from Kim and Choi's work (2023), taken from a different cultural setting, in which the Us–Them divide may not be as clear as in the previous examples. Shown below is an excerpt of an editorial published 2 July 2018[10] by Chosŏnilbo, a South Korean centre-right mainstream broadsheet newspaper popular in terms of circulation numbers in Korea.

The 1,000 attendees raised their voice saying, "[what we do is] not racism. [We] want safety". A protest group against 'against refugees', although much smaller in size [...] chants "against racism" and "there is no fake refugee" slogans [...]. It was noticeable that there were many young women in masks at the rally against [the refugees]. It seems anxiety over 'security' worked [...] disparate Islam culture and refugee crimes have even changed the social atmosphere in European society that was friendly to 'political refugees'.

The discoursal strategy employed to justify the anti-refugee movement in Europe is clearly shown, although no effort has been made to provide any evidence to support the claim that Europe has changed its position towards Muslim refugees. Furthermore, the media's polarised discourse clearly shows a 'negative Other' representation, which is employed to construct a negative image of refugees. Discourse against refugees is justified by bringing 'security' to the fore (i.e., 'our' decision to anti-refugee is because of 'security' reasons caused by 'Them'), in which refugees are constructed as threats to society.

As with any theory/approach/model, the ideological square model is often criticised for "its closed coding approach [that] may prevent more nuanced ideological critiques" and "overlook[ing] how Othering develops in media longitudinally" (Reynolds 2019, 51). Nevertheless, this model is certainly influential and has been widely used in studies examining, for example, the ideological construction of Iran's nuclear programme in American newspaper editorials (Izadi and Saghaye-Biria 2007), news headlines (Kharbach 2020), and even textbooks (van Dijk and Atienza 2011). Scholars of translation studies have also adopted this model, as discussed in the following chapter.

Practice essay questions

1 Can you think of any other examples in which language has changed because of shifts in social norms and standards, and vice versa?
2 Choose two different news reports on the same topic, preferably one from a centre-right-wing media and the other being centre-left on the socio-political spectrum. Identify the principal discourse constructed in each newspaper and discuss the discourse strategies and linguistic devices used.
3 Choose one language-learning textbook, identify any ideological polarisation patterns, see how others or other cultures are presented and discussed, and discuss them using van Dijk's ideological square model.
4 Choose one media report from a mainstream, centre-right source, and find an alternative, progressive media report with a different political slant. Compare the two, focusing on how their discourses and discourse strategies differ.

Notes

1 Other lesser-used (or lesser-known) approaches include Ruth Wodak's discourse-historical model (Wodak 1996; Hodge and Kress 1993) and Theo van Leeuwen's social actor framework (2014); however, they will not be discussed due to space restrictions.
2 The application of appraisal theory to translation studies is discussed in more depth in Chapter 3.
3 For discussions about Halliday's work and further development, see Martin and White (2005), Hasan (2014), Manfredi (2008, 2011) and Di Bari (2013).
4 'Field' is divided into further categories, as SFL views language as realised through the system of subjectivity, via participants, process, and circumstances. Thus, the 'content' of discourse concerns who is involved and what is happening in what situation. However, I do not go into each of these in detail as they are not the focus of this book. SFL is discussed here only to allude to appraisal theory, which has also been adopted in discourse analysis within the field of translation studies.
5 Mayo and Taboada's data are interesting, as much as their study itself. They examined discourse featured on *CosmoVotes*, a new website created by Cosmopolitan prior to the US midterm elections in November 2014 to encourage readers to vote and get engaged in various issues concerning women's rights, including "labour rights, abortion, contraception, health, minimum wage and social equity" (Mayo and Taboada 2017, 40).
6 www.grammatics.com/appraisal/(last accessed 5 April 2022)
7 Breeze (2011, 496) explains that the origins of this politicised concern with society can be traced to scholars within a Marxist or neo-Marxist tradition, like Frankfurt school – most notably Adorno.
8 See Chapter 5 of Catalano and Waugh (2020) for more detailed discussion of the criticisms of CDA.
9 See van Dijk (1993; 2006a; 2006b; 2011; 2012) for more details.
10 The translation is the authors'. Available at: https://news.chosun.com/site/data/html_dir/2018/07/01/2018070101359.html (accessed 06.15.20.). Korean ST: Ch'amsŏkcha 1000 myŏngŭn 'injongch'abyŏri anida. anjŏnŭl wŏnhanda'myŏ sorirŭl nop'yŏtta. Kyumonŭn hwŏlssin chakchiman 'nanmin pandae'e pandaehanŭn siwido […] "injongch'abyŏre pandaehanda", "katcha nanminŭn ŏpta"nŭn kuhorŭl oech'yŏtta. […] Masŭk'ŭrŭl ssŭn chŏlmŭn yŏsŏngdŭri pandae chiphoee manhŭn kŏtto nune ttŭiŏtta. 'Anjŏn'e taehan puran'gamjagyonghan kŏt kat'ta. […] Ijiljŏgin isŭllam munhwawa nanmin pŏmjoenŭn chŏngch'i nanmin'e uhojŏgidŏn yurŏp sahoe punwigikkaji pakkwŏnohatta.

Suggestions for further reading

Angermuller, Johannes, Dominique Maingueneau, and Ruth Wodak, eds. 2014. *The Discourse Studies Reader: Main Currents in Theory and Analysis*. Amsterdam & Philadelphia: John Benjamins.
Bax, Stephen. 2011. *Discourse and Genre: Analysing Language in Context*. London: Palgrave Macmillan.
Fairclough, Norman. 1989. *Language and Power*. London: Longman.
Hatim, Basil. 1998. "Discourse Analysis." In *Routledge Encyclopedia of Translation Studies*, edited by Mona Baker and Kirsten Malmkjaer, 88–92. Routledge.
Hatim, Basil. 2009. "Discourse Analysis." In *Routledge Encyclopedia of Translation Studies*, edited by Gabriela Saldanha and Mona Baker, Second edition, 88–92. Routledge.
Hatim, Basil, and Ian Mason. 1990. *Discourse and the Translator*. London: Longman.

Stubbs, Michael. 1983. *Discourse Analysis: The Sociolinguistic Analysis of Natural Language*. Chicago: The University of Chicago Press.
Widdowson, Henry G. 1995. "Discourse Analysis: A Critical View." *Language and Literature* 4 (3): 157–72.
Widdowson, Henry G. 2004. *Text, Context, Pretext: Critical Issues in Discourse Analysis*. Edited by Kirsten Malmkjaer. Oxford: Blackwell.
Wodak, Ruth, and Michael Meyer. eds. 2001. *Methods of Critical Discourse Analysis*. First edition. London: Sage.

References

Breeze, Ruth. 2011. "Critical Discourse Analysis and its Critics". *Pragmatics* 21 (4): 493–525.
Catalano, Theresa, and Linda R. Waugh. 2020. *Critical Discourse Analysis, Critical Discourse Studies and Beyond*. Berlin: Springer.
Fairclough, Norman. 1989. *Language and Power*. London: Longman.
Fairclough, Norman. 1992. *Discourse and Social Change*. Cambridge: Polity.
Fairclough, Norman. 1995. *Critical Discourse Analysis*. London: Sage.
Fairclough, Norman. 1996. "A Reply to Henry Widdowson's 'Discourse Analysis: A Critical View.'" *Language and Literature* 5 (1): 49–56.
Fairclough, Norman. 2003. *Analysing Discourse: Textual Analysis for Social Research*. London: Routledge.
Fairclough, Norman. 2013. *Critical Discourse Analysis: The Critical Study of Language*. 2nd edition. London and New York: Routledge.
Fairclough, Norman, and Ruth Wodak. 1997. "Critical Discourse Analysis." In *Discourse as Social Interaction*, edited by Teun A. van Dijk, 258–84. London: Sage.
Firth, John Rupert. 1957. "A Synopsis of Linguistic Theory 1930–1955." In *Selected Papers of J.R. Firth 1952–1959*, edited by Frank Robert Palmer, 168–205. London: Longman.
Gales, Tammy. 2009. "Identifying Interpersonal Stance in Threatening Discourse: An Appraisal Analysis." *Discourse Studies* 13 (1): 27–46.
González Rodríguez, María José. 2006. "Tracing Context in the Discourse of the Media: Features of Language-in-Use in the British Press." *Revista Alicantina de Estudios Ingleses* 19: 149–68.
Halliday, Michael Alexander Kirkwood, and Ruqaiya Hasan. 1985. *Language, Context and Text: Aspects of Language in a Social Semiotic Perspective*. Oxford: Oxford University Press.
Hasan, Ruqaiya. 2014. "Towards a Paradigmatic Description of Context: Systems, Metafunctions, and Semantics." *Functional Linguistics* 1 (9): 1–54. https://doi.org/10.1186/s40554-014-0009-y.
Hodge, Robert, and Gunther Kress. 1993. *Language as Ideology*. London: Routledge.
Huan, Changpeng. 2016. "Journalistic Engagement Patterns and Power Relations: Corpus Evidence from Chinese and Australian Hard News Reporting." *Discourse & Communication* 10 (2): 137–56.
Izadi, Foad, and Hakimeh Saghaye-Biria. 2007. "A Discourse Analysis of Elite American Newspaper Editorials: The Case of Iran's Nuclear Program." *Journal of Communication Inquiry* 31 (2): 140–65.
Kharbach, Mohamed. 2020. "Understanding the Ideological Construction of the Gulf Crisis in Arab Media Discourse: A Critical Discourse Analytic Study of the Headlines of Al Arabiya English and Al Jazeera English." *Discourse & Communication* 14 (5): 447–65.

Kim, Kyung Hye, and Jinsil Choi. 2023. "Discourses on Islamic Refugees in the South Korean News: A Corpus-Based Approach." *Journal of Immigrant & Refugee Studies* 21 (3): 349–362.

Leeuwen, Theo van. 2014. "The Representation of Social Actors." In *The Discourse Studies Reader: Main Currents in Theory and Analysis*, edited by Johannes Angermuller, Dominique Maingueneau and Ruth Wodak, 273–81. Amsterdam & Philadelphia: John Benjamins.

Li, Tao, and Fang Xu. 2018. "Re-Appraising Self and Other in the English Translation of Contemporary Chinese Political Discourse." *Discourse, Context & Media* 25: 106–13.

Li, Tao, and Yifan Zhu. 2020. "How Does China Appraise Self and Others? A Corpus-Based Analysis of Chinese Political Discourse." *Discourse & Society* 31 (2): 153–171.

Malinowski, Bronislaw. 1994. "The Problem of Meaning in Primitive Languages." In *Language and Literacy in Social Practice: A Reader*, edited by Janet Maybin, 1–10. Clevdon: Multilingual Matters, The Open University.

Martin, James R. 2000. "Beyond Exchange: Appraisal Systems in English." In *Evaluation in Text*, edited by Susan Hunston and Geoff Thompson, 142–75. Oxford: Oxford University Press.

Martin, James R. 2003. "Introduction." *Text* 23 (2): 171–181.

Martin, James R., and Peter R. R. White. 2005. *The Language of Evaluation: Appraisal in English*. New York: Palgrave Macmillan.

Mayo, María Aloy, and Maite Taboada. 2017. "Evaluation in Political Discourse Addressed to Women: Appraisal Analysis of Cosmopolitan's Online Coverage of the 2014 US Midterm Elections." *Discourse, Context & Media* 18: 40–48.

Mills, Sara. 2003. *Michel Foucault*. London & New York: Routledge.

Munday, Jeremy. 2001. *Introducing Translation Studies*. London and New York: Routledge.

Munday, Jeremy. 2015. "Engagement and Graduation Resources as Markers of Translator/Interpreter Positioning." *Target* 27 (3): 406–21. https://doi.org/10.1075/target.27.3.05mun.

Oteíza, Teresa. 2017. "The Appraisal Framework and Discourse Analysis." In *The Routledge Handbook of Systemic Functional Linguistics*, edited by Tom Bartlett and Gerard O'Grady, 457–72. London: Routledge.

Oxford Reference. 2021. "OVERVIEW: Context of Situation." Oxford University Press. www.oxfordreference.com/view/10.1093/oi/authority.20110803095634862.

Ozier, Owen. 2019. "Gendered Languages May Play a Role in Limiting Women's Opportunities, New Research Finds." The World Bank. 2019. www.worldbank.org/en/news/feature/2019/01/24/gendered-languages-may-play-a-role-in-limiting-womens-opportunities-new-research-finds.

Piser, Karina. 2021. "Aux Armes, Citoyen·nes!: Gender-Neutral Terms Have Sparked an Explosive Battle over the Future of the French Language." Foreign Policy. 2021. https://foreignpolicy.com/2021/07/04/france-gender-language-ecriture-inclusive-aux-armes-citoyennes/.

Reynolds, Chelsea. 2019. "Building Theory from Media Ideology: Coding for Power in Journalistic Discourse." *Journal of Communication Inquiry* 43 (1): 47–69.

Stubbs, Michael. 1997. "Whorf's Children: Critical Comments on Critical Discourse Analysis (CDA)." In *Evolving Models of Language*, edited by Ann Ryan and Alison Wray, 100–116. Clevedon: Multilingual Matters.

van Dijk, Teun A. 1987. *Communicating Racism: Ethnic Prejudice in Thought and Talk*. London: Sage.

van Dijk, Teun A. 1990. "Social Cognition and Discourse." In *Handbook of Language and Social Psychology*, edited by W. Peter Robinson and Howard Giles, 163–83. Chichester: John Wiley & Sons.
van Dijk, Teun A. 1991. *Racism and the Press*. London and New York: Routledge.
van Dijk, Teun A. 1993. "Principles of Critical Discourse Analysis." *Discourse & Society* 4 (2): 249–83.
van Dijk, Teun A. 1996. "Discourse, Power and Access." In *Texts and Practices: Readings in Critical Discourse Analysis*, edited by Carmen Rosa Caldas-Coulthard and Malcolm Coulthard, 84–104. London and New York: Routledge.
van Dijk, Teun A. 1998. *Ideology: A Multidisciplinary Approach*. London: Sage.
van Dijk, Teun A. 2000. "New(s) Racism: A Discourse Analytical Approach." In *Ethnic Minorities and the Media: Changing Cultural Boundaries*, edited by Simon Cottle, 33–49. Maidenhead and Philadelphia: Open University Press.
van Dijk, Teun A. 2001. "Critical Discourse Analysis." In *The Handbook of Discourse Analysis*, edited by Deborah Schiffrin, Deborah Tannen and Heidi E. Hamilton, 1st edition, 352–71. Oxford: Blackwell Publishers.
van Dijk, Teun A. 2006a. "Discourse and Manipulation." *Discourse & Society* 17 (3): 359–383.
van Dijk, Teun A. 2006b. "Ideology and Discourse Analysis." *Journal of Political Ideologies* 11 (2): 115–40.
van Dijk, Teun A. 2011. "Discourse and Racism: Some Conclusions of 30 Years of Research." Paper presented at *17th International Workshop on Critical Discourse Analysis*. Madrid / Short version: 2016. In *Interdisciplinary Studies in Pragmatics, Culture and Society* edited by Alessandro Capone and Jacob L. Mey, 285–295. Heidelberg: Springer.
van Dijk, Teun A. 2012. *Ideology and Discourse: A Multidisciplinary Introduction*. Online source. Available at: https://discourses.org/wp-content/uploads/2022/06/Teun-A.-van-Dijk-2012-Ideology-And-Discourse.pdf
van Dijk, Teun A. 2015a. "Context." In *The International Encyclopedia of Language and Social Interaction*, edited by Karen Tracy, Cornelia Ilie and Todd Sandel, 198–209. London: Wiley-Blackwell.
van Dijk, Teun A. 2015b. "Critical Discourse Analysis." In *The Handbook of Discourse Analysis*, edited by Deborah Tannen, Heidi E. Hamilton and Deborah Schiffrin, 2nd edition, 466–85. Oxford: John Wiley & Sons, Inc.
van Dijk, Teun A. 2016. "Racism in the Press." In *The Routledge Handbook of Linguistic Anthropology*, edited by Nancy Bonvillain, 383–92. New York and London: Routledge.
van Dijk, Teun A. 2017. "Socio-Cognitive Discourse Studies". In *Routledge Handbook of Critical Discourse Studies*, edited by John Flowerdew and John E. Richardson, 26–43. Oxon and New York: Routledge.
van Dijk, Teun A., and Encarna Atienza. 2011. "Knowledge and Discourse in Secondary School Social Science Textbooks." *Discourse Studies* 13 (1): 93–118.
White, Peter Robert Rupert. 2001. "Appraisal: An Overview. Manuscript (Word Processor Version)." 2001. www.grammatics.com/appraisal/appraisalguide/appraisalguidewpfiles.html.
White, Peter Robert Rupert. 2015. "Appraisal Theory." In *The International Encyclopedia of Language and Social Interaction*, edited by Karen Tracy, Cornelia Ilie and Todd Sandel, 1st edition, 1–7. New York: JohnWiley & Sons.
Widdowson, Henry G. 1995a. "Book Review: Norman Fairclough Discourse and Social Change." *Applied Linguistics* 16 (4): 510–16.

Widdowson, Henry G. 1995b. "Discourse Analysis: A Critical View." *Language and Literature* 4 (3): 157–72.

Widdowson, Henry G. 1996. "Reply to Fairclough: Discourse and Interpretation: Conjectures and Refutations." *Language and Literature* 5 (1): 57–69.

Wodak, Ruth. 1996. "The Genesis of Racist Discourse in Austria since 1989." In *Text and Practices: Readings in Critical Discourse Analysis*, edited by Carmen Rosa Caldas-Coulthard and Malcolm Coulthard, 107–28. New York and London: Routledge.

Wodak, Ruth. 2011. "Critical Linguistics and Critical Discourse Analysis." In *Discursive Pragmatics*, edited by Jan Zienkowski, Jan-Ola Östman and Jef Verschueren, 50–70. Amsterdam & Philadelphia: John Benjamins Publishing.

Wodak, Ruth, and Michael Meyer. 2009. "Critical Discourse Analysis: History, Agenda, Theory, and Methodology." In *Methods for Critical Discourse Analysis*, edited by Michael Meyer and Ruth Wodak, second rev, 1–33. London: Sage.

Xiao, Han, and Lei Li. 2021. "A Bibliometric Analysis of Critical Discourse Analysis and Its Implications." *Discourse & Society* 32 (4): 482–502.

Zhang, Meifang. 2002. "Language Appraisal and the Translator's Attitudinal Positioning." *Foreign Languages and Their Teaching* 7: 15–18.

3 CDA in translation studies

Key points of learning

- Halliday's SFL model has prompted scholars in translation studies to consider various other pragmatic approaches for translation when situational and cultural contexts change rather than limiting their choices to abide by the 'faithfulness' and 'translator's invisibility' mantras.
- Applying appraisal theory to identify translation shifts and interventions has primarily been restricted to 'attitude' in translation studies.
- van Dijk's ideological square has enabled translation studies scholars to examine ideological shifts in translation or translators' intervention in either reinforcing or challenging the ideology presented in the source text.
- Several scholars in interpreting studies have demonstrated how CDA helps reveal the ideological positioning of interpreters, interpreters' agency, mediation, intervention in ideologically laden conference interpreting, and how discourse analysis can be used to investigate how political discourse is reconstructed through interpreting in diplomatic settings.

In Chapter 2, I discussed critical discourse analysis (CDA) in depth, by reviewing various proposed definitions. I then considered three main approaches – M.A.K. Hallidayan, Norman Fairclough's, and Teun van Dijk's. When discussing these approaches in the current chapter, I will focus on how they have been adopted and employed in translation studies research. As I will demonstrate below, the three CDA-informed analytical frameworks, which are distinct from each other, have prompted translation studies scholars to explore a broader range of translation research avenues, such as the translation process, products, and the role of mediating agents.

In the first section, I will introduce how the three approaches have been applied to the study of translation and interpreting. In the second section, I will discuss the

DOI: 10.4324/9781003029083-4

application of CDA in translation studies, focusing on text types. I will demonstrate how the three theoretical and analytical frameworks discussed in the first section are applied to examine the three most widely examined text types (political, institutional, and media texts) and interpreting.

3.1 The three different approaches

As earlier alluded to, I will focus on the three main approaches in the first section of this chapter. However, I must clarify that these are not the only approaches adopted in translation studies. Those approaches, such as Ruth Wodak's discourse-historical approach, have also been employed by scholars to examine the translation and interpreting products and processes. However, because of space restrictions, I will have to focus on the following three. I do not intend to encourage readers to follow suit and adopt the same approaches; instead, I wish to demonstrate how each approach offers theoretical insights to translation and interpreting research scholars. Thus, I hope that readers of this book gain analytical and methodological insights from previous studies to apply alternative approaches to their research. The discussion begins by applying Halliday's SFL and the appraisal theory framework in translation studies.

3.1.1 M.A.K. Halliday's SFL-informed discourse analysis and appraisal framework-informed discourse analysis in translation studies

> "Translation (translating/interpreting) is meaning-making activity, and we would not consider any activity to be translation if it did not result in the creation of meaning [...] What is distinct about translation is that it is not just creation of meaning; it is guided creation of meaning"
>
> (Halliday 1992, 15)

As discussed in Chapter 2, Halliday's understanding of text and context was inspired by Malinowski's understanding of text, situation, and culture and Firth's understanding of context. However, Halliday further developed Firth's system into SFL. Considering language contextually, the SFL framework has inspired numerous translation studies scholars who deal with context-shifting texts. SFL focuses on how different meanings are constructed and how they reflect on language use in both form and meaning in various contexts. The Hallidayan SFL considerably influenced Norman Fairclough's work, whose CDA this book is based on, as he explains as follows:[1]

> In contrast with the more influential Chomskyan tradition within Linguistics, SFL is profoundly concerned with the relationship between language and other elements and aspects of social life, and its approach to the linguistic analysis of texts is always oriented to the social character of texts [...] This makes it a

valuable resource for critical discourse analysis, and indeed, major contributions to critical discourse analysis have developed out of SFL.

(Fairclough 2003, 5)

In particular, the view that text, the context of a situation, and the context of culture are intertwined has inspired discourse analysts, such as Fairclough, and helped scholars of translation and interpreting research to investigate why a particular word has been chosen for a corresponding translation over others. Moreover, it encourages them to consider various other pragmatic approaches for translation when the context of the situation and culture changes rather than limiting their choices to abide by the 'faithfulness' and 'translator's invisibility' mantras. SFL considers both the form and meaning of a text within a context and, more specifically, is a model that explains how meaning and society are intertwined and are reflected in linguistic choices through linguistic devices and various forms of language. Additionally, it helps translation studies scholars explain both translation products and processes. Kim and Matthiessen (2017, 11–12) aptly explain how SFL inspires translation studies scholars in terms of meaning:

> If we see translation as centrally involving the *recreation of meaning* through *choices* made by the translator in the interpretation of the source text and through choices in the generation of the translated text […], it follows that all modes of meaning are equally implicated: translation involves recreating ideational meanings of the logical kind, ideational meanings of the experiential kind, interpersonal meanings and textual meanings. Each metafunctional mode of meaning involves particular meaning-making resources — particular sets of systems in any language — and part of the difficulty translators face is that different languages may have evolved somewhat or even fairly different sets of *systems* for each metafunction.
>
> (Kim and Matthiessen 2017, 11–12, emphasis in original)

Similarly, Mira Kim, who provides an in-depth discussion of the application of SFL to translation and interpreting analysis, explains that SFL has been influential and is a highly effective tool for translator training since the metafunctional modes of meaning in SFL that "sees meaning as a multi-dimensional phenomenon – experiential, logical, interpersonal and textual" equip translators with a "formative assessment tool" (Kim 2016a, 6). In addition, SFL that describes language as a 'system of choices' can be used as a tool researchers can use to interpret "the different modes of meaning on the basis of lexis and grammar" (Kim 2016a, 6). Therefore, translation studies scholars could also examine translation choices "in each specific mode of meaning systemically on the basis of hard evidence found in texts" (Kim 2016a, 7). Manfredi summarises why and how the SFL-inspired translation studies:

> In an SFL paradigm, a speaker makes choices from within the total meaning potential of the language, i.e., its system. Each utterance encodes different kind of meanings, which are related to the functions of language. However, the grammatical resources responsible for realizing such meanings most often work differently across languages. Thus a translator, in order to accomplish his/her delicate task of interpreting and rendering a source text (henceforth ST) into a meaningful and effective target text (henceforth TT), needs to understand all these meanings, and reproduce them in another language.
> (Manfredi 2011, 51)

Perhaps one of the most well-known applications of SFL in translation studies is Mona Baker's textbook *In Other Words* (1992), in which, by adopting primarily the perspectives from pragmatics and SFL, Baker offers a vast array of examples to explain the equivalence of meaning in translation. Some other translation studies scholars who have adopted Halliday's systemic functional model for their analyses have focused on three components – field, tenor, and mode, which are associated with the metafunctions (i.e., experiential, interpersonal, and textual).[2] Hatim and Manson's work *Discourse and the Translator* (Hatim and Mason 1990) and *The Translator as Communicator* (Hatim and Mason 1997) are well-known examples of the application of SFL to translation and interpreting and are more relevant to this book's discussion of discourse analysis. The intertwined relationship between text and society and the crucial role that context plays in determining meaning and meaning-making processes in a communicative setting are acknowledged in Hatim and Mason's studies, where several SFL concepts, such as 'register', 'intertextuality', 'field', 'tenor', and 'mode', are adopted. These concepts have also been adopted by Juliane House, who developed a translation quality assessment model by applying Halliday's SFL theories of language. She first proposed the model in 1977 (shown in Figure 3.1) but later revised and refined the original model in 1997. In 2015, House updated the model again to reflect the growth and development of translation studies (Figure 3.2). In her 1997 model, House used the representative concepts of Halliday's 'register' (i.e., 'field', 'mode' and 'tenor'; see Chapter 2 for more details). In her 2015 work, House discussed the relevance of corpus studies for translation quality assessment and demonstrated that corpus studies offer "empirical substance to the previously rather vague notion of Genre" (2015, 126). Thus, she added 'corpus studies' to the updated model to establish the individual textual function and to compare and evaluate ST and TT for translational equivalence, as shown in Figure 3.2. Corpus studies and the corpus-based CDA approach are discussed in Chapter 4.

52 *Critical Discourse Analysis in Translation Studies*

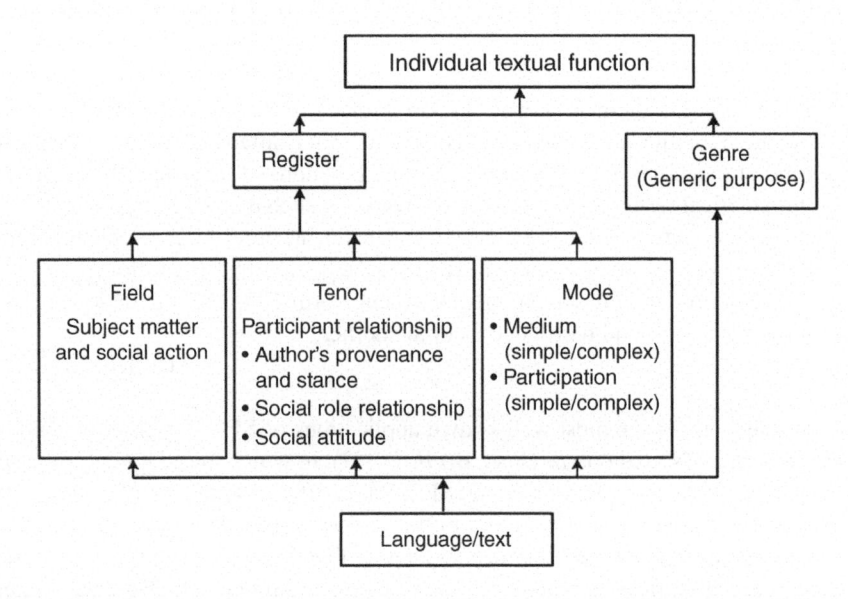

Figure 3.1 A scheme for analysing and comparing original and translation texts.
Source: House (1997, 108).

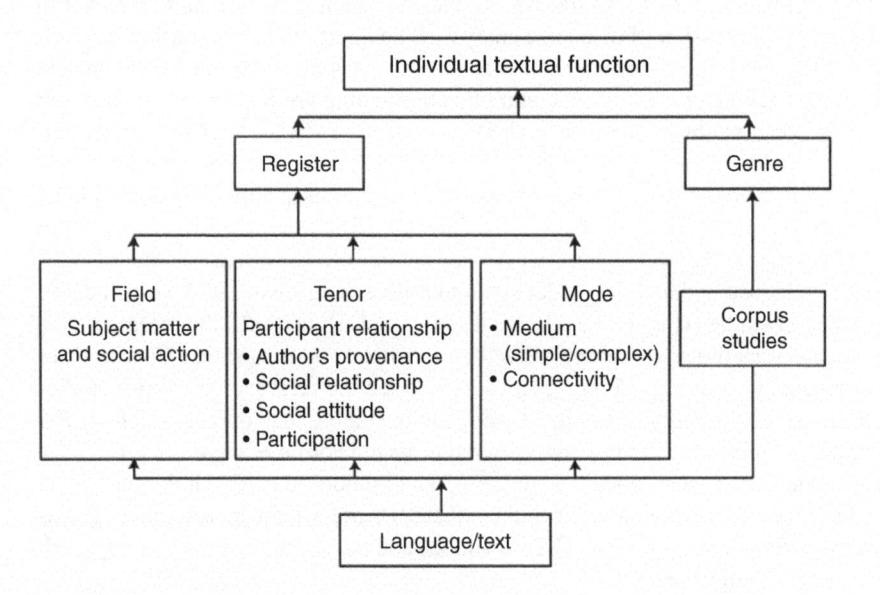

Figure 3.2 A revised model for analysing and comparing original and translation texts.
Source: House (2015, 127).

Textbooks and monographs, such as those discussed above, inspired several translation studies scholars by showing them the potential for applying SFL frameworks. This resulted in many special issues in academic journals, such as *Discourse Analysis in Translation Studies* edited by Munday and Zhang (2015) and *The Journal of Translation Studies special issue* in 2016 edited by Kim (2016b), which offer case studies that demonstrate how SFL is applied to the study of translation and examine translation choices and strategies that have different impacts on (re)creating meaning. Some of the most recent example studies that adopt the SFL model can be found in the special issue of *Meta: New Contexts in Discourse Analysis for Translation and Interpretation* (2020), edited by Munday and Calzada-Pérez. However, as Trosborg's (1997) detailed discussion of categories and terminologies (e.g., discourse, text, register, genre, text type) in the Hallidayan SFL approach shows, different scholars and different disciplines have used SFL terminologies in subtly different ways. Thus, it is crucial to define the SFL terminologies explicitly prior to the use of SFL in translation analysis.

A body of research articles that employ the SFL can also be found, with most of them analysing translations at three levels: experiential, interpersonal, and textual. For example, Mah (2018) showed that translation studies students enhanced their translation skills after they had been trained in the systematic categorisation of differences between English and Korean texts based on SFL's three meaning levels: experiential, interpersonal, and textual. Jing and White (2016) examined how interpersonal elements are translated in audiovisual translation. SFL's three strands of meaning also inspired Yu and Wu (2016) to investigate the construction of meaning in a narrative written in Chinese, with shifts in meaning in four English translations of the same Chinese tale. Lee (2020, 129) adopted the notion of 'theme' and 'rheme' in SFL when examining the thematic choices of the English translations of Korean statutes to identify the extent to which source text (hereafter ST) and target text (hereafter TT) clauses match in relation to the contents and grammatical functions.

The intriguing pattern found in SFL-informed studies within translation studies is that they also draw on other concepts to provide more holistic perspectives. For example, Othman (2020) employed it to develop a model for investigating explicitation-related phenomena in translation by focusing on an English-to-Arabic translation of the manner of motion verbs. Li (2020) used other concepts, such as voice, theme, and modality, and SFL's transitivity system as an analytical tool for investigating translation agency, ideology, characterisation, and narratives in text.

The SFL-inspired approach has also been adopted in corpus-based translation studies, and one of the most recent corpus-based works to adopt it is Calzada-Pérez (2020).[3] Notably, while most SFL-inspired translation studies research has been qualitative, Calzada-Pérez (2020) employed a quantitative approach (i.e., a corpus method) to identify patterns that are elusive to the human eye. She combined corpus linguistics and SFL-inspired discourse analysis in her recent work to examine 'individuation', the less-explored SFL perspective but where "meaning potential is specialised according to people" (Calzada-Pérez 2020, 146).

Practice essay question

Choose a ST and its corresponding translation. First, explain the rationale for the choice of your text. Next, identify and discuss translation shifts in three metafunctions and lexicogrammatical realisations from the Hallidayan SFL perspective.

You will need to provide a proper rationale for the text choice. Therefore, the essay should clearly present an in-depth analysis of both ST and TT in terms of context, meaning, and lexicogrammar. First, the definitions of the field, tenor, and mode should be provided, as a discussion of ideational, interpersonal, and textual meanings will follow this. On the one hand, for the analysis of ideational meanings, wording systems, such as transitivity, can be focused. On the other hand, mood, modality, and appraisal systems can be investigated to analyse meanings. Thematic structure and cohesion may be consulted when examining textual meanings. Subsequently, you will need to identify translation shifts through a comparative analysis of what you have identified.

Appraisal theory, which was developed within an SFL framework, has also increasingly been adopted in translation studies, as demonstrated in Munday (2018) and Zhang (2002). Munday and Zhang are probably the two scholars who observed the strengths of appraisal theory early on. Considering "all [translational] intervention to be evaluative" (Munday 2012a, 20), they analysed how values and attitudes expressed in the text are mediated through a translator (Munday 2012a, 101). Munday has shown, and demonstrated, how the system of appraisal (Martin and White 2005) can help identify a translator's intervention and subjective evaluation in much of his work (Munday 2010, 2012a, 2012b, 2015, 2018) and some academic journal special issues with Zhang (Zhang and Munday 2018).

However, among the three domains of appraisal, 'attitude', 'engagement', and 'graduation', as Munday (2012a, 31) observes, the application of appraisal theory to identify translation shifts and interventions has been restricted primarily to 'attitude', which Munday calls the "central pillar of the appraisal system" (2012b, 102). The concept of attitude has been used to explain evaluative resources of language, particularly in the analysis of news media texts. This is illustrated in the case of Zhang (2013), where the attitudes and values of media institutions in different cultures and how they are featured in translations are discussed through the analysis of trans-edited news headlines. The appraisal system has also been an effective tool for analysing translations of political discourse. Drawing on an appraisal framework, Pan and Huang (2021) analysed English articles and translations of Chinese President Xi Jinping's speeches delivered at international conferences. Their study is distinctive in that the research focus was on the political metaphors that Xi frequently used. Specifically, examining stance mediation in media translations of political metaphors, their study revealed that the value positions featured in Xi's use of metaphors are shifted when only parts are translated and contextualised, thus, "mediation of stance can be facilitated by contextual evaluation, such as that in the headlines and the surrounding words of the metaphors and other parts of news reports" even when metaphors are faithfully translated and quoted (Pan and Huang 2021, 147).

A Chinese scholar, Tao Li, has employed the appraisal system to examine English translations of Chinese political discourses. Li employed the appraisal system and van Dijk's ideological square to explain shifts in political discourse translation (this work will be discussed later in Section 3.1.3 on the application of van Dijk's models and 3.2.1). However, some of his studies (e.g., Li and Xu 2018; Li and Zhu 2020; Li and Pan 2021) have filled the research gap identified by Munday by focusing specifically on evaluative epithets in 'graduation' featured in Chinese–English translations of Chinese political discourse. Souza's (2010) study is also a key reference for the application of appraisal in translation studies. Pan and Liao (2021), who focused on a 'graduation' subsystem of appraisal theory, also demonstrated how appraisal theory, together with Fairclough's CDA, specifically the three-dimensional analytical procedure, can be employed to reveal news translators' mediation of (re)positioning, motivated by ideologies.

3.1.2 Norman Fairclough's three-dimensional model-informed research in translation studies

Valdeón (2007) was an earlier scholar who observed the benefit of adopting Fairclough's model for the analysis of translations – particularly media texts. He demonstrated how Fairclough's CDA framework can be applied in analysing the articles by BBC's Mundo, its Spanish service, and *CNN en Español*, CNN's Spanish version, alongside their English translations. Iețcu-Fairclough (2008) is another scholar who discussed translation practising CDA concepts, such as recontextualisation, strategy, and ideology. Based on Fairclough's CDA, she suggested viewing translation as "recontexualization of source-language texts in new social and cultural contexts [...in that] it is text producers and text receptors that attribute *illocutionary intentions to texts* in relation to their own strategies of action, background knowledge or worldview" (Iețcu-Fairclough 2008, 67, emphasis added). Her understanding of translation demonstrates the potential of applying the CDA framework to translation analysis, as shown in the following explanation:

> Whatever significances are intended by text-producers or inferred by audiences, these will be based on features of the (translated) text, and interpreted in relation to a social, cultural, political context. For instance, a translator may choose to translate a particular text and intend the translation to function as an act of protest and resistance against the political establishment, but these subversive intentions may be relatively alien to the source-language text.
>
> (Iețcu-Fairclough 2008, 67)

This will sound overtly straightforward to anyone in the current translation studies field. However, some scholars outside translation studies, particularly discourse studies scholars such as Isabela Ieţcu-Fairclough, have acknowledged the role played by translation. They have sought to understand translation activities through the CDA lens and have understood that political and ideological constraints can influence translations.

Among the body of CDA-informed translation studies conducted to date, such as those cited above, Bandar Al-Hejin's (2012) study is worth discussing in detail. He is a CDA scholar but proposed three main discourse analytical models for translation studies after reviewing several discourse studies conducted in translation studies. Although some studies focus more on translation practices or processes, others focus more on discursive and social practices. However, CDA-informed research in translation studies has primarily examined textual shifts in translation processes to examine the extent to which they are ideologically motivated (Al-Hejin 2012, 317). Based on previous literature that drew on the CDA framework in the field of translation studies, Al-Hejin proposed the following three models: (1) Model 1, where translation as a rewriting is emphasised; (2) Model 2, where translation as an intertextual chain is highlighted; and (3) Model 3, which emphasises translation as multiple versions. The first analytical model considers translation as a re-write. The first model conducts

> a textual analysis of a translation and then analyse the discursive and socio-cultural practices of the translator operating in the target language domain [...] Assuming that translators, like authors, are both ideological agents and subject to orders of discourse that impact their work, a translation can be viewed as a text in its own right which reflects the interests of a particular culture or group.
> (Al-Hejin 2012, 317)

Note that Fairclough's three-dimensional model appears in this model. Fairclough's model is applied particularly to the target culture environment, where the translation (target text) is considered within discursive practices and social practices.

Bandar Al-Hejin's second CDA-informed translation analysis model considers translation as an intertexual chain, where both a source text and a target text are examined at three levels – text, discursive and social practices. In this second model, Fairclough's model applies to both source and target texts. As Al-Hejin rightly explains, although it requires further analysis, it helps researchers consider particular linguistic choices in the source culture and language context and enables them to better understand any "intended function and discursive impact" (2012, 318).

Note that Al-Hejin also acknowledges retranslation in this second model. As Fairclough's model explains, a text is inextricably intertwined with various contexts (e.g., historical, economical, socio-political...). Indeed, the exact text can be retranslated for multiple reasons, one of which is led by shifts in the historical, socio-political context, as shown in much of the previous literature on retranslation (e.g., Koskinen and Paloposki 2003; Tahir Gürçağlar 2009; Deane-Cox 2014; Alvstad and Rosa 2015; Kim 2018; Charlston 2020).

The third model views translation as multiple versions. This third type of analytical model is for comparative CDA analyses of a single text's multiple translations. Al-Hejin (2012) explained that what makes the third model different from the second one is that the target texts are "all primary translations of the same SL [source language] text rather than forming an intertextual chain based on retranslations" (2012, 319). Here, CDA analysis is applied to different translation contexts of the same source text. Thus, multiple translations in multilingual and multicultural settings, as is the case in international organisations, such as the European Union (EU), the United Nations (UN), and the World Health Organisation (WHO), can be examined using the third analytical model. *Life and Death in Shanghai* by Cheng (1987), for example, was originally written in English and has been translated into several languages, from simplified to traditional Chinese, Korean and Japanese, all of which can be examined using the third model.

However, these three models are not the only CDA-informed translation analytical models; there is room for further development and refinement. For example, Baumgarten (2007, 2009) drew on CDA to analyse eleven English translations of Hitler's *Mein Kampf*. Baumgarten examined eleven English translations produced by different mediating agents in various cultural, temporal, and geographical settings; thus, it fell under Al-Hejin's third analytical model type. However, compared with Al-Hejin's model, the analytical steps Baumgarten (2007) undertook in his study provided more pronounced attention to the issue of agency in the translation process. Baumgarten (2007, 43) first investigated socio-cultural, political, and ideological preconditions for translation events. The study subsequently examined situative-agentive practices employed within individual translation events, as well as the paratexts and structural and textual features of individual translation profiles. Finally, it considers context and text variables, such as human agency. Furthermore, the three models of the CDA framework applied to translation analysis, as proposed by Al-Hejin, do not consider the relationships among different translations, even when previous translations may have impacted the subsequent translations, as shown in the discussion of the translation hypothesis (Berman 1990; Koskinen and Paloposki 2003; Brownlie 2006). Nevertheless, Al-Hejin's proposal remains one of the first attempts to establish analytical models for CDA-applied translation analysis.

Practice essay question

Drawing on the CDA framework, Baumgarten (2007) examines eleven English translations of Hitler's *Mein Kampf* written in German to identify strategies employed by institutions in ideologically inspired and institutionally translated political discourse.

> Employing Al-Hejin's third analytical model, discuss what discursive and socio-cultural practices surrounding the German source text (*Mein Kampf*) and translations published in the USA and the UK, for example, must be considered when analysing translations.

3.1.3 Teun van Dijk's ideological square: structures and strategies of communicative events, ideology, and identity

Chapter 2 mentioned that the key to van Dijk's discourse analysis approach is that it **emphasises** what happens in the human mind and society. His approach concerns how social power controls people's minds, where discourse is understood to be a key mediator. His analytical model, therefore, explains how discourse and society influence each other, such as how social structures are affected by discourse structures and how discourse structures are influenced by social structures through the mind (cognition/ideology). His model focuses on "the discursive proliferation of ideologies as cognitive representations shared by different social groups", whereby "the interpretation of ideology and language is thought to be most fruitfully examined on the three analytical levels of discursive activity, human cognition and social value orientations" (Baumgarten 2007, 39). Thus, 'ideology', the "foundational beliefs that underlie the shared social representations of specific kinds of social groups" (van Dijk 2006, 120), is one of the core concepts in his CDA model, particularly his ideological square (1998), one of the most representative analytical models in his CDA approach proposal. van Dijk's CDA model has been applied to the study of the translation of discourses that serve specific ideological interests, such as "colonial and hegemonic power relations [...], nationalist agitation [...], and the politics of resistance" (Baumgarten and Schröter 2017, 139). In particular, van Dijk's ideological square has enabled translation studies scholars to examine ideological shifts in translation or translators' intervention in reinforcing or challenging the ideology presented in the source text.

Representing, constructing, challenging, and reshaping a national image through translation has been subject to continual research. In recent years, scholars in mainland China have actively conducted such research. They adopt various analytical frameworks and research methodologies to identify how the national image of China is constructed by itself ('Self') and the extent to which it has been challenged or reshaped in the translation process ('Other') (see Chapter 2 – Section 3 for more details). Among the approaches widely employed is van Dijk's ideological square, which focuses on different social group ideologies and cognitive representations. Li has frequently adopted van Dijk's ideological square model in his analysis of discourse shifts in translation (e.g., Li and Pan 2021; Li and Xu 2018). In one of his recent studies, Li and his co-author Pan examined English translations of Chinese political discourse, drawing both on the ideological square model and the appraisal system, and argued that both approaches share common ground (Li and Pan 2021, 357) because "ideologies feature *evaluative beliefs or opinions*" (van Dijk 1998, 33, emphasis in original). Li and Pan's study is worth discussing in more detail because its findings present what contrasts with the ideological square.

In their work, they identify and investigate translation shifts in Chinese political discourses, comprising ninety files (1,469,213 Chinese characters and 1,090,850 English words) in reports by the National Congress of the Communist Party of China, work reports and white papers issued by the central Chinese government, and their translations.

Because translation is an "ideology-governed social practice" (Li and Pan 2021, 365), they examine the agency of translators and discuss their findings regarding the political and social systems of translation values in the translation community. Since the translators and mediators in their study were government officials, Li and Pan regard them as the "institutionalised part of the Chinese government, and thus are subservient to the authoritative source authorship" (Li and Pan 2021, 366). Interestingly, contrary to the expectation that translators, who are government officials, would strictly adhere to canonical translation guidelines and principles, certain translators who do not share the ideological translation principles of Chinese political discourse appear to present more translation shifts and emphasise on the norms and target readers of the receiving culture (Li and Pan 2021, 366). Consequently, any positive image constructed in the Chinese source text was shifted, in translation, to negative, whereas a negative image of China (Self) was emphasised. Consequently, this created a pronounced contradiction to van Dijk's ideological square structure of positive self-presentation. Li and Pan (2021, 367–68) explain that it is almost impossible that such translation shifts received no attention in several rounds of translation and editing processes given the "authoritative China's voice [in the Chinese political documents examined in this study] that requires extremely cautious translation and the translation participants are top-ranked translators and editors, including native speakers of English, with professional expertise in both Chinese and English".

Based on such a pronounced shift, which conflicts with van Dijk's ideological square model, Li and Pan suggested refining the existing model by proposing that two layers be applied to it based on Chinese diplomatic principles. See below how they developed the argument.

[t]he negative image of China is discursively presented in the TTs within a superficial layer of Ideological Square Model, but translation shifts and variations in China's image mediated by the translators, we argue, have a deeper purpose of serving China's interests within a deeper layer of Ideological Square Model to meet the requirement of the governing self-serving principle. This proposal can trace its evidence from the governing principles of China's diplomatic policies, particularly those established by Mr Deng Xiaoping, the general designer of China's Reform and Opening-up, which were followed by subsequent generations of Chinese leaders. These principles can be summarised and are known as 'Keep a low profile and make a contribution'. […] the discursive fact

of a more negative image of China in the TTs is attributed to the translators' aim to ultimately achieve an implicitly positive image of China within a deeper layer of Ideological Square model governed by the self-serving principle.

(Li and Pan 2021, 367)

Li and Pan's study is an excellent example of how a proposed model can be further developed. Several other interesting studies such as this have been undertaken to showcase how the ideological square model can be used to explain translation shifts involving ideology, although I cannot comprehensively discuss this here, due to space restrictions. However, van Dijk's framework of CDA has been used to elucidate ideological manipulation in subtitling (Joz, Ketabi, and Dastjerdi 2014), to investigate ideo-political manipulation in political TV documentary subtitling (J. Li 2019), and to examine the diachronic analysis of ideological shifts identified in political press conference interpreting in China (Gu and Tipton 2020).

Practice essay question

Daghigh, Sanatifar, and Awang (2018) examined 31 Persian news opinion articles, which were translated from English and published in *Diplomacy-e-Irani* [Iranian Diplomacy] between 1 April and 30 June 2013. They intentionally chose the article that discussed the controversies over Iran's nuclear programme. The following is one of the examples provided in the study (emphasis added).

ST1
It would have to agree to completely open all Iranian nuclear facilities to regular inspections by the IAEA (**which has thus far refused to do so**) (Purzycki, 2013).

TT1
.نخست ایران باید مجوز ورود بازرسان به تمامی سایت های هسته ای اش را بدهد

Back Translation
First, Iran would give permission to inspectors to enter all its nuclear sites.

Here is another example:

ST2
And Obama's decision last week to send small arms to the rebels in Syria is hardly a step likely to make Iran feel better about Washington's regional objectives (Walt 2013).

TT2
برای مثال تصمیم هفته گذشته اوباما به منظور ارسال سلاح برای معترضان سوری قطعا بدبینی بیشتری را در نگاه ایران نسبت به اهداف منطقه ای واشنگتن حاکم کند.

Back Translation
For example, the last week decision by Obama to send arms for Syria rebels absolutely sheds more pessimism on Iran's view toward Washington's regional objectives.

The following is the historical background provided in the study (Daghigh, Sanatifar, and Awang 2018):

1 Since the establishment of the Islamic Republic of Iran in 1979, following the Islamic revolution and a referendum, Iran has had conflicts with the USA, the UK, and Israel. Iran's nuclear programme increased the degree of conflict and tension between Iran and those countries, particularly the USA and the UK.
2 "Article 56 of Chapter 8 of the Iranian constitution categorizes a number of countries, mainly the USA and Israel, as hostile governments"
3 "Chapter 2 of the law states the missions of the media. Among the missions described in this chapter are those that
    1 promote the goals stated in the constitution of the Islamic Republic of Iran;
    2 disclose the hostile nature and position of Western governments, including their hegemonic policies; and
    3 promote the policies of the Islamic Republic of Iran worldwide."
4 "Chapter 4 of the [Iranian media] law bans several cases, among which are those that noticeably
    1 promote ideas that negatively affect the Islamic Republic of Iran;
    2 insult the officials of the country, specifically the Supreme Leader; and
    3 violate political, social, economic, and cultural policies of the Islamic Republic of Iran."

Considering the above socio-political context, identify translation shifts in the examples provided and explain them using van Dijk's ideological square.

3.2 Text types

In the previous section, I discussed how the three main CDA frameworks and models – SFL/ appraisal theory-informed approach, Fairclough's three-dimensional model, and van Dijk's ideological square – are used to investigate ideologically motivated discourse shifts in translation. However, it is also useful to understand how CDA analysis has been undertaken in translation studies in relation to the genre of the examined text.

Topics such as racism, institutional discourse, capitalism, genre, immigration, and media language have been the subject of primary CDA research. Regarding these topics, the main interest of CDA has been to reveal hidden ideologies and to discover how certain discursive structures have been employed to control or bring changes to social structures and interactions, such as through domination, oppression, and power control. Thus, the most widely studied text genres in CDA-informed translation analysis have been political texts, such as political speeches, and institutional texts, such as news media. This is not surprising, considering that political figures who deliver political speeches and institutions have the power to disseminate discourses and influence, control, oppress, and dominate society through discourses. Such power is reflected in language use and is exercised through discourses.

In what follows, I will discuss how a CDA framework can provide theoretical insight for translation and interpreting research by focusing on studies examining political and institutional discourses and their translations. Moreover, I will spare some space in the concluding section of this chapter for CDA-informed research into interpreting studies. Admittedly, it is challenging to categorise previous studies into political and institutional discourses, because political discourses are often disseminated through political institutions, such as foreign offices, international relations offices, and global news media institutions like *CNN*. Nevertheless, given the large body of literature on political discourse analysis in translation studies, I will discuss studies of political text genre and political discourse translations in a separate section.

3.2.1 Research on the political and diplomatic settings in translation studies

Translations in political and diplomatic contexts are critical in either strengthening or weakening political ties. For example, the documentation of the USA foreign relations between 1977 and 1980 highlights discussions about translation problems encountered while translating the Shanghai Joint Communique (Office of the Historian, n.d.). The memorandum states that "we never saw the Chinese translation of the joint normalisation communique. We worked entirely in English. We were assured by Leonard that the translation posed no problems. I have now learned that the Chinese text departs from the Shanghai communique", where the English word 'acknowledge' was translated initially as 'jen shih tao' [认识到] to 'cheng-jen' [承认]. The reports add that a few linguists say the latter "denotes a stronger acceptance of the Chinese position" than does the former. This is followed by some suggestions for the USA's responses "should this line of attack materialize" (Office of the Historian, n.d.). This example demonstrates that translation is salient and conspicuous in elevating or diffusing conflicts.

Indeed, as Chilton and Schäffner (2002, VII) rightly mentioned, language plays a vital role in politics and communication, and politics and language are intimately intertwined. Moreover, it can be observed from the example above that it is not surprising that one of the most widely studied text types in CDA-informed research is the political text genre. At face value, political discourse analysis may sound straightforward. However, considering this in greater depth raises a series of questions, such as what is political discourse?", "what are the characteristics of political discourse?", "what forms of features does political discourse have?", and "how can we define political discourse?". These questions require a profound understanding of political discourse, together with some comprehension of related concepts, including 'institution', 'power', 'inequality', 'manipulation', 'ideology' and 'media'. This is why much CDA research in translation studies that examine political discourse examines ideology, a translator's agency and power, and the mediatory role of a translator (e.g., Schäffner 2003; Kuo and Nakamura 2005; Munday 2007; Doerr 2017; Li and Xu 2018; Li and Pan 2021).

A bibliometric analysis by Lijuan Du and Wenliang Chen (2022) provides an overview of research on political discourse and translation. To examine English translations of Chinese political discourses, they examined previous studies published in international academic journals between 1990 and 2020, including the geographical areas where political discourse in translation was most prevalent. The result reveals that while political discourse in and of translation was first mentioned in 1994, research in this area was sporadic until 2010, with only six articles published. The number of articles increased to twelve by 2014 and further to thirty by 2018, marking the highest number of articles published between 1990 and 2010.

Du and Chen's study is distinct from all the other studies because it presents the keyword clusters of political discourse research. The 758 keywords from the 155 articles examined in their study were investigated to identify patterns using the visualisation and clustering technique in the VOSviewer tool. It returned the eight most prominent keyword clusters in political discourse analysis (Du and Chen 2022, 7–9): the first cluster related to linguistic analysis where transitivity and translation shifts are examined. Corpus-based discourse analysis, Chinese political discourse, and journalism are other terms strongly associated with the first cluster. Li and Pan's corpus-based discourse analysis work, mentioned earlier, which drew heavily on Martin and White's appraisal system and van Dijk's ideological square model to examine the English translations of Chinese political discourses, provided a representative example of this cluster. The second cluster concerned ideology and manipulation. Here, media, ideology, and political discourses were most frequently discussed. The third cluster related to social media, power, and political communications mediated by translation. The fourth cluster concerned political discourse and interpreting, the fifth cluster involved political discourse and recontextualisation, and the sixth cluster encompassed translation and diplomacy. The seventh cluster concerned diplomatic translation. Finally, cluster eight involved conflict and politics. These eight keyword groupings enable us not only to understand the concepts and themes examined together (e.g., 'ideology, manipulation, and media', 'political discourse in interpreting', and 'political discourse and recontextualization') but also to identify research gaps, such as political discourse interpreting in a diplomatic setting.

64 *Critical Discourse Analysis in Translation Studies*

These scholars also investigated cocitation ties among the articles on political discourse and translation, which revealed Christina Schäffner's numerous studies as a central reference point. As a translation scholar, Schäffner has worked on diverse topics, mostly discourse-related, such as text and discourse, metaphors, news translation, and institutional discourses (Schäffner 1997b, 2004, 2008, 2012, 2015a, 2015b; Schäffner and Bassnett 2010; Schäffner, Tcaciuc, and Tesseur 2014).

Schäffner has worked extensively on political discourses and translation, inspiring numerous fellow scholars by demonstrating how the CDA framework can be exploited in research. At the same time, she showed discourse studies scholars how translation can play a significant role in re/deconstructing political discourses. Much of Schäffner's work has revealed a link between translation and mediating agents, such as translators embedded in socio-political and ideological contexts and mediated institutional forms of political discourse. She has also enhanced the understanding of the political consequences of translating political discourses through continued discussions about translation and interpreting practices and their influence on the dissemination and reception of translated political discourses and the power relations exercised in political settings. Some of her work on political discourse and translation is worth reviewing, at least briefly, because she has made a significant contribution to the field and beyond.

In her early work in 2004, Schäffner demonstrated how combined political discourse and translation analysis synergised. She indicated the lack of understanding in discourse studies of translation in general and the role of translation in discourse construction, in particular, where translated or interpreted political discourses, such as political speeches, are analysed in discourse studies without acknowledging that "translators work in *specific socio-political contexts*, producing target texts for *specific purposes*" (Schäffner 2004, 137, emphasis added). She focused on the relationship between discourse and social and political structures and stressed that textual features must be analysed in relation to the "social and ideological contexts of text production and reception" because "texts and discourses are framed by social and political structures and practices" (Schäffner 1997a, 131–32). She emphasises that more attention needs to be paid to the nature of translation because it operates in a new socio-cultural and political context, as translations "have their own profiles which came about by decisions that were taken by a translator who was working in specific conditions" (Schäffner 2004, 138). She explained that the analysis of translations also helps identify universal or culture-specific metaphors and ideological and socio-cultural values. See the following example from her work (Schäffner 2004, 138, also available Baumgarten and Gagnon 2016, 198), which illustrates this point.

  a Source Text (English)
     "In this election, the parties of the Left challenge those of the Right on two fronts. [...] We reject the posture of the Right [...] reject the short-sighted focus of the Right on narrow national interest [...]" (PES Manifesto 1999)

b Target Text (German)
"Bei dieserWahl werden die sozialdemokratischen und sozialistischen Parteien sich besonders in zwei Bereichen mit der Politik der Konservativen auseinander zu setzen haben. [...] wir lehnen es ab [...] wir lehnen die kurzsichtige Ausrichtung auf nationale Interessen ab [...]"

c Back translation (literal translation)
In this election the Social-Democratic and Socialist parties will have to challenge the policies of the Conservatives especially in two areas. [...] we reject [...] we reject the short-sighted focus on narrow national interest [...]

This example clearly shows the translator's intervention, or translational shift: the German translation avoids the political labels used in the source text, such as 'the Left', 'the Right', where the ideologically charged labels are replaced by 'Socio-Democratic and Socialist parties", and 'the Conservatives'.

Similarly, in the volume Schäffner edited with Susan Bassnett in 2010, she emphasised another less-explored area – multilingual government websites. These are increasingly multilingual, but as many have already noticed, multilingual versions are often vastly different from sources and each other. Many reasons exist for such discrepancies, from economic, such as limited resources or funds, to the target-audience approach, whereby information of most interest is placed in the foreground. Some information may not be available in multilingual versions of a government website for political and ideological reasons (which involve power). For example, snapshots from the Tourism Authority of Thailand, which appear in multilingual versions, present pronounced differences: Figure 3.3–3.6. Different images foregrounded on the main page show what the institution considers of interest to the respective target audience.

Figure 3.3 The snapshot of the Thai Government website in Thai (captured 2 December 2023).

Figure 3.4 The snapshot of the Thai Government website in Korean (captured 2 December 2023).

Figure 3.5 The snapshot of the Thai Government website in Polish (captured 2 December 2023).

Interestingly, even when there are hundreds of Aboriginal languages and Indigenous Australians in Australia, the Australian government website is presented only in English, which provides many discussion points regarding language, power, and inequality. See Figure 3.7.

Figure 3.6 The snapshot of the Thai Government website in Spanish (captured 2 December 2023).

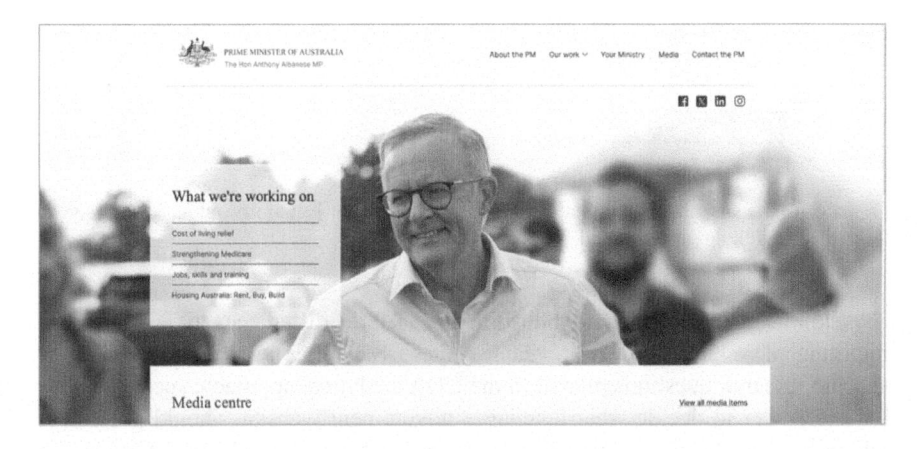

Figure 3.7 The snapshot of the Australian government website, offered only in English, http://australia.gov.au (captured 2 December 2023).

Another example is taken from the State Information Service of Egypt's website, which is available in five languages: Arabic, English, French, Spanish, and Chinese. These targets tell us who the government considers the most important; however, they each receive different picture layouts and amounts of information: Figures 3.8–3.11.

Figure 3.8 The snapshot of the State Information Service of Egypt in Arabic, www.sis.gov.eg/?lang=ar (captured 2 December 2023).

Acknowledging the marked, but sometimes subtle, differences in translation on multilingual government websites such as these, Schäffner poses some translation-specific research questions related to the CDA analytical approach, such as: "who has the power to decide what languages government websites should present?", "Who decides what is to be translated, and for what reasons?", "Who translates the texts?" Additionally,

> Are they in-house translators or is translation out-sourced? [...] "Are some texts translated by politicians and/or political advisors and/or staff themselves? [...] For example, on the basis of which criteria are speeches by the UK Prime Minister translated into which language(s) and by whom, and on the basis of which criteria are speeches by foreign politicians translated into English and by whom? Are the criteria the same, and if not, why not?
>
> (Schäffner 2012, 119)

Figure 3.9 The snapshot of the State Information Service of Egypt in English (captured 2 December 2023).

Schäffner's interest in political discourse has not been limited to the mode of translation but has extended to interpreting. She has investigated interpreter-mediated press conferences and political communication across national borders, where political reality has been (re)constructed (Schäffner 2015a, 2015b). Apart from drawing our attention to the imbalance in the power of political actors (e.g., some political actors are heard more often than others are), she demonstrates that translation is not a value-free activity but is embedded in institutional practices, "which in turn are determined by institutional policies and ideologies" (Schäffner 2012, 121). Some research questions she suggested for translation studies still provide us with a number of critical lenses through which translation and interpreting

70 *Critical Discourse Analysis in Translation Studies*

of political discourses: "What actually are the translation practices in political institutions, what is their translation policy, who are the actual agents who take all these decisions?", which includes sub-questions such as "Who produces the different language versions of joint policy statements?", "Who decides on the form of interpreting to be chosen? Is the interpreters' performance monitored? If yes, by whom?" (Schäffner 2012, 121–122).

Figure 3.10 The snapshot of the State Information Service of Egypt in French (captured 2 December 2023).

As alluded to earlier, there is much common ground between media and political discourses, as they fall under the institutional discourse umbrella. This explains why Schäffner has also actively worked on media discourses. In the subsequent section, I also mention her work when discussing how CDA work is applied to the study of translations of media discourses.

Figure 3.11 The snapshot of the State Information Service of Egypt in Chinese (captured 2 December 2023).

3.2.2 Institutional discourses in translation studies

'Institution' is a complex concept that is widely used and loosely defined. However, institutional translation mostly refers to "the act or product of linguistic mediation carried out by individual or collective actors on behalf of or for the benefit of institutions" (Kang 2020, 256). In translation studies, as Kang (2020, 257) observes, it has been used more concretely, where institutional translation refers to translations conducted at an institutional level, such as "international or supranational organization, national governments, news organizations and private companies" (cf. see Theo Hermans' work in 1997, who used 'institution' in his work 'Translation as Institution'). In that sense, studies of courtroom translation and interpreting, translation and interpreting in a medical setting, and (news) media translation all fall under the 'institutional translation research' category. The interest in translation activities and translation products within institutional settings has resulted in several interesting studies to date (e.g., Kang 2014 and Zhang and Pan 2015).

Kang, who has also worked extensively on news translation in Korea from a CDA perspective (e.g., 2007 2008, 2010), explains that two major developments have impacted both institutional translation in particular and translation studies in general (2020, 257–58): (1) the expansion of translation and interpreting services at the EU and (2) the increased interest in sociological aspects of translation. The studies I referred to in Section 3.2, which consider translation as socio-cultural and political acts and focus on its impact, were mostly the result of the second development. The main research questions addressed in such studies include who is translating what, when and for whom?', and 'what has (not) been translated and why?' (Kang 2020, 257–58). Spiessens (2015) addressed similar research questions when she analysed the news coverage of the Russian–Ukrainian confrontation in Crimea in 2014, including "how is the news presented on the website? Which articles are selected for translation? To which textual and extratextual strategies do the translators resort? How are the opponents in the conflict identified? Which voices are heard and which muted?".

Kang (2020) grouped the studies of institutional translations into three categories. Notably, in this context, they enable us to have a general idea of the copious research on translations of institutional discourse. The first group focuses on *institutional culture*, where the norms, regulations and policies related to translation, institutional procedures and roles, and the networks of related institutions and activities (Kang 2020, 258) are examined. Examples include translation activities at national translation bureaus and the way in which official institutional document translations are framed and regulated at the European Commission. The second group of research Kang identifies focuses on "the *process and product* of translation undertaken in institutions" (2020, 258, emphasis added). From text selection to the way in which translation activities de/recontextualise the source text is subject to research in this second strand of research. The third group, which focuses on "[d]ifferent forms of agency and their impact on the institutional order" (Kang 2020, 259), concerns the *actors* – translators and interpreters within the institutional setting.

Not all these groups of studies have drawn on the CDA framework. Koskinen (2000, 2008, 2009, 2014) has worked extensively on institutional translation and most of her studies have been part of Kang's first group that examines institutional culture. However, none of these studies have drawn on the CDA framework. Even when media discourse is frequently mentioned in studies of the latter two groups, CDA is not explicitly used as theoretical insight.

Much of institutional discourse analysis in translation studies has examined media discourses (e.g., Al-Hejin 2012; Kamyanets 2021, 2022; Kang 2007, 2008a, 2008b, 2012; Pan 2014, 2015; Pan and Liao 2021; Schäffner and Bassnett 2010; Valdeón 2007). Although not all these studies have necessarily adopted the CDA framework, the use of Fairclough's CDA model and Martin and White's appraisal theory is noticeable. Alongside Al-Hejin (2012), who vividly demonstrated what Fairclough's CDA model offers textual analyses of the translations of media texts (as discussed in 3.1.2), Li Pan has used Fairclough's three-dimensional model in her analyses of the translations of news media discourses. Pan (2014) focuses on institutional practices in news translation, using *Reference News*, a Chinese state-run newspaper, as an example. Her work offers new insight into the institutional practices of a state-run news organisation, as opposed to private types, by showing a marked agency of translators at a state-run media institution. According to Pan, translators who are "expected to be information transmitters" were found to have expressed their own beliefs regarding news translations; hence, they "function as part of the gatekeeping institution in the mediation between the different social contexts" (2014, 557). In a 2015 study, Pan employed Fairclough's three-dimension model of CDA (Fairclough 1995a, 1995b) alongside Martin and White's (2005) appraisal theory. Pan investigated the ideologically different positioning featured in Chinese translations of English news reporting on China's human rights issues published in the same state-run media institution, *Reference News*. Fairclough's CDA framework has also been used by Angela Kamyanets (2021, 2022), who examined Ukrainian and Russian translations of three news reports, initially published in English on BBC News, to identify translation shifts and ideological implications.

Spiessens and van Poucke (2016) used CDA when examining discourses constructed in news reports about the Crimean crisis in 2014, when the disputed Crimean status referendum was held concerning the status of Crimea. Articles by *The Guardian*, *Wall Street Journal*, *Le Monde*, and *Le Figaro* and their Russian translations by *InoSMI* (Inostrannye sredstva massovoi informacii or foreign media) were investigated. Translational shifts, including omissions, downgrading, and selective appropriation, were identified, and the research finding was in line with van Dijk's ideological square model, where *InoSMI* "mitigates Russia's aggressive behaviour, downplays alarming reports on the region's economic health and endorses a strong president image, while at the same time discrediting oppositional forces and excessively foregrounding existing criticism on the West's handling of the conflict" (2016, 336).

Practice Essay Question

Shown below is taken from Spiessens and van Poucke's (2016, 327–328) work:

Example 1 French ST (*Le Figaro*, 8 March)
(Poutine) a mené une opération de 'gesticulation calculée', comme disent les militaires

Gloss
[(Putin) engaged in an operation of 'calculated posturing', as the military say]

74 *Critical Discourse Analysis in Translation Studies*

> **Russian TT (*InoSMI*)**
> Президент России сделал просчитанный ход
>
> **Gloss**
> The Russian president made a well-calculated move
>
> **Example 2 English ST (*Wall Street Journal*, 14 March)**
> … we are living in a time of uprisings, from the Mideast to Africa to the streets of Kiev …
>
> **Russian TT (*InoSMI*)**
> … мы вступили в эпоху восстаний, охвативших Ближний Восток, Африку, и
>
> И теперь перекинувшихся на Украину …
>
> **Gloss**
> we have entered a time of uprisings, covering the Middle East, Africa, and nowmoving over to Ukraine
>
> *'Kiev' in the English ST refers to Ukrainians rally on Maidan Nezalezhnosti (Independent Square) in Kiev, protesting against Russia's intervention.
>
> Identify translation shifts in these examples, focusing on word choices and the use of quotation marks, and discuss the shifts in terms of the discourse constructed in each media.

3.2.3 Discourse studies in interpreting studies

Interpreting is another area where such dynamic interactions are conducted. It involves face-to-face human interaction in various in-situ contexts, frequently in international and transnational contexts concerning regional or global issues, such as diplomatic, press, and presidential/prime ministerial press conferences. The foreign media briefing at a time of crisis in Korea is an example of such a context. A prime ministerial international media briefing was arranged following the deadly Halloween crowd crush incident in Itaewon, Seoul, in 2022, when almost 160 people, including Koreans and non-Koreans, were crushed to death, whereas 200 others were injured. This is an example of a press conference where interpreting services are essential.

Many scholars in interpreting studies have demonstrated how CDA helps to reveal the ideological positioning of interpreters, interpreters' agency, mediation, and intervention in (particularly ideologically laden) conference interpreting. They have also indicated how CDA can be used to investigate how political discourse is reconstructed through interpreting in diplomatic settings (Fu and Chen 2019; Gao 2021; Gao and Munday 2023; Gao and Wang 2021, 2019; Gu 2018; Gu and

Tipton 2020; Gu 2021). Mason (2015) and Okoniewska and Wang (2021) present in detail an overview of the development of the discourse analytical approach in interpreting and its application in various settings. Mason (2015) overviewed the previous scholarship in relation to the main methodological approaches: mainstream discourse analysis, conversational analysis, and CDA, whereas Okoniewska and Binhua Wang (2021) identified the following six topics and approaches of research on discourse analysis in conference interpreting while reviewing previous literature: (1) cognitive processing of discourse: knowledge-based comprehension and mental models; (2) the pragmatic perspective of discourse analysis: context, agency, and facework; (3) the socio-interactional perspective of discourse analysis; (4) critical and systemic functional analysis of interpreted discourse; (5) discourse analysis as applied to interpreting strategies; and (6) discourse analysis applied in interpreter training pedagogy. The intersection between discourse analysis and interpreting studies was also discussed by Binhua Wang and Jeremy Munday (2021). Given the focus of this book – CDA in translation studies – and due to its limited space, I will restrict my discussion in this section to CDA-informed interpreting research.

Generally, the two analysis steps are systematically undertaken in studies of CDA-based interpreting research. First, interpreters' intervention through linguistic means is identified at the micro level. Subsequently, the discourse de(re) construction led by such intervention is discussed at the macro level (e.g., Gu 2018; Gu and Tipton 2020).

Morven Beaton-Thome (2007, 2013, 2020) has extensively worked on discussing ideological shifts in simultaneous interpreting in the European Parliament context using CDA. In her 2013 work, she examined German and English simultaneously interpreted plenary debate in 2009 from the European Parliament on the potential resettlement of Guantánamo detainees. Focusing on the choice of the lexical labels in the ST used to refer to those detained, such as 'criminals', 'inmates', 'illegal detainees' and 'innocents' and interpreted texts, she discussed interpreters' negotiation and contestation strategies. In the 2020 work, she also discussed lexical labelling and evaluative language featured in the plenary debates on Brexit and simultaneous interpreting practice in the European Parliament. Her study expanded the application of CDA by using it in examining the agency and role of interpreters in multilingual settings/discourse.

Gu has also continuously researched ideological interventions made by interpreters and shifts in discourses in the interpreter-mediated conference interpreting settings by drawing on a CDA framework. In much of his research to date, he adopts a quantitative analytical method, called corpus-based analysis, to overcome the CDA framework limitations that CDA examines a limited number of texts (see Chapter 2 for a discussion of the limitations of CDA; also, see Chapter 4 for more on corpus-based analysis). Gu worked with Tipton (2020), using the CDA framework to examine the government-affiliated interpreters' mediation of the Chinese government's discourse. Some of Gu's work draws particularly on van Dijk's ideological square. In his 2018 work, Gu investigated interpreter-mediated premier press conferences in mainland China and revealed how interpreters from Chinese into English mediated the government's discourses on its past accomplishments. He specifically focused on the use of the present-perfect structure in interpreting political press conferences when discussing China's past actions and achievements. Interestingly, the results demonstrated interpreters' habitual tendency in the interpreted discourse to use present perfect – which implied continuity – structures when reporting the government's accomplishments. Even when the Chinese ST allowed interpreters to select between the simple past and the present perfect, the interpreters actively chose the latter. This disproportionate use of present-perfect structures in the interpreting "leads to a stronger level of achievement, positive self-portrayal, and resultantly, political legitimisation" (Gu 2018, 137). This aligned with what van Dijk (1997) identified as 'positive self-representation' and 'national self-glorification'.

Gu and Wang (2021), still employing the CDA framework but moving beyond micro lexico-grammatical analysis, emphasised the act of interpreting in various political-institutional contexts that can create new meaning potentials. They argue that interpreters are "important (re)tellers of the Chinese story in English amid a major push for Beijing to have its voice heard internationally and to counterbalance the dominant Western-centric ideological discourse" (Gu and Wang 2021, 391). However, it is essential to note that Gu and Wang further acknowledged the possibility that what is already mediated interpreted discourses are being (re)contextualised again by different agents for diverse purposes in multi-semiotic ways and modalities (Gu and Wang 2021, 391). They added:

> The act of (re)contextualising and (re)enacting the interpreted discourse is inevitably selective and subjective in nature, which might involve foregrounding and backgrounding […] certain elements over others and the placement of certain interpreted discourse in a new context for certain effects […] The involvement of various subjective actors highlights how the (re)packaged interpreted product might be used to serve the ideological goals and institutional agendas of certain media outlets. Possibly, the interpreted discourse might be (re)contextualised and quoted to weaken or strengthen certain party/actors' position and legitimacy and to defame or undermine the ideological other.
>
> (Gu and Wang 2021, 391)

Unlike Gu's work, Li and Zhang (2021) employed CDA to examine consecutive interpreted Chinese foreign minister's annual press conferences between 2016 and 2018 to investigate interpreters' gatekeeping practices (a custom-made corpus was built for this study, and this will be discussed further in Chapter 4). Other studies that draw on van Dijk's ideological square to analyse interpreting include Gao (2021) and Gao and Munday (2023), in which appraisal theory is employed as well. Bartłomiejczyk (2022) employed appraisal theory when investigating ideological shifts in Polish and English simultaneously interpreted Eurosceptic discourse, but the shifts introduced by interpreters during plenary debates in the European Parliament were discussed in relation to the constraints and characteristics of simultaneous interpreting.

Political and media discourses are not the only discourse types that interest scholars in interpreting studies. For example, Claudia Angelelli applied the CDA framework to investigate interpreted communicative events in a healthcare setting. In her 2011 work, she investigated healthcare-provider-patient conversation about chronic illness during a medical interview at a public hospital on the west coast of the USA. She investigated interaction dynamics, including the power differentials between the healthcare provider and the patient. In this case, the CDA framework enabled Angelelli to examine the power shift between the two within the interpreting process by focusing more on the interpreters' role in mitigating or reinforcing the power differentials. She also interviewed the interpreter, further strengthening the main argument.

However, like any research, CDA is not immune to criticism, and this has already been discussed in Chapter 2. A similar limitation has also been highlighted for CDA-informed research of interpreting. Ian Mason explains that:

> One problem involved in all such studies arises from the tenets of CDA itself. Precisely because CDA posits that power relations in society control discourse and discourse shapes power relations in society, there is a danger of circularity in analysis: talk is explained by pre-existing power relations and the power relations are explained by talk. In many cases of CDA, no independent evidence is presented.
>
> (Mason 2015, 115)

A quantitative analytical approach is employed alongside CDA-informed research to counter such limitations. We can also transcend this limitation by offering "triangulation of the findings and a source of evidence external to the analyst" (Mason 2015, 115). For example, interviews with interpreter informants, as shown in Angelelli's work (2011), can be one way to address this issue. Then, how can we provide a 'source of evidence' to support our findings of the CDA-informed translation analysis? A typical quantitative analytical method called corpus-based analysis can be one of the keys, and this approach will be comprehensively discussed in the next chapter.

Notes

1 However, Fairclough also makes it clear that the aim of SFL and CDA is different, and highlights that there is a need to develop a "transdisciplinary" dialogue between the study of language and discourse within social theory "in order to develop our capacity to analyse texts as elements in social processes" (2003, 5–6).
2 See Section 2.1 for more details.
3 See Chapter 4 for more about 'corpus'.

Suggestions for further reading

Al-Hejin, Bandar. 2012. "Linking Critical Discourse Analysis with Translation Studies: An Example from BBC News." *Journal of Language and Politics* 11 (3): 311–35. https://doi.org/10.1075/jlp.11.3.01alh.

Baumgarten, Stefan, and Melani Schröter. 2017. "Discourse Analysis, Interpreting and Translation." In *The Routledge Handbook of Translation Studies and Linguistics*, edited by Kirsten Malmkjær, 135–50. Oxon and New York: Routledge.

Hatim, Basil, and Ian Mason. 1990. *Discourse and the Translator*. London: Longman.

Hatim, Basil, and Ian Mason. 1997. *The Translator as Communicator*. London and New York: Routledge.

House, Juliane. 2015. *Translation Quality Assessment: Past and Present*. London: Routledge.

Li, Tao, and Feng Pan. 2021. "Reshaping China's Image: A Corpus-Based Analysis of the English Translation of Chinese Political Discourse." *Perspectives* 29 (3): 354–70.

Manfredi, Marina. 2011. "Systemic Functional Linguistics as a Tool for Translation Teaching: Towards a Meaningful Practice." *Rivista Internazionale Di Tecnica Della Traduzione = International Journal of Translation* 13: 49–62.

Mason, Ian. 2015. "Discourse Analytical Approaches." In *Routledge Encyclopedia of Interpreting Studies*, edited by Franz Pöchhacker, 111–16. London: Routledge.

Munday, Jeremy. 2010. "Evaluation and Intervention in Translation." In *Text and Context*, edited by Mona Baker, Maeve Olohan and Maria Calzada-Pérez, 77–94. Manchester: St. Jerome.

Schäffner, Christina. 2004. "Political Discourse Analysis from the Point of View of Translation Studies." *Journal of Language and Politics* 3 (1): 117–50.

Schäffner, Christina, and Susan Bassnett, eds. 2010. *Political Discourse, Media and Translation*. Newcastle upon Tyne: Cambridge Scholars Publishing.

References

Al-Hejin, Bandar. 2012. "Linking Critical Discourse Analysis with Translation Studies: An Example from BBC News." *Journal of Language and Politics* 11 (3): 311–35. https://doi.org/10.1075/jlp.11.3.01alh.

Alvstad, Cecilia, and Alexandra Assis Rosa. 2015. "Voice in Retranslation: An Overview and Some Trends." *Target* 27 (1): 3–24.

Angelelli, Claudia. 2011. "'Can You Ask Her about Chronic Illnesses, Diabetes and All That?'" In *Methods and Strategies of Process Research: Integrative Approaches in Translation Studies*, edited by Cecilia Alvstad, Adelina Hild and Elisabet Tiselius, 231–46. Amsterdam: John Benjamins.

Baker, Mona. 1992. *In Other Words: A Course Book on Translation*. London and New York: Routledge.

Bartłomiejczyk, Magdalena. 2022. "Interpreting Nonmainstream Ideology (Euroscepticism) in the European Parliament." *Perspectives* 30 (4): 678–94. doi:10.1080/0907676X.2021.1939740.

Baumgarten, Stefan. 2007. *Translation as an Ideological Interface: English Translations of Hitler's Mein Kampf*. PhD Thesis. Birmingham: Aston University.

Baumgarten, Stefan. 2009. *Translating Hitler's "Mein Kampf": A Corpus-aided Discourse-analytical Study*. Saarbrücken: VDM Verlag Dr Müller.

Baumgarten, Stefan, and Chantal Gagnon, eds. 2016. *Translating the European House: Discourse, Ideology and Politics – Selected Papers by Christina Schäffner*. Newcastle upon Tyne: Cambridge Scholars Publishing.

Baumgarten, Stefan, and Melani Schröter. 2017. "Discourse Analysis, Interpreting and Translation." In *The Routledge Handbook of Translation Studies and Linguistics*, edited by Kirsten Malmkjær, 135–50. Oxon and New York: Routledge.

Beaton, Morven. 2007. *Intertextuality and ideology in interpreter-mediated communication: The case of the European Parliament*. Doctoral thesis, Heriot-Watt University.

Beaton, Morven. 2013. "What's in a word? Your 'enemy combatant' is my 'refugee'. The role of simultaneous interpreters in negotiating the lexis of Guantánamo in the European Parliament." *Journal of Language and Politics* 12 (3): 378–399. https://doi.org/10.1075/jlp.12.3.04bea

Beaton, Morven. 2020. "Flagging the homeland: Interpreting Brexit à la Nigel Farage in the European Union." In *Multilingualism and Politics. Revisiting Multilingual Citizenship*, edited by Katerina Strani, 105–127. Palgrave Macmillan.

Berman, Antoine. 1990. "La Retraduction Comme Espace de Traduction." *Palimpsestes* 13 (4): 1–7.

Brownlie, Siobhan. 2006. "Narrative Theory and Retranslation Theory." *Across Languages and Cultures* 7 (2): 145–70.

Calzada-Pérez, María. 2020. "A Corpus-Assisted SFL Approach to Individuation in the European Parliament: The Case of Sánchez Presedo's Original and Translated Repertoires." *Meta* 65 (1): 142–67.

Charlston, David. 2020. *Translation and Hegel's Philosophy: A Transformative, Socio-Narrative Approach to A.V. Miller's Cold-War Retranslations*. London and New York: Routledge.

Cheng, Nien. 1987. *Life and Death in Shanghai* . New York: Grove Press.

Chilton, Paul, and Christina Schäffner. 2002. *Politics as Text and Talk: Analytic Approaches to Political Discourse*. Amsterdam and Philadelphia: John Benjamins.

Daghigh, Ali Jalalian, Mohammad Saleh Sanatifar, and Rokiah Awang. 2018. "Modeling van Dijk's Ideological Square in Translation Studies: Investigating Manipulation in Political Discourse Translation." *InTRAlinea* 20. www.intralinea.org/archive/article/modeling_van_dijks_ideological_square_in_translation_studies.

Deane-Cox, Sharon. 2014. *Retranslation: Translation, Literature and Reinterpretation*. London: Bloomsbury-Continuum.

Doerr, Nicole. 2017. "Bridging Language Barriers, Bonding against Immigrants: A Visual Case Study of Transnational Network Publics Created by Far-Right Activists in Europe." *Discourse & Society* 28 (1): 3–23.

Du, Lijuan, and Wenliang Chen. 2022. "Political Discourse and Translation Studies. A Bibliometric Analysis in International Core Journals." *Sage Open* 12 (1). https://doi.org/10.1177/21582440221082142

Fairclough, Norman. 1995a. *Critical Discourse Analysis: The Critical Study of Language*. London and New York: Longman.

Fairclough, Norman. 1995b. *Media Discourse*. London: Arnold.

Fairclough, Norman. 2003. *Analysing Discourse: Textual Analysis for Social Research*. London: Routledge.

Fu, Rongbo, and Jing Chen. 2019. "Negotiating Interpersonal Relations in Chinese–English Diplomatic Interpreting: Explicitation of Modality as a Case in Point." *Interpreting* 21 (1): 12–35.

Gao, Fei. 2021. "Making Sense of Nationalism Manifested in Interpreted Texts at 'Summer Davos' in China." *Critical Discourse Studies* 18 (6): 688–704.

Gao, Fei, and Jeremy Munday. 2023. "Interpreter Ideology: 'Editing' Discourse in Simultaneous Interpretin." *Interpreting* 25 (1): 1–26.

Gao, Fei, and Binhua Wang. 2021. "Conference Interpreting in Diplomatic Settings: An Integrated Corpus and Critical Discourse Analysis." In *Empirical Studies of Translation and Interpreting: The Post-Structuralist Approach*, edited by Caiwen Wang and Binghan Zheng, 95–113. London: Routledge.

Gu, Chonglong. 2018. "Forging a Glorious Past via the 'Present Perfect': A Corpus-Based CDA Analysis of China's Past Accomplishments Discourse Mediat(Is)Ed at China's Interpreted Political Press Conferences." *Discourse, Context & Media* 24:137–49.

Gu, Chonglong. 2019. "Mediating 'Face' in Triadic Political Communication: A CDA Analysis of Press Conference Interpreters' Discursive (Re)Construction of Chinese Government's Image (1998–2017)." *Critical Discourse Studies* 16 (2): 201–21.

Gu, Chonglong. 2021. " 'The Main Problems in China-Japan Relations Lie in the FACT That Some Leaders in Japan Keep on Visiting the Yasukuni Shrine': A Corpus-Based CDA on Government Interpreters' Metadiscursive (Re)Construction of Truth, Fact and Reality." In *Advances in Discourse Analysis of Translation and Interpreting: Linking Linguistic Approaches with Socio-Cultural Interpretation*, edited by Binhua Wang and Jeremy Munday, 40–63. London and New York: Routledge.

Gu, Chonglong, and Rebecca Tipton. 2020. "(Re-)Voicing Beijing's Discourse through Self-Referentiality: Acorpus-Based CDA Analysis of Government Interpreters'discursive Mediation at China's Political Press Conferences (1998–2017)." *Perspectives* 28 (3): 406–23.

Gu, Chonglong, and Binhua Wang. 2021. "Interpreter-Mediated Discourse as a Vital Source of Meaning Potential in Intercultural Communication: The Case of the Interpreted Premier-Meets-the-Press Conferences in China." *Language and Intercultural Communication* 21 (3): 379–94.

Halliday, Michael Alexander Kirkwood. 1992. "Language Theory and Translation Practice." *Rivista Internazionale Di Tecnica Della Traduzione* no 0: 15–25.

Hatim, Basil, and Ian Mason. 1990. *Discourse and the Translator*. London: Longman.

Hatim, Basil, and Ian Mason. 1997. *The Translator as Communicator*. London and New York: Routledge.

Hermans, Theo. 1997. "Translation as Institution." In *Translation as Intercultural Communication*, edited by Mary Snell-Hornby, Zuzana Jettmarová and Klaus Kaindl, 3–20. Amsterdam/Philadelphia: John Benjamins.

House, Juliane. 1977. *A Model for Translation Quality Assessment*. Tübingen: Narr.

House, Juliane. 1997. *Translation Quality Assessment: A Model Revisited*. Tübingen: Narr.

House, Juliane. 2015. *Translation Quality Assessment: Past and Present*. London: Routledge.

Ieţcu-Fairclough, Isabela. 2008. "Critical Discourse Analysis and Translation Studies: Translation, Recontextualization, Ideology." *Bucharest Working Papers in Linguistics* 10 (2): 67–72.

Jing, Yi, and Peter R. R. White. 2016. "Why Audiovisual Translators Downplay the Interpersonal: The Case of 'Interjections' in English-to-Chinese Movie Subtitling." *Journal of Translation Studies* 17 (4): 107–42.

Joz, Rasool Moradi, Saeed Ketabi, and Hossein Vahid Dastjerdi. 2014. "Ideological Manipulation in Subtitling: A Case Study of a Speech Fragment by Mahmoud Ahmadinejad (President of the Islamic Republic of Iran)." *Perspectives* 22 (3): 404–18.

Kamyanets, Angela. 2021. "Ideological Shifts in the BBC Headlines Translated into Ukrainian and Russian." *Perspectives* 30 (1): 86–102. doi:10.1080/0907676X.2021.1891269.

Kamyanets, Angela. 2022. "Selective Appropriation in the BBC News Translated into Ukrainian and Russian." *Journalism* 23 (7): 1548–66.

Kang, Ji-Hae. 2007. "Recontextualization of News Discourse." *The Translator* 13 (2): 219–42.

Kang, Ji-Hae. 2008a. "Pŏnyŏkkisaŭi chemoge kwanhan yŏn'gu [An Analysis of Headlines of Translated News Magazine Articles]." *Pŏnyŏkhagyŏn'gu [The Journal of Translation Studies]* 9 (2): 7–43.

Kang, Ji-Hae. 2008b. "'Pŏnyŏgesŏ inyongŭi munje: CNN.com nyusŭt'eksŭt'ŭrŭl chungsimŭro' [Speech Representation in News Translation]." *Pŏnyŏkhagyŏn'gu [The Journal of Translation Studies]* 9 (4): 7–40.
Kang, Ji-Hae. 2012. "Translating Mad Cow Disease: A Case Study of Subtitling for a Television News Magazine." *Meta: Journal Des Traducteurs* 57 (2): 439. https://doi.org/10.7202/1013955ar.
Kang, Ji-Hae, ed. 2014. *Translation in Institutions: Special Issue of Perspectives.* Vol. 22, 469–628. Routledge.
Kang, Ji-Hae. 2020. "Institutional Translation." In *Routledge Encyclopedia of Translation Studies*, edited by Mona Baker and Gabriela Saldanha, 3rd edition, 256–61. Oxon and New York: Routledge.
Kim, Kyung Hye. 2018. "Retranslation as a Socially Engaged Activity: The Case of The Rape of Nanking." *Perspectives: Studies in Translatology* 26 (3): 391–404. https://doi.org/10.1080/0907676X.2017.1388413.
Kim, Mira. 2016a. "SFL, an Empowering Tool for Translation Studies." *Pŏnyŏkhagyŏn'gu [The Journal of Translation Studies]* 17 (4): 5–10.
Kim, Mira, ed. 2016b. *The Journal of Translation Studies Special Issue.* 4th edition,. Vol. 17. The Korean Association for Translation Studies.
Kim, Mira, and Christian M. I. M. Matthiessen. 2017. "Ways to Move Forward in Translation Studies: A Textual Perspective." In *Discourse Analysis in Translation Studies*, edited by Jeremy Munday and Meifang Zhang, 11–26. Amsterdam/Philadelphia: John Benjamins Publishing Company.
Koskinen, Kaisa. 2000. "Institutional Illusions: Translating in the EU Commission." *The Translator* 6 (1): 49–65.
Koskinen, Kaisa. 2008. *Translating Institutions: An Ethnographic Study of EU Translation.* London and New York: Routledge.
Koskinen, Kaisa. 2009. "Going Localised – Getting Recognised. The Interplay of the Institutional and the Experienced Status of Translators in the European Commission." *Hermes: Journal of Languages and Communication in Business* 42: 93–110.
Koskinen, Kaisa. 2014. "Institutional Translation: The Art of Government by Translation." *Perspectives* 22 (4): 479–92.
Koskinen, Kaisa, and Outi Paloposki. 2003. "Retranslations in the Age of Digital Reproduction." *Cadernos* 11 (1): 19–38.
Kuo, Sai-hua, and Mari Nakamura. 2005. "Translation or Transformation? A Case Study of Language and Ideology in the Taiwanese Press." *Discourse & Society* 16 (3): 393–417.
Lee, Jieun. 2020. "Hanyŏng pŏmnyul pŏnyŏgesŏ chuje (theme) sŏnt'aege kwanhan sarye yŏn'gu: ch'egyeginŭngjuŭi ŏnŏhakchŏk kwanjŏmesŏ [A Case Study on the Thematic Choices of English Translations of Korean Statutes from the Theoretical Perspectives of Systemic Functional Linguistics]." *T'ongyŏkkwa pŏnyŏk [Interpretation and Translation]* 22 (2): 129–56.
Li, Jingjing. 2019. "Political TV Documentary Subtitling in China: A Critical Discourse Analysis Perspective." *Perspectives* 28 (4): 554–74. https://doi.org/https://doi.org/10.1080/0907676X.2019.1609533.
Li, Long. 2020. "Shifts of Agency in Translation: A Case Study of the Chinese Translation of Wild Swans." *Meta* 65 (1): 168–92.
Li, Tao, and Feng Pan. 2021. "Reshaping China's Image: A Corpus-Based Analysis of the English Translation of Chinese Political Discourse." *Perspectives* 29 (3): 354–70.
Li, Tao, and Fang Xu. 2018. "Re-Appraising Self and Other in the English Translation of Contemporary Chinese Political Discourse." *Discourse, Context & Media* 25: 106–13.

Li, Tao, and Yifan Zhu. 2020. "How Does China Appraise Self and Others? A Corpus-Based Analysis of Chinese Political Discourse." *Discourse & Society* 31 (2): 153–71.

Li, Xin, and Ranran Zhang. 2021. "Interpreting as Institutional Gatekeeping: A Critical Discourse Analysis of Interpreted Questions at the Chinese Foreign Minister's Press Conferences." In *Advances in Discourse Analysis of Translation and Interpreting*, edited by Binhua Wang and Jeremy Munday, 106–27. London: Routledge.

Mah, Seung-Hye. 2018. "Developing SFL-Based Language Awareness on Differences between English and Korean Writing Styles and Its Implications for Literary Translation." *Pŏnyŏkhagyŏn'gu [The Journal of Translation Studies]* 19 (5): 7–41.

Manfredi, Marina. 2011. "Systemic Functional Linguistics as a Tool for Translation Teaching: Towards a Meaningful Practice." *Rivista Internazionale Di Tecnica Della Traduzione = International Journal of Translation* 13: 49–62.

Martin, James R., and Peter R. R. White. 2005. *The Language of Evaluation: Appraisal in English*. New York: Palgrave Macmillan.

Mason, Ian. 2015. "Discourse Analytical Approaches." In *Routledge Encyclopedia of Interpreting Studies*, edited by Franz Pöchhacker, 111–16. London: Routledge.

Munday, Jeremy. 2007. "Translation and Ideology: A Textual Approach." *The Translator* 13 (2): 195–217. https://doi.org/10.1080/13556509.2007.10799238.

Munday, Jeremy. 2010. "Evaluation and Intervention in Translation." In *Text and Context*, edited by Mona Baker, Maeve Olohan, and Maria Calzada-Pérez, 77–94. Manchester: St. Jerome.

Munday, Jeremy. 2012a. *Evaluation in Translation: Critical Points of Translator Decision-Making*. Abingdon: Routledge.

Munday, Jeremy. 2012b. "The Expression of Attitude in Translation." *Revista Canaria de Estudios Ingleses* 65: 101–14.

Munday, Jeremy. 2015. "Engagement and Graduation Resources as Markers of Translator/Interpreter Positioning." *Target* 27 (3): 406–21. https://doi.org/10.1075/target.27.3.05mun.

Munday, Jeremy. 2018. "A Model of Appraisal: Spanish Interpretations of President Trump's Inaugural Address 2017." *Perspectives* 26 (2): 180–95.

Munday, Jeremy, and María Calzada-Pérez, eds. 2020. *New Contexts in Discourse Analysis for Translation and Interpretation: Special Issue of Meta*. 65 (1).

Munday, Jeremy, and Meifang Zhang, eds. 2015. *Discourse Analysis in Translation Studies: Special Issue of Target*.27 (3). Target. John Benjamins.

Office of the Historian, Foreign Service Institute, United States Department of State. n.d. "186. Memorandum From Michel Oksenberg of the National Security Council Staff to the President's Assistant for National Security Affairs (Brzezinski)." Accessed December 2, 2023. https://history.state.gov/historicaldocuments/frus1977-80v13/d186#fn:1.5.4.4.14.11.14.2.

Okoniewska, Alicja M., and Binhua Wang. 2021. "Discourse Analysis in Conference Interpreting." In *The Routledge Handbook of Conference Interpreting*, edited by Michaela Albl-Mikasa and Elisabet Tiselius, 428–42. Abingdon: Routledge.

Othman, Waleed. 2020. "An SFL-Based Model for Investigating Explicitation-Related Phenomena in Translation." *Meta* 65 (1): 193–210.

Pan, Li. 2014. "Investigating Institutional Practice in News Translation: An Empirical Study of a Chinese Agency Translating Discourse on China." *Perspectives* 22 (4): 547–65.

Pan, Li. 2015. "Ideological Positioning in News Translation: A Case Study of Evaluative Resources in Reports on China." *Target: International Journal on Translation Studies* 27 (2): 215–37.

Pan, Li, and Chuxin Huang. 2021. "Stance Mediation in Media Translation of Political Speeches: An Analytical Model of Appraisal and Framing in News Discourse" In *Advances in Discourse Analysis of Translation and Interpreting*, edited by Binhua Wang and Jeremy Munday, 131–49. London: Routledge.

Pan, Li, and Sixin Liao. 2021. "News Translation of Reported Conflicts: A Corpus-Based Account of Positioning." *Perspectives* 29 (5): 722–39.

Purzycki, Michael. 2013. "War with Iran: Full Diplomatic Relations Are the Best Option for the U.S. and Iran." *MIC*. 8 June. Accessed March 15, 2025. www.mic.com/articles/45447/war-with-iran-full-diplomatic-relations-are-the-best-option-for-the-u-s-and-iran

Schäffner, Christina. 1997a. "Metaphor and Interdisciplinary Analysis." *Journal of Area Studies* 11 (1): 57–72.

Schäffner, Christina. 1997b. "Strategies of Translating Political Texts." In *Text Typology and Translation*, edited by Anna Trosborg, 119–45. Amsterdam and Philadelphia: Benjamins Publishing Company.

Schäffner, Christina. 2003. "Third Ways and New Centres: Ideological Unity or Difference?" In *Apropos of Ideology*, edited by Maria Calzada-Pérez, 23–43. Manchester and Northampton: St. Jerome Publishing.

Schäffner, Christina. 2004. "Political Discourse Analysis from the Point of View of Translation Studies." *Journal of Language and Politics* 3 (1): 117–50.

Schäffner, Christina. 2008. "'The Prime Minister Said...': Voices in Translated Political Texts." *Synaps* 22: 3–25.

Schäffner, Christina. 2012. "Unknown Agents in Translated Political Discourse." *Target: International Journal on Translation Studies* 24 (1): 103–125.

Schäffner, Christina. 2015a. "Follow-Ups in Interpreter-Mediated Interviews and Press Conferences." In *Discourse Approaches to Politics, Society and Culture*, edited by Elda Weizman and Anita Fetzer, 205–30. Amsterdam and Philadelphia: John Benjamins Publishing Company.

Schäffner, Christina. 2015b. "Speaker Positioning in Interpreter-Mediated Press Conferences." *Target* 27 (3): 422–39.

Schäffner, Christina, and Susan Bassnett, eds. 2010. *Political Discourse, Media and Translation*. Newcastle upon Tyne: Cambridge Scholars Publishing.

Schäffner, Christina, Luciana Sabina Tcaciuc, and Wine Tesseur. 2014. "Translation Practices in Political Institutions: A Comparison of National, Supranational, and Nongovernmental Organisations." *Perspectives: Studies in Translatology* 22 (4): 493–501.

Souza, Ladjane Maria Farias de. 2010. "Interlingual re-instantiation: A model for a new and more comprehensive systemic functional perspective on translation." Doctor of Philosophy, Universidade Federal de Santa Catarina and University of Sydney.

Spiessens, Anneleen and Piet Van Poucke. 2015. "News Reporting and Translation of the Crimean Conflict: The Relevance of Critical Discourse Analysis for Translation Studies." In *Book of Abstracts of the 5th IATIS Conference: Innovation Paths in Translation and Intercultural Studies*, 267. Belo Horizonte: FALE/UFMG.

Spiessens, Anneleen, and Piet Van Poucke. 2016. "Translating News Discourse on the Crimean Crisis: Patterns of Reframing on the Russian Website *InoSMI*." *The Translator* 22 (3): 319–39. doi:10.1080/13556509.2016.1180570.

Tahir Gürçağlar, Şehnaz. 2009. "Retranslation." In *Routledge Encyclopedia of Translation Studies*, edited by Mona Baker and Gabriela Saldanha, 2nd edition, 233–35. London and New York: Routledge.

Trosborg, Anna. 1997. "Text typology: Register, genre and text type." In *Text Typology and Translation*, edited by Anna Trosborg, 3–23. Amsterdam and Philadelphia: John Benjamins.

Valdeón, Roberto A. 2007. "Ideological Independence or Negative Mediation: BBC Mundo and CNN En Español's (Translated) Reporting of Madrid's Terrorist Attacks." In *Translating and Interpreting Conflict*, edited by Myriam Salama-Carr, 99–118. Amsterdam and New York: Rodopi.

van Dijk, Teun A. 1997. *Discourse as Structure and Process*. London: SAGE Publications.

van Dijk, Teun A. 1998. *Ideology: A Multidisciplinary Approach*. London: Sage.

van Dijk, Teun A. 2006. "Ideology and Discourse Analysis." *Journal of Political Ideologies* 11 (2): 115–40.

Walt, Stephen M. 2013. "Another Opportunity to Squander." *Foreign Policy*. 17 June. Accessed March 15, 2025. https://foreignpolicy.com/2013/06/17/another-opportunity-to-squander/

Wang, Binhua, and Jeremy Munday, eds. 2021. *Advances in Discourse Analysis of Translation and Interpreting: Linking Linguistic Approaches with Socio-Cultural Interpretation*. Oxon and New York: Routledge.

Yu, Hailing, and Canzhong Wu. 2016. "Same Chan Master, Different Images: Multi-Functional Analysis of the Story of Huineng and Its Translations." *The Journal of Translation Studies* 17 (4): 143–80.

Zhang, Meifang. 2002. "Language Appraisal and the Translator's Attitudinal Positioning." *Foreign Languages and Their Teaching* 7: 15–18.

Zhang, Meifang. 2013. "Stance and Mediation in Transediting News Headlines as Paratexts." *Perspectives* 21 (3): 396–411.

Zhang, Meifang, and Jeremy Munday. 2018. "Innovation in Discourse Analytic Approaches to Translation Studies." *Perspectives* 26 (2): 159–65.

Zhang, Meifang, and Hanting Pan. 2015. "Institutional Power in and behind Discourse: A Case Study of SARS Notices and Their Translations Used in Macao." *Target* 27 (3): 387–405. https://doi.org/10.1075/target.27.3.04zha.

4 Corpus-based critical discourse analysis in translation studies

Key points of learning

- A combined methodology enables CDA scholars to go beyond intuitive interpretations and formulate reliable generalisations about recurrent lexical choices.
- Concordance lines and collocates enable scholars to identify dominant patterns that contribute to the construction of certain discourses and to explain them in relevant socio-political and cultural contexts.
- Not only does a corpus-based method provide objective figures on whose basis an argument can be established, but it also accords further weight to the argument made in relation to the ideological orientations of news outlets.
- Any translational shifts or deviations and recurrent patterns identified through the comparative analysis of ST and TT are discussed in terms of the historical, political, and societal contexts in which both of these texts are embedded.
- A growing number of translation studies have employed the corpus-based CDA approach, whereby optional translation shifts are identified and discussed in terms of the historical and socio-political contexts where each ST and TT are embedded.

CDA studies view language as a powerful means that provides "a finely articulated vehicle for establishing differences in power in hierarchical social structures" (Wodak and Meyer 2009: 10). As mentioned in Chapter 2, CDA has been criticised for its perceived lack of objectivity in text selection, resulting in a failure to achieve an acceptable level of representativeness. Because CDA is a typically qualitative approach that focuses on close textual analysis, it needs to be supplemented with a different method to strengthen the claims made based on it and enable the generalisation of its findings. Although many CDA scholars conduct manual analyses that enable them to unravel covert ideological elements, some computer software packages that allow for a more systematic examination of concordance lines and scrutiny of hidden ideologies are currently available. The existence of such software has meant that scholars can now conduct quantitative analysis and that CDA scholars and others can examine how specific lexical items are associated with particular social issues.

Using corpora as supplementary sources to support CDA analyses would, to some extent, resolve the representativeness issue and the problem of selecting materials. A corpus-based analytical method is useful, as it is grounded in corpus linguistics[1] data consisting of texts or samples of texts chosen with reference to explicit, transparent and largely objective criteria for text selection. This method also offers the opportunity to support the close textual analysis of specific stretches of data with statistical findings drawn from a larger corpus; thus, the findings increased in credibility. Such holistic analyses reveal patterns that are often unpredictable and unavailable to *a priori* intuition (Hunston 2002; Louw and Chateau 2010).

The continued criticism of CDA has encouraged scholars to search for a new analytical method that can complement it. A recommended strategy is to borrow an approach from corpus linguistics (CL), a branch of linguistics that entails the exploration of a vast collection of authentic electronically stored texts. CL and CDA indeed share a common ground in the sense that CL is "the study of language based on examples of 'real life' language use" (McEnery and Wilson 2001, 1).

Some CDA scholars have felt the need to adopt a quantitative approach in working with broader and more representative empirical data and accordingly strengthening their arguments (for instance, van Dijk 1988; Fairclough 1992; Hardt-Mautner 1995; Stubbs 1996, 1997). For example, van Dijk seems to have been the first scholar to realise the necessity of adopting such an approach within a CDA framework, employing CDA and corpus-based studies in his early work on international and national news analysis. He predicted the role of computers in linguistic analysis when he said that "only the work of large teams or, in the future, of computers would enable the qualitative analysis to be quantified" (1988, 66). However, his predictions were abstract since he did not specify how a corpus-based method might be adapted to CDA research.

A few years later in 1992, Fairclough also raised the potential for using corpora in CDA. He encouraged discourse analysts to collaborate with other scholars from relevant disciplines, echoing van Dijk's suggestion on the work of large teams, to decide on which samples are typical or representative. Although Fairclough discussed the various ways by which a corpus can enhance discourse analysis, his discussion of employing a corpus-based method in CDA was still limited to relatively brief comments on its potential. Another early attempt to explore the usefulness of corpora in CDA analysis in detail was made by Hardt-Mautner (1995, 3–5), who stresses the need to combine qualitative and quantitative techniques by arguing that "what is gained in terms of depth is usually lost in terms of breadth". In reality, one cannot generate a detailed and holistic analysis of voluminous data manually, but it is humans, not computer programs, who can conduct meaningful examinations.

Thus, Hardt-Mautner (1995) proposed a procedure for integrating a quantitative approach (CL) with a qualitative approach (CDA). First, the author argued that a particular feature, revealed through qualitative analysis, can be investigated using corpora. A case in point is the use of large corpora to investigate collocational behaviour, including semantic prosodies (see section 4.3). Second, a particular pattern found in corpora can be studied qualitatively in a broader context. Third, the findings derived through both procedures can be compared against the backdrop of an extensive reference corpus, such as the British National Corpus or the COBUILD corpus. Hardt-Mautner can be regarded as a pioneer of corpus-based CDA because she explicitly argued for the possibility of a merger between the two methods and showed how they can be combined productively. She also alerted scholars to the need to move constantly between two antithetical views of data by shedding light on the merits and limitations of each and modelling a procedure for better research.

In 1996 and 1997, Stubbs expressed support for Hardt-Mautner's argument and conducted an in-depth analysis in which he showed how CDA could be improved by using corpora. He also casts doubt on several CDA studies by pointing out that they were largely focused on short texts or text fragments. Stubbs stressed that:

Analyses must be comparative: individual texts must be compared with each other and with data from corpora. Analyses *must not be restricted to isolated data fragments*: a much wider range of data must be sampled before generalisations are made about typical language use. And a much wider range of linguistic features must be studied, since varieties of language use are defined, not by individual features, but by clusters of co-occurring features: this entails the use of quantitative and probabilistic methods of text and corpus analysis.

(Stubbs 1997, 111, emphasis added)

The 1990s saw the first suggestions for combining corpus techniques and CDA (Subtirelu and Baker 2017, 107). The advances in technology and the common use of personal computers have allowed more CDA scholars to adopt computer-aided analytical method and see its benefit. As detailed analytical steps for corpus-based CDA have been suggested by Subtirelu and Baker (2017, 110), corpus-based CDA analysis generally includes corpus collection, keyword analysis, qualitative analysis, and collocation analysis, and similar patterns are undertaken for corpus-based CDA translation analysis.

In translation studies, scholars are already both open to and accustomed to using computer software programs in translation analysis (M. Baker 1993, 1995, 1996). In addition to the textual analysis of translations (e.g., Chen 2006; Fattah 2010; Ji 2010; Hu 2016; Hu and Li 2016; Choi 2020; Jones 2020; Buts 2020b), the method has also been used to examine interpreting activities (Hu and Tao 2013; F. Pan and Zheng 2017; X. Li 2018; Hu and Meng 2018; Gu 2018, 2019a, 2019b; F. Pan 2020; and Y. Pan 2021). Thus, it is not surprising that corpus-based CDA has found its place in translation studies.

Against this backdrop, this chapter discusses how such a relatively new analytical approach – corpus-based CDA – is currently being used in translation research. It first explains what the corpus-based method brings to CDA-informed analysis before proceeding to a detailed discussion of how this method is used in translation analysis. Some specific examples are also provided.

4.1 Corpus-based CDA: the benefits

In analysing language in use, various scholars, including those mentioned above, have attempted to achieve a balance between quantitative and qualitative approaches, as well as between objective statistical data and subjective individual interpretations, by incorporating the two aforementioned approaches. A typically quantitative, corpus-based approach is most illuminating for describing collocational and other recurrent patterns associated with specific lexical items across an entire corpus, whereas a typically qualitative, CDA-informed approach is best suited for scrutinising specific stretches of text at various levels. Hence, drawing on a methodology that combines these approaches enables CDA scholars to transcend intuitive interpretations and move towards reliable generalisations about recurrent lexical choices. This also allows them to trace more extensive and intricate discursive patterns that cannot be revealed through corpus analysis alone.

A corpus-based methodology is instrumental in gaining a considerable degree of consensus about what is found in the examination of texts with statistical findings drawn from a larger corpus. Corpus analysis software tools process several batches of text at a time; thus, a corpus-based software program dedicated to analysis rapidly presents manually unmanageable numbers of occurrences of a given object (Kim 2014). Hence, a specific pattern of ten years of news articles on a specific topic, for instance, can be investigated more easily, and the identified pattern can be discussed against a specific cultural, social, and economic background. The methodological synergy this combined methodology produces has been widely discussed, particularly in Baker et al. (2008) (see the summary in Figure 4.1).

CDA	*Corpus-based methodology*
Qualitative	Quantitative
Step outside the textual boundaries	Best tool for the identification of typical linguistic behaviour or words in texts
Fails to acknowledge the significance of the issue of representativeness	Objective results
Limited amounts of texts	Large volumes of data

Figure 4.1 Dialogue between the two approaches: Interdisciplinary synergy.

N	Concordance	File
1	he possibility of a ballistic missile attack from rogue states like NK, Iran or Iraq no longer a distant threa	NYT_5.txt
2	se it of being nuclear scofflaw whose actions aid rogue states like NK and Iran; Brazil has resisted allowing	NYT_56.txt
3	t week that the threat of a missile strike from a rogue state like NK, Iraq or Iran justified building a limit	NYT_5.txt
4	rts of being a nuclear scofflaw whose actions aid rogue states like NK and Iran? Ever since it began observing	NYT_56.txt
5	s. While Mr. Bush has tended to focus narrowly on rogue states like NK and Iran, Mr. Kerry wisely favors a mor	NYT_55.txt
6	defense system, because everyone recognized that rogue states like NK and Iran posed a threat to Europe, to R	CNNEE_57.txt
7	world today is not from Moscow but from so-called rogue states like NK, Iran and Iraq which are not party to t	CNNEE_4.txt
8	world today is not from Moscow but from so-called rogue states like NK, Iran and Iraq which are not party to t	CNNEE_3.txt
9	threat of a small number of missiles launched by rogue states like NK, Iraq and Iran, all of whom have shown	NYT_12.txt
10	se, which proponents say would defend against ''rogue'' states like NK and Iran, has called the treaty into qu	NYT_12.txt
11	n says is necessary to defend the USA against ''rogue'' states like NK and Iran. National missile defense syst	NYT_12.txt
12	ian leader that the ballistic missile threat from rogue states like NK, Iran and Iraq warrants an adjustment t	NYT_12.txt
13	he defended Russia's continuing involvement with rogue states like NK, Iraq and Iran in distinctly lukewarm t	NWE_15.txt
14	ncerned about a potential new missile threat from rogue states like NK, Libya, Iraq and Iran--which, according	NWE_16.txt

Figure 4.2 A recurrent pattern of 'rogue state* like North Korea' which feature 'Iran'.

Corpus-based critical discourse analysis in translation studies 89

Figure 4.2 was taken from my manually built corpus consisting of texts about North Korea and published in American mainstream news media outlets – *Newsweek*, *New York Times*, and *CNN* from 1998 to 2010. The figure shows that North Korea is strongly associated with Iran (as well as with Iraq) in the American media chosen for investigation. These countries are described as 'rogue states', as shown in the strong pattern identifiable in the figure. This polarised view was revealed through recurrent patterns, wherein the entire world was divided into 'rogue states' and 'others'. This phenomenon can be explained using van Dijk's ideological square model, which is discussed in Chapter 2. Such patterns are difficult to capture with manual analysis, but the argument can be supported by objective, explicit patterns identified during corpus-based data analysis.

The corpus-based method enables researchers to conduct an extended longitudinal analysis. A manual analysis of the ten years' news articles would take an inordinate amount of time to identify recurrent patterns. Moreover, by adopting a corpus-based method, we can analyse specific lexical items statistically, thus enabling a clearer presentation of statistics to strengthen arguments.

This combined empirical approach enables scholars both to identify media institution-specific patterns and to compare journalistic practices. For example, Figure 4.3 shows the different uses of 'dictator' and 'President', referring to Kim Jong Il[2], the late leader of North Korea and the son of Kim Il Sung, the founder of North Korea, across the three news outlets – *CNN*, *Newsweek* and *The New York Times*, covering the same period (1998–2010).

It reveals *Newsweek*'s sparing use of the 'president' in referring to Kim Jong Il. *NYT*, on the other hand, shows more instances of 'President' rather than 'Dictator'. Among the 7,446 concordances of 'Kim Jong Il', he is referred to as the 'President' (including 'President' and 'Pres', the shorter form of 'President') in 120 instances (2%). Of these 120 instances, 55 concordance lines are from *CNN*, 57 from *NYT*, and only eight from *Newsweek*.

	Instances		
	CNN	Newsweek	NYT
Dictator	94 (52%)	46 (26%)	40 (22%)
President	55 (46%)	8 (7%)	57 (47%)

Figure 4.3 The different uses of 'dictator' and 'President', referring to Kim Jong Il, in The New York Times (North American daily newspaper), *CNN* (the 24-hour TV news in the US), and *Newsweek* (a weekly magazine published in the US).

Figures 4.4 and 4.5 show that 'President' is overwhelmingly used in referring to Kim Dae Jung, the late South Korean president, as opposed to Kim Jong Il, where the former is described as 'President' 880 times, accounting for 69% of all occurrences, whereas the latter is referred to only as 'leader Kim Dae Jung' 25 times. While Kim Jong Il is described as a 'dictator' and 'leader', the late South Korean president Kim Dae Jung is more frequently referred to as the 'South Korean President' or the 'former South Korean President'.

90   *Critical Discourse Analysis in Translation Studies*

The use of 'President'	News outlets	Number of concordance lines	% of total occurrences
	NYT	571	65%
	CNN	236	27%
	Newsweek	73	8%

Figure 4.4 The use of 'President', referring to Kim Dae Jung across all news outlets.

The use of 'leader'	News outlets	Number of concordance lines	% of total occurrences
	NYT	13	52%
	CNN	9	36%
	Newsweek	3	12%

Figure 4.5 The use of 'leader', referring to Kim Dae Jung across all news outlets.

These figures, which were obtained from objective data, enable scholars to easily identify differences in reporting practices through the choice of lexical items when referring to various political figures. These practices ultimately help scholars produce arguments that are supported by factual data. For example, based on Figure 4.6, we can argue that the US media considers Kim Dae Jung to be the 'President', i.e., the *official* leader of South Korea, whereas they bestow less on Kim Jong Il the official title of 'President' and that *Newsweek* maintained a negative attitude towards Kim Jong Il, most frequently by using the term 'Dictator' rather than 'President'.

	Kim Dae Jung	Kim Jong Il
leader	2% (25 occurrences out of 1,273)	27% (1,995 occurrences out of 7,446)
President	69% (880 occurrences out of 1,273)	2% (120 occurrences out of 7,446)

Figure 4.6 The use of 'leader' and 'President', referring to Kim Dae Jung and Kim Jong Il, in The New York Times (North American daily newspaper), CNN (the 24-hour TV news in the US), and Newsweek (a weekly magazine published in the US).

4.2 Analytical methodology for corpus-based CDA research: frequency lists, collocates, and concordances

This section discusses the practicality of a corpus-based method by elaborating on analytical software programs and language-specific issues – the tools and functions widely used in corpus-based CDA studies. A number of software programs, or web corpora, are used in corpus-based CDA research, including *WordSmith* and *Sketch Engine*. Although the manner in which each program presents discourse patterns and collocates lists may differ, the list of items for analysis and the steps that must be taken are very similar.

4.2.1 Analysing frequency lists

A common way to identify a discursive pattern when a corpus-based method is used is to consult a *frequency list* that represents all linguistic items used in the text in question in order of their frequency. While different software programs have different features and functions, they mostly have a frequency function (see Figures 4.7 and 4.8). A frequency list provides a useful starting point for linguistic analysis, although the output needs to be refined and supplemented with other types of analysis. For WordSmith, a frequency list can be obtained by using the 'WordList' function.

In an English text, most discourse analysis research, which typically involves an examination of texts longer than a sentence, starts with the elimination of all the function items, such as the articles such as 'a', 'an', and 'the'; all the pronouns, such as 'he', 'she', 'they' and 'we'; all the possessives, such as 'hers', 'his', 'theirs', and 'ours', and all the coordinating conjunctions, such as 'and', 'but' and 'then'. Owing to the nature of English, these items, particularly the articles, need to be removed, since even when they are not part of a meaningful pattern, 'a', 'an', or 'the' are the most repetitive words in an English text, as seen from Figures 4.8 and 4.9. However, if the analysis involves an in-depth linguistic investigation of a particular item, they, of course, should be kept.

N	Word	Freq.	%	Texts	% Lemmas Set
1	THE	11,466	8.74	508	100.00
2	#	8,535	6.51	508	100.00
3	OF	5,460	4.16	508	100.00
4	AND	4,893	3.73	508	100.00
5	TO	3,864	2.95	506	99.61
6	IN	3,076	2.35	490	96.46
7	ON	2,167	1.65	482	94.88
8	FOR	1,758	1.34	507	99.80
9	ROK	1,739	1.33	434	85.43
10	A	1,473	1.12	421	82.87
11	MINISTER	1,431	1.09	503	99.02
12	AS	1,233	0.94	392	77.17
13	WILL	1,174	0.90	387	76.18
14	WITH	991	0.76	419	82.48
15	S	917	0.70	370	72.83
16	KOREA	837	0.64	418	82.28
17	FOREIGN	820	0.63	303	59.65
18	RELATIONS	777	0.59	501	98.62
19	COUNTRIES	690	0.53	310	61.02
20	DEPUTY	659	0.50	500	98.43
21	COOPERATION	617	0.47	236	46.46
22	MOFAT	603	0.46	500	98.43
23	MEETING	599	0.46	222	43.70
24	PUBLIC	591	0.45	500	98.43
25	BY	573	0.44	328	64.57
26	TWO	572	0.44	230	45.28
27	GOVERNMENT	563	0.43	255	50.20
28	SPOKESPERSON	536	0.41	500	98.43
29	DATE	535	0.41	508	100.00
30	FROM	506	0.39	275	54.13
31	TRANSLATION	504	0.38	500	98.43
32	UNOFFICIAL	502	0.38	501	98.62
33	INTERNATIONAL	499	0.38	227	44.69
34	IS	485	0.37	286	56.30
35	ITS	468	0.36	248	48.82
36	THAT	460	0.35	236	46.46
37	AT	457	0.35	266	52.36
38	REPUBLIC	450	0.34	349	68.70
39	AN	440	0.34	272	53.54

Figure 4.7 Frequency list example (Wordsmith).

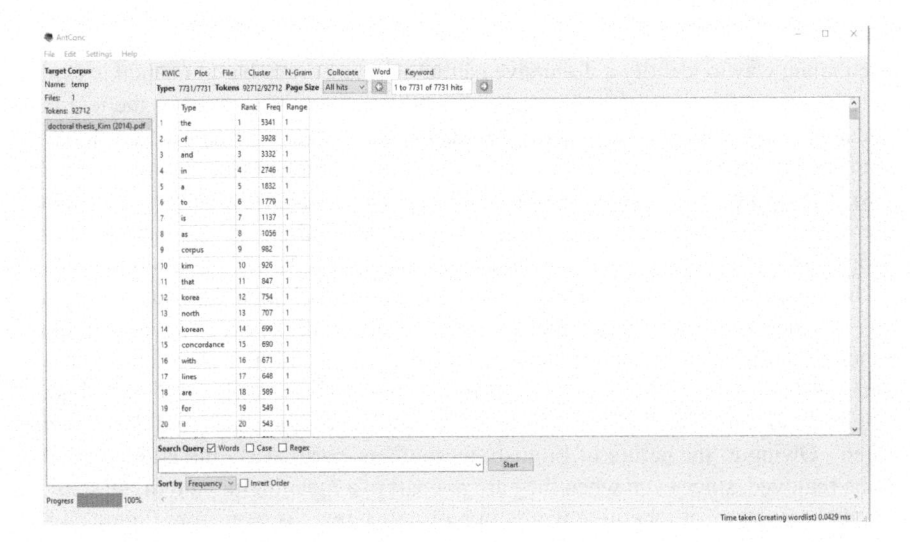

Figure 4.8 Frequency list example (AntConc).

Other functional words can also be eliminated from the list; for example, prepositions, 'of' and 'in'; modal verbs, such as 'will', 'should' and 'may'; relative pronouns, such as 'which' and 'how'; determiners, such as 'other'; demonstratives, such as 'this' and 'these'; and auxiliary verbs, such as 'was', 'have' and 'does'. This process is not carried out manually since some software tools, such as WordSmith, offer a 'stop list' function that enables researchers to exclude specific words in the analysis. These items should remain on the list if the analysis needs to examine them; hence, they can be added in a plain text (.txt) file to enable the software program to read and process them (see Figure 4.9).

```
; removed
the, of, in, to, into,
an, an, will, should,
may, which, how, that,
other, was, be, is,
does ,been, it, here,
there, and, but,
or ,then, this, as, by,
its, on, with, for,
from, at, these, those,
do, have, has, had,
another, would, shall,
might, are, were, about
```

Figure 4.9 The stop list example.

Other languages also feature functional words. This observation is supported by the work of Wang and Feng (2018), who used an extended version of the bilingual parallel corpus of Chinese–English Interpreting for Premier Press Conferences (CEIPPC). Built by Wang, this extended version of the bilingual parallel corpus of the CEIPPC consists of fifteen interpreted press conferences held between 1998 and 2002 and between 2003 and 2012. To identify the attitude and ideology-laden 'critical points' in interpreting, they first generated the frequency list using AntConc, another corpus analysis software, and used it as a starting point of analysis. In its frequency list, Chinese function words, such as 的 ['s], 是 [is], and 在 [(there) is], appear higher. These words are therefore disregarded in the analysis unless research questions specifically relate to them.

The characteristics of a specific genre also need to be taken into account. For example, for corpus-based CDA studies of news articles, the frequency list needs to be refined further because news articles often feature elements such as headers, including dates that incorporate the days of the week, which push these items up to a higher position on the collocate list than is warranted by their contribution in elaborating the meaning of the main text (Kim 2014).

After all these processes have been undertaken, a final 'refined' frequency list featuring all content words that have semantic meaning can be examined. A refined frequency list can be useful for translation analysis, which itself can be subject to scrutiny. The list can also serve as complementary data for confirming what has been revealed. For example, as part of their investigation into how the subfield of translation studies has developed and changed, Federico Zanettin, Gabriela Saldanha, and Sue-Ann Harding (2015, 175) probed content words on a frequency list that they obtained through an analysis of the Translation Studies Abstracts (TSA) online database. They filtered out function words, including articles, from the list and compared the refined list to a frequency list on the basis of a larger reference corpus. This process enables the authors to obtain keywords. The list of the most common content words and keywords in the TSA corpus reaffirmed what the authors predicted – the dominant position of English and literary translation (Zanettin, Saldanha, and Harding 2015, 175), with the word 'English' positioned third, after 'translation' (first) and 'language' (second). On the basis of the presence of keywords such as 'language(s)', 'text(s)', 'linguistics', and 'discourse', the authors argued that the pattern suggested a preference for text-based analysis as a method of conducting translation studies research. Similarly, Jan Buts (2020) explored the linguistic patterns of the online political journal *ROAR* (*Reflections on a Revolution*) *Magazine* using the Genealogies of Knowledge software suite[3]. Buts confirmed the prominent status of 'democracy' – the central keyword governing *ROAR Magazine* – by using a frequency list.

Such a list can be used to identify the most discursive semantic groups, not only an individual semantic word. Gallego (2018), for instance, pinpointed the most frequently occurring verbs and categorised them semantically. A frequency list can likewise be adopted for other types of research to determine the type-token ratio and lexical density. This use, however, is touched upon briefly in this chapter because the corpus-based approach discussed here is not intended to demonstrate how linguistic analysis can be conducted but rather to describe the preliminary steps necessary prior to the discourse analysis of translations.

Looking solely at a frequency list is inadvisable because high frequency in a corpus is not always equivalent to an item's representative status and can thus be misleading. For example, Buts (2020, 6) revealed that 'representative', which he found to be one of the strong collocates[4] of 'democracy', "shares a grammatical space with *direct, participatory, real* and *radical*, but is located outside the compatible set constituted by these terms […] despite its high frequency in the corpus, *representative* tends not to co-occur with its modifying counterparts (*direct, real, participatory* and *radical*)". This is one of the reasons why a frequency list is used as a primary observed variable, but other statistical techniques and measures can also be employed in corpus-based discourse analysis. One of the frequently used measures in this regard, not only in translation studies but also in the social sciences and linguistics, is collocation, which is discussed below.

Activity

Find at least two available corpus analysis software tools and compare them, particularly in terms of the extent to which they support the linguistic/translation analysis of a text written in the language(s) of your choice.

4.2.2 Analysing a collocate list

A collocate list, which Scott (2022) defines as a list of words that appear in the vicinity of a search word, also helps researchers conduct quantitative analyses. When words tend to recur more often than at random, collocation, or collocational behaviour, is established. Thus, the meaning that these words carry may be more than the sum of the meanings of their individual parts. For example, 'the bed' collocates strongly with the verb 'make' so that 'make the bed' creates a new meaning: to 'prepare the bed to sleep in'. Another example is found in the work of Milani, who has examined profiles registered in an online space for men seeking other men for companionship in a South African online community (see Milani 2013, 623 for further details). Milani has shown that the word 'guy' is associated with "racial descriptors (white, black, Indian), physical attributes (hot, slim, good-looking) and general characteristics (decent, nice, fun, next-door)", whereas 'man' retains its racial undertones, as evidenced by it being strongly collocated with 'black'. While 'guy' is linked to youth (young, younger), 'man' is tied to maturity (older, mature).

Collocational behaviour can be ideologically laden, which is one of the reasons why analysing collocational profiles has attracted the attention of many CDA scholars. For example, Baker, Gabrielatos, and McEnery (2013), using Sketch Engine to analyse the collocates of 'Muslim', ascertain how this word was represented in British newspaper articles published between 1998 and 2009. One of their findings was that "Muslims were frequently constructed in terms of homogeneity and connected to conflict" (ibid., 275). 'Community' and 'world' were found to be two of the most frequent noun collocates of the adjective 'Muslim' and that "Muslim community and Muslim world were frequently characterised as distinct, reasonably homogeneous entities that are quick to take offence, in tension with the UK or 'the West', rather than integrated, contain dangerous radical 'elements', and are threatened by a backlash" (ibid.).

Fairclough (2000) also conducted a corpus-based CDA study by compiling a computerised corpus of New Labour texts, together with a small corpus of earlier old Labour texts. Inspired by the idea that "managerial government is partly managing language" (ibid. : viii), he investigated not only newspaper articles written by New Labour leaders but also Labour party documents from their election manifesto, books, pamphlets, and other government documents to investigate particular words and phrases. Comparing both New Labour and 'earlier' Labour material, as well as New Labour material with large corpora of contemporary English, he explored patterns of linguistic behaviour in a specifically political context and identified particular words, such as 'we', 'welfare', 'Britain', 'new', 'reform' and 'young', as occurring at particularly high frequencies in the New Labour context. By this means, he identified a strong pattern associated with the use of 'new', as in 'new labour', 'new deal', 'new politics', 'new Britain', 'new Europe', 'new era', and even the 'new world'.

Fairclough argued that the word 'new' is used "quite selectively for national, political, and governmental renewal in 'new times', which generate new opportunities and challenges and call for new approaches, ideas, and attitudes" (Fairclough 2000, 19). His corpus analysis also reveals that 'modernisation' is overwhelmingly used with reference to the UK, whereas references to 'reform' tend to be restricted to the EU. The collocation 'economic reform' occurs very often, and 'reform' tends to collocate with items such as 'labour', 'capital' and 'product', always with reference to the EU. On the other hand, 'modernise' occurred only once in the context of markets and the economy. Interpreting these results from the perspective of a CDA scholar, Fairclough argued that "economic change is 'reform' not 'modernisation', and it applies only at the EU level, not in Britain" (ibid.).

All these studies are based on the analysis of collocational patterns and profiles, which were obtained using software programs in a manner similar to how frequency lists are derived. However, some steps need to be taken to retrieve a collocate list of meaningful items before this list can be analysed. Like words in a frequency list, these items appear in the text in question, but the strength of the relationship between each item and a search item is also determined. For example, the

96   *Critical Discourse Analysis in Translation Studies*

N	Word	With	Relation	Set	Texts	Total	Total Left	Total Right	L5	L4	L3	L2	L1	Centre	R1	R2	R3	R4	R5
1	THE	korea	0.000		390	861	615	246	39	43	429	26	78		11	94	43	40	58
2	KOREA	korea	0.000		418	858	11	11	6	2	3			836		3	2	6	
3	OF	korea	0.000		382	826	739	87	20	228	18	36	437			7	26	35	19
4	REPUBLIC	korea	0.000		344	414	406	8	1			405					5	1	2
5	AND	korea	0.000		188	294	74	220	16	12	19	18	9		127	18	22	27	26
6	TO	korea	0.000		196	270	105	165	18	40	6	21	20		42	17	57	16	33
7	NORTH	korea	0.000		71	172	166	6	2				164			1	2		3
8	GOVERNMENT	korea	0.000		104	144	135	9	131	3	1					5	3	1	
9	ON	korea	0.000		105	127	51	76	8	6	4	26	7		50	3	8	8	7
10	IN	korea	0.000		87	111	55	56	7	16	1	26	5		20	8	9	12	7
11	A	korea	0.000		84	109	20	89	5	6	2	5	2		6	12	21	33	17
12	S	korea	0.000		69	95	16	79	4	8	4				65	3	1	3	7
13	WILL	korea	0.000		84	92	27	65	22	1		4			28	2	20	11	4
14	VISIT	korea	0.000		56	89	69	0	27	19		15	8						
15	BETWEEN	korea	0.000		54	60	57	3	1	46		2	8						3
16	FOR	korea	0.000		43	52	19	33	3	5	2	7	2		10	5	7	1	10
17	LAUNCH	korea	0.000		30	49	10	39	3	2	3	2				22	8	5	4
18	AS	korea	0.000		39	49	15	34	1	4	2	7	1		10	2	13	4	5
19	COOPERATION	korea	0.000		32	45	15	30	8	2	5					21	6	1	2
20	HAS	korea	0.000		43	44	0	44							39	1	1	1	2
21	WITH	korea	0.000		35	42	14	28	5	4	1	4			2	4	7	7	8
22	US	korea	0.000		31	40	15	25	1	2	1	11			4	6	11	2	2
23	FROM	korea	0.000		36	40	20	20	1	13	1	5			11	1	3	1	4
24	ITS	korea	0.000		34	35	3	32	1		2					15	5	6	6
25	INTERNATIONAL	korea	0.000		30	34	7	27		6	1				19	1	4	2	1
26	JAPAN	korea	0.000		24	34	4	30	1			3			7	13	2	3	5
27	THAT	korea	0.000		27	34	21	13	1	4	1	14	1		2	3	4	3	1
28	BY	korea	0.000		27	33	16	17	1	1		13	1		4	1	3	4	5
29	CHINA	korea	0.000		20	32	7	25	2	2	3				9	12	2	2	
30	DECIDED	korea	0.000		31	31	0	31							4	27			
31	MINISTRY	korea	0.000		28	30	27	3	22		5						1	2	
32	2012	korea	0.000		25	28	2	26	1				1		1	7	11	2	5
33	INSTITUTE	korea	0.000		16	27	3	24		2			1		9	11	2	1	1
34	NUCLEAR	korea	0.000		26	27	4	23	1	3						2	11	3	7
35	TRADE	korea	0.000		15	26	12	14	7		2	3			3	5	4	1	1
36	AT	korea	0.000		22	25	3	22	2			1			3	2		4	13
37	PROVIDE	korea	0.000		24	24	0	24								1	1	22	
38	IS	korea	0.000		22	24	10	14	6			4			9		2	2	1
39	AGENCY	korea	0.000		18	23	4	19		1	1	2				17	2		

Figure 4.10 A snapshot of a collocate list of 'North Korea', using WordSmith Tools.

	Word	Cooccurrences	Candidates	T-score	MI	LogDice ↓	
1 ☐	cup	829	3,598	28.79	11.99	11.42	•••
2 ☐	coffee	409	5,034	20.21	10.49	10.20	•••
3 ☐	cups	137	1,022	11.70	11.21	9.25	•••
4 ☐	pot	100	1,478	9.99	10.23	8.71	•••
5 ☐	mug	74	616	8.60	11.05	8.44	•••
6 ☐	drank	68	1,270	8.24	9.89	8.19	•••
7 ☐	drinking	74	2,922	8.58	8.81	8.03	•••
8 ☐	sipped	49	499	7.00	10.76	7.87	•••
9 ☐	afternoon	85	6,238	9.18	7.91	7.79	•••
10 ☐	tray	51	1,212	7.13	9.54	7.79	•••
11 ☐	poured	51	1,575	7.13	9.16	7.72	•••

Figure 4.11 An example collocate list example 'tea', using Sketch Engine.

list of collocates of 'North Korea' in Figure 4.10 shows that 'the' has the strongest relational score with 'North Korea', which is expected considering the English language. However, content words, such as 'government', 'cooperation', and 'Japan', appear to be strong collocates, suggesting that they have a more robust link with the node word ('North Korea'). Figure 4.11 illustrates the word that appears most often in the vicinity of 'tea' in an English corpus. 'Cup', 'pot', and 'tray' are strong collocates of 'tea', implying, for example, that 'tea' is considerably associated with 'cup' or 'pot' in the English language.

Analysing a collocate list helps researchers identify major collocation patterns (i.e., repetitive patterns of lexical association) across substantial volumes of texts. A list of collocates can be semantically grouped for discourse to be identified. For example, 'Korea', 'Japan' and 'China' in Figure 4.10 can be grouped together semantically under 'countries'. 'Drank', 'drinking', 'sipped' and 'poured' in Figure 4.11 can be categorised as 'verbs', whereas 'cups', 'pot', 'cup', 'mug', and 'tray' can fall under 'dishware'. Groups of collocates can then be investigated further in larger stretches of texts to examine what types of discourses are constructed through these collocates. The same analytical steps can be used for the translation analysis. Collocate lists of STs and TTs can also be examined to identify the extent to which the lists deviate from each other. In what follows, a case study used to indicate how collocate list analysis can efficiently advance CDA-informed translation studies is illustrated.

4.2.2.1 Analysing collocates for translation analysis: a case study

Figure 4.12 lists country and city collocates in the English ST corpus and the Korean TT corpus built for a study conducted in 2013 (Kim 2013). The English ST corpus consisted of news media texts about North Korea published by US news institutions (*The New York Times*, *Newsweek*, and *CNN*), which were then chosen for translation by Korean media institutions. The Korean TT corpus comprises the corresponding Korean translations. As discussed below, the corpus-based CDA-informed analysis of collocational profiles helps researchers uncover discursive shifts in translations.

In Figure 4.12, the country and city collocates that appear in the top 300 collocates are ordered according to the relation score. The relation score of each collocate can be reached by using the calculation technique and function in the software (WordSmith 5.0 in this case), and the relation score is used merely as an instrument for selecting a manageable number of collocates. For ease of reference and analysis of the sets of countries and cities, 'Yeongpyeong Island', the name of the island in South Korea, is relocated to appear directly under 'South Korea', and the collocate list of the English ST corpus is provided for comparison purposes.

98 *Critical Discourse Analysis in Translation Studies*

N	English ST sub-corpus collocates			Korean TT sub-corpus collocates			
	English word	Relation score	Total frequency	Korean word	Gloss	Relation score	Total frequency
1	NK PYONGYANG YONGBYON	0.999 0.017 0.006	2,234 27 7	북한	NORTH KOREA	1.081	6,383
2	USA WASHINGTON AMERICAN	0.061 0.021 0.015	120 27 19	미국	USA	0.055	675
3	SK SEOUL SKN YEONPYEONG	0.059 0.029 0.023 0.008	87 38 32 9	중국	CHINA	0.042	446
4	CHINA CHINESE BEIJING	0.057 0.009 0.010	92 12 13	한국	KOREA	0.038	259
5	IRAN	0.051	66	일본	JAPAN	0.023	143
6	JAPAN JAPANESE	0.025 0.008	34 10	이란	IRAN	0.015	76
7	IRAQ	0.023	32	남한 연평도	SOUTH KOREA YEONPYEONG ISLAND	0.014 0.014	155 42
8	RUSSIA	0.014	18	한반도	KOREAN PENINSULA	0.011	34
9	KOREAN	0.009	12	러시아	RUSSIA	0.009	54
10	LIBYA	0.008	9	이라크	IRAQ	0.007	22
11	PAKISTAN	0.008	9	남북한	SOUTH AND NORTH KOREA	0.006	17

Figure 4.12 Comparison of the collocate list of English ST and Korean TT sub-corpora.

The collocational profile of the Korean TT corpus is similar, to an extent, to that of the English ST corpus: it reveals that North Korea strongly collocates with 'USA/US', 'China', 'Korea' and 'Japan'. However, there are some differences in terms of the order of collocates, as well as the presentation of countries and cities. For example, 'Iran' is a strong collocate of North Korea and appears before 'Japan' in the English ST corpus top 300 collocate list; however, it appears in a lower position than Japan in the Korean TT corpus collocate list (fifth position), occupying sixth place. The differences between the English ST corpus and the Korean TT corpus can largely be reduced to two main points: (1) some countries, cities and people either disappear or appear for the first time, and (2) some countries and cities appear higher up, or lower down, the list.

Starting with the first group, a few countries, cities, and people that appear among the top collocates of the English ST corpus are not found at all in the Korean TT corpus collocate list. Specifically, 'Libya' and 'Pakistan' do not appear on the Korean list. These countries have little in common with North Korea; specifically, they have no evident historical, geographical, cultural, or political connection with North Korea. There is no history of conflict between North Korea or South Korea and these countries. The relationship of Libya and Pakistan with South Korea is not only non-conflictual but also close enough to support mutual agreements. South Korea established consular relations with Libya in 1980 and signed a trade agreement with Pakistan in 1968. Since then, there have been consistent exchanges of high-profile diplomatic figures, diplomatic ties have strengthened, and cooperation has been extended between Libya and Korea. Pakistan has signed a number of agreements with South Korea. According to a report by the Ministry of Foreign Affairs and Trade (2012), Pakistan has consistently sought to strengthen its diplomatic relations with South Korea since the 1980s; at the same time, it has maintained its distance from North Korea since 2002, when that country's nuclear ambitions came to the forefront.

The fact that North Korea does not have close historical, geographical, and political ties with Libya and Pakistan and that South Korea has built fairly good relations with those countries goes some way towards explaining why they do not appear as strong collocates of North Korea on the Korean TT corpus collocate list. The assumption here is that the process of selecting material for translation into Korean will be subject to the usual constraints on newsworthiness from the perspective of the target rather than the source culture.

Interestingly, '남북한 (nambukhan)' [South and North Korea] did not appear on the English ST corpus collocate list but did appear on the Korean TT corpus collocate list as a single collocate. This may indicate that the Korean media are more concerned about North Korean issues that might affect the relationships between North Korea and South Korea, in particular, and that they select or supplement news from a South Korean perspective.

Notably, specific cities – 'Pyongyang', 'Yongbyon', 'Washington' and 'Beijing', and people – 'American', 'Chinese' and 'Japanese' – are not found at all in the top 300 collocates of the Korean TT corpus. 'Yeonpyeong Island' is the only province that appears on the list. Close investigations of concordance lines and specific texts would need to be carried out to find plausible explanations for these patterns. However, a tentative explanation for the absence of cities might be as follows. Whereas capital cities are widely used in the media as a substitute for countries – for example, 'Pyongyang announced' might be assumed to mean 'North Korea announced', and 'Washington', where the White House is located, is routinely used as a substitute for 'the US' – North Korean issues tend to be reported at a national level, thus reducing the various aspects of 'North Koreanhood' (such as people and cities) to a single, abstract actor.

Turning now to the second set of countries and cities, some countries moved higher up, whereas others appeared lower down the list. China and Japan, two of the countries 'expected' to collocate strongly with North Korea because of their historical, geographical and political ties, feature higher up the list, whereas Iran and Iraq, who belong to the set of 'unexpected alliances', the same set in which Libya and Pakistan were placed, appear in lower positions, below China and Japan. 'China' appeared below 'South Korea' in the English ST corpus collocate list but appears above 'South Korea' in the Korean TT corpus collocate list. Moreover, Iran is not as strongly associated with North Korea as it is in the English ST corpus. Its position dropped to 6th place, below Japan. Iraq, similarly, moved way down the list, below Russia.

As one of the major diplomatic players in East Asia, South Korea has built strong relationships with China and Japan. Moreover, historical enmity during World War II, when Japan invaded several East Asian countries, including China and Korea, continued to make diplomatic relations between China, both North Korea and South Korea, and Japan newsworthy. Similarly, South Korea also has an ongoing interest in Russia, since Russia is a long-standing ally of North Korea. Such historical, political and diplomatic realities explain, to some degree, the changes in the order of those countries in the Korean TT corpus collocate list, which might be reflected in the selection of STs again.

The differences between the English ST corpus and the Korean TT corpus discussed thus far can be summarised as follows: (1) the countries identified as 'expected collocates' of North Korea, including China and Japan, hold prominent positions or even appear higher on the collocate list of the Korean TT corpus; (2) whereas Iran and Iraq appear further down the list, compared with their positions in the English ST corpus, Libya and Pakistan, which were strongly associated with North Korea in the English corpus and appear on the collocate list of the English ST corpus, do not appear at all in the Korean TT corpus collocate list; (3) '남북한 (nambukhan)' [South and North Korea], which did not appear on the collocate list of the English ST corpus, is a strong collocate of North Korea in the Korean TT corpus; (4) specific cities (Pyongyang', 'Yongbyon', 'Washington' and 'Beijing') and the people of relevant countries ('American', 'Chinese' and 'Japanese'), which are also strongly associated with North Korea in the English ST corpus, do not appear at all in the 300 Korean TT corpus collocate list. These differences reflect what Korean media institutions value most. At the same time, they reveal interesting discursive shifts in the Korean translations.

This case study of collocate lists reveals how media institution constructs, reconstructs, and deconstructs discourses through selecting and translating news materials. In selecting news materials to be translated, Korean media institutions appear to have given preference to texts that focus more directly on countries that are more closely connected with North Korea. This is particularly evident in the appearance of 'Yongbyon' and 'Yeonpyeong' at the top of the list. The appearance of Yongbyon, a county in a North Korean province where a major nuclear complex is situated, was introduced in the collocate list of North Korea in the English ST corpus. Furthermore, Yeonpyeong, the name of an Island in South Korea that was subjected to artillery bombardment launched by North Korea in 2010, also occupied a prominent position in the English ST corpus collocate list. These lend support to the argument that news translation is not merely a process of objective transfer of a text from one language to another but also a complex, multi-layered process whereby a text is carefully selected, mediated and tailored to the interests and values of audiences in the target society.

A similar analytical method can be used to identify the extent to which patterns that contribute to the construction of discourse (identified in the ST chosen for translation) differ from those in a larger corpus (e.g., reference corpus). Not every news report can be translated, but advances in technology have enabled journalists and other media-based practitioners to produce and disseminate work beyond their own geographical boundaries more easily and frequently than they did before. Despite continued attempts by both individuals and institutions to produce translations of news items at great speed, the volume of material available for translation far exceeds the resources accessible for this purpose. News translation thus always involves extensive processes of selection. Different media institutions have their own views, sets of criteria, political and sociological orientations and voices, all of which heavily influence the choice of STs to be translated.

For example, Figure 4.13 shows the list of countries appearing in the top 300 collocate list in the English corpus (larger corpus) and the English ST corpus of US news reports about North Korea. As seen from the table, there are a number of differences in terms of the order of collocates between the collocate list of the English corpus and the English ST corpus. Some appear higher on the collocate list, and some new items that did not appear on the collocate list of the English corpus are introduced. For example, 'Iran' occupies a second position, just after North Korea, on the collocate list of the English corpus. However, 'USA/US', 'South Korea' and 'China' occupy higher positions on the collocate list of the English ST corpus, demoting 'Iran' to fifth place. Iraq and Libya, too, appear lower on the English ST corpus collocate list than on the English corpus. Iraq appeared in fifth place, between China and South Korea, in the English corpus; however, as shown in Table 4.13, Iraq's position dropped to seventh place, below both China and South Korea, in the English ST corpus. Whereas it occupied a higher position than Japan in the English corpus collocate list, it now appears to be in a lower position than Japan. Similarly, Libya, which had appeared above Russia in the previous analysis, now appears below Russia. Finally, Syria and Cuba, originally appearing in tenth and twelfth positions on the 300 collocate list of the English corpus, do not appear at all among the 300 top collocates of the English ST corpus.

These differences reflect what Korean media institutions value most. The fact that the USA, South Korea and China collocate more strongly with North Korea than with other countries, especially Iran, in the English ST corpus reflects what the South

102 *Critical Discourse Analysis in Translation Studies*

Korean media institutions consider to be important. The prominent position of the USA, South Korea and China is to be expected, and it is no surprise to see more news reporting on these countries being selected to be translated into Korean than news involving other countries such as Iran, Iraq, Libya and Pakistan, considering their historical and political relations with North Korea and that South Korea is inextricably linked to North Korea in every respect. Thus, news about countries that have more direct relationships with both North Korea and South Korea, such as China and the USA, must have been placed at the forefront of the items to be translated.

N	English Corpus			English ST Sub-corpus		
	Word	Relation	Total	Word	Relation	Total
1	NK	1.015	86,350	NK	0.999	2,234
	PYONGANG	0.014	629	PYONGYANG	0.017	27
				YONGBYON	0.006	7
2	IRAN	0.084	5,464	USA	0.061	120
				WASHINGTON	0.019	27
				AMERICAN	0.015	19
3	USA	0.039	5,066	SK	0.059	87
	AMERICAN	0.013	1,007	SEOUL	0.029	38
	WASHINGTON	0.007	440	SKN	0.023	32
				YEONPYEONG	0.008	9
4	CHINA	0.038	2,309	CHINA	0.057	95
	CHINESE	0.007	366	CHINESE	0.009	12
	BEIJING	0.007	319	BEIJING	0.010	13
5	IRAQ	0.031	2,849	IRAN	0.051	66
6	SK	0.030	1,550	JAPAN	0.025	34
	SKN	0.009	442	JAPANESE	0.008	10
	SEOUL	0.008	387			
7	JAPAN	0.020	1,007	IRAQ	0.023	32
	JAPANESE	0.006	293			
8	LIBYA	0.014	613	RUSSIA	0.014	18
9	SYRIA	0.013	607	KOREAN	0.009	12
10	RUSSIA	0.011	554	LIBYA	0.008	9
11	CUBA	0.009	401	PAKISTAN	0.008	9

Figure 4.13 Countries and cities appearing in the top 300 collocate list in the English corpus and the English ST corpus, ordered by relation score.

4.2.3 Some corpus techniques to consider

To retrieve a collocate list, first, the 'collocate' function in software programs or corpus analysis software tools can be used; then, the 'stop list' can be used to remove function words and pronouns, similar to how the 'frequency list' is retrieved. The collocate function only recognises orthographic words separated by spaces on each side. Hence, multi-word lexical items are broken down into individual words that appear separately in the collocate list. For example, 'North

Korea' is a compound word consisting of 'North' and 'Korea'; each of these items is counted separately by software programs such as WordSmith. The two items occur with different frequencies, mainly because 'North Korea' is also referred to in the corpus as 'the North', and because 'Korea' is mentioned in relation to 'South Korea'. These differences are not meaningful in the context of a corpus-based CDA study, where the focus is not on variation in ways of referring to North Korea. Similar examples include 'Kim Jong Il', the North Korean leader, and 'the US'. Moreover, most software programs do not distinguish between singular and plural forms, thus showing separate counts for words such as 'Korean' and 'Koreans'. In this case, multi-word lexical items that are likely to be broken down by the software programs and presented separately in the word and collocate lists can be replaced with something else. For example, 'North Korea' needs to be replaced with 'NK' in the collocate list to determine the relationship score (as described below). 'United States', 'United Nations' and 'South Korea' need to be replaced by 'USA', 'UN', and 'SK'. In the specific case of the 'United States', the 'U. S', 'U S' and 'U.S.' can be replaced by 'USA'.

Some software programs, such as WordSmith, have the 'auto remove duplicate' function, which automatically removes duplicate concordance lines. Whether to use this function is ultimately each individual researcher's decision. However, in regard to the corpus-based CDA analysis of news articles, not activating this function is suggested since news outlets repeat items, such as interviews in full or in part, at different times, and this repetition, especially of text fragments, is highly significant in CDA terms since repetitions in discourse create, reinforce, and strengthen ideas and statements. Johnstone (1994) focused specifically on repetitions in discourse. Repetition functions in a number of ways, such as playfully, emotionally and expressively; however, as he explains, it is "a great aid to memory, and repeating a text evokes associations from every time you have participated in that type of event through your whole life" (1994, 8). Thus, repetitions found in persuasive speech or media by a powerful person can be inevitable since "propaganda is one example of a use of repetition by someone in a powerful position" (Johnstone 1994, 19). Repetition is also a powerful rhetorical device that encourages audiences to retain information and make the speech more memorable (e.g., "I have a dream" speech by Martin Luther King Jr.). For example, Fairclough (2000) examined the use of the word 'new' (mentioned earlier) in the then Prime Minister Tony Blair's speeches, in which 'new' occurred 609 times in 53 speeches between 1997 and 1999, whereas 'modern' occurred 89 times, 'modernise/modernisation' 87 times, and 'reform' 143 times (Fairclough 2000, 18).

The next step is to produce a relation score via statistical techniques. Many corpus tools provide a function that automatically calculates the statistical significance of words included in the collocate list. Although this does not reduce the overall size of the list, it does provide the means to reduce it, since it orders collocates by significance, showing the stronger ones at the top and the weaker ones at the bottom. For example, WordSmith 5.0 offers six different statistical testing options – 'Specific Mutual Information' (or MI), 'MI3', 'T-score', 'Log Likelihood' (L.L), 'Dice Coefficient' (DC), and 'Z-score', with each using a different algorithm. Nevertheless, across the different statistical tests, the strongest and weakest collocates are measured according to their relation scores: the higher the score is, the stronger the collocation. This is generally calculated by examining (1) the frequency of occurrence of each collocate in the vicinity of the search item; (2) the relative number of occurrences, both next to and away from the search word, which requires access to a full frequency list of the corpus (Baker 2009, 101); and (3) the overall size of the corpus.[5]

Figure 4.14 shows six snapshots of the collocate outputs for 'NK' (North Korea) acquired using the different statistical techniques, with each listing item in order of collocation strength.[6] In terms of the relation score, higher scores indicate strong collocations and are calculated down to three places of decimals. First, Baker (2009, 102) points out that specific mutual information (MI) tends to assign high scores to relatively low-frequency words, which is reflected in the MI output in the list with items such as 'A-ARMS' and 'ONJUNG-RI' featuring near the top.

Dice Coefficient (DC)				Specific Mutual Information			
N	Word	Relation score	Total frequency	N	Word	Relation score	Total frequency
1	NK	1.015	86,350	1	NK	9.684	86,350
2	NUCLEAR	0.135	10,128	2	A-ARMS	9.663	6
3	IRAN	0.084	5,464	3	ONJUNG-RI	9.400	10
4	TALKS	0.053	2,758	4	RESTARTS	9.248	15
5	PROGRAM	0.043	2,488	5	TAEPODONGS	9.149	7
6	MISSILE	0.040	2,065	6	TEST-LAUNCH	9.149	7
7	WEAPONS	0.040	2,489	7	TEST-FIRES	9.104	19
8	USA	0.039	5,066	8	YONG-HYUN	9.035	11
9	CHINA	0.038	2,309	9	GRAPHITE-MODE-RATED	8.859	8
10	TEST	0.034	1,684	10	DEFECTING	8.773	41

MI3				Z-score			
N	Word	Relation score	Total frequency	N	Word	Relation score	Total frequency
1	NK	42.440	86,350	1	NK	2,632.857	86,350
2	NUCLEAR	33.584	10,128	2	NUCLEAR	327.987	10,128
3	S	31.577	15,674	3	IRAN	209.645	5,464
4	IRAN	31.468	5,464	4	TALKS	165.825	2,758
5	TALKS	29.753	2,758	5	MISSILE	126.342	2,065
6	USA	29.164	5,066	6	TEST	116.410	1,684
7	MISSILE	28.614	2,065	7	PROGRAM	108.359	2,488
8	PROGRAM	28.600	2,488	8	SANCTIONS	107.158	1,298
9	WEAPONS	28.252	2,489	9	KIM	97.542	1,676
10	TEST	28.073	1,684	10	LIBYA	92.892	613

Figure 4.14 An example of the output of all six statistical options.

Log Likelihood (L.L)				T-score			
N	Word	Relation score	Total frequency	N	Word	Relation score	Total frequency
1	NK	1,327,054.875	86,350	1	NK	293.920	86,350
2	NUCLEAR	80,655.625	10,128	2	S	125.041	15,674
3	S	54,438.469	15,674	3	NUCLEAR	100.454	10,128
4	IRAN	40,491.762	5,464	4	IRAN	74.018	5,464
5	USA	22,675.334	5,066	5	USA	70.761	5,066
6	TALKS	21,399.635	2,758	6	NOT	55.913	3,155
7	PROGRAM	16,199.842	2,488	7	IRAQ	53.453	2,849
8	MISSILE	15,079.412	2,065	8	TALKS	52.075	2,758
9	WEAPONS	14,976.497	2,489	9	SAID	50.990	2,579
10	CHINA	13,895.954	2,309	10	PROGRAM	50.369	2,488

Figure 4.14 (Continued)

Although the Z-score seems to place more frequently occurring items at the top than MI does, it also returns lower frequency items near the top, thereby pushing more meaningful items down the list. Although Clear (1993, 282) argued that the T-score statistic identifies very reliable collocations by offering "a semantic profile of the node word and a set of particular fixed phrases, grammatical frames and typical stereotyped combinations", as Figure 4.14 reveals –, at least in this example, the T-score test tends to prioritise grammar and hence scores the possessive form of 's (i.e., 'SK's', 'NK's', and 'USA's'), which is higher than 'nuclear', for instance; it also returns items such as 'not'.

As Baker (2009) argues, L.L. and MI3 also seem to focus more on grammar. The remaining three options – DC, MI3, and L.L. – show little difference in output, and all three options include 'NK' and 'nuclear' as the first and second items on the list and share the rest of the items, albeit in a different order: 'talks', 'USA', 'Iran', 'program' and 'missile'. However, both L.L. and MI3 return 's' as a meaningful item. This suggests that DC focuses more on orthographic words than the other options do. However, depending on the type of text, this pattern may change. Therefore, it is suggested that researchers try different techniques before opting for a particular technique.[7]

4.2.3.1 A point to consider assembling a collocate list in languages other than English

Another issue that should be considered when generating a collocate list is that foreign characters need to be replaced with equivalent symbols in the language under investigation for analysis to be facilitated. This requirement is important because some software programs, such as WordSmith Tools, count the same words in various languages differently if both forms are maintained. What follows is an example of how this treatment affects collocate analysis. Although the example provided covers Korean, Chinese, and English, the same can apply to other languages where different scripts are used as part of the national language. A case in point is Japanese, where kanji (the Chinese script used in Japanese writing) is used alongside hiragana and katakana.

In Korea, particularly in media texts, Chinese characters are often found alongside Korean characters since Chinese ideographs are useful for clarifying the meanings of Korean words, especially when two or more terms are pronounced similarly. For example, a foreign, or polysemous, term in Korean is typically followed by corresponding Chinese characters enclosed in brackets. For example, President Lee [이 대통령 (i taet'ongnyŏng)] features as 李 대통령 or 이 (李) 대통령 in some cases because the Korean 이 대통령 can be understood either as this president or President Lee. Another reason behind the largely pervasive use of Chinese characters in Korean media is that ideographic language takes up less space. For example, the Korean equivalent of the US is 미국 (miguk); its corresponding Chinese character is 美國. However, the first character, 美, also means the US. Hence, in some Korean newspapers, 美, which requires only one space for one character, is preferred to 미국, which requires two spaces. Other examples include the Korean translations of 訪韓 [visit South Korea] and 訪美 [visit the US], where the Korean translations are 한국을 방문하다 (han'gugŭl pangmunhada) or 한국방문 (han'gukpangmun) and 미국을 방문하다 (migugŭl pangmunhada) or 미국방문 (migukpangmun), respectively.

However, maintaining both forms in texts means that they appear in a collocate list separately and are also counted separately, even when they refer to the same idea. This is problematic particularly when comparing collocate lists of a ST and a TT because while for example, a ST collocate list shows 100 instances of 'visit', its corresponding Korean translation (방문 (pangmun)) may appear only 40 times. Simply comparing the number of times a word under examination appears in a ST with that in a TT, without considering the nature of the language and the possibility that other words are used to refer to the same English ST, may skew the result. Therefore, either all derivatives are searched and counted together, or they are rendered consistent before software is used for counting. In the case of the use of Chinese characters in Korean media, all these characters can be changed to Korean; otherwise, software tools count them as different words, even when their referential meanings remain the same.

Therefore, depending on the nature of the language under examination, a supplementary measure may need to be adopted prior to retrieving a collocate list given how software processes it. For example, in Korean, the language features various types of Korean particles and suffixes, such as *-eun*, *-neun*, *-ga* and *-eneun*, which have various grammatical functions; however, the referential meanings of the nouns to which they are attached remain the same.[8] For example, although '정부는 (chŏngbunŭn)' and '정부를 (chŏngburŭl)' both refer to '정부 (chŏngbu)' [government], the former functions as a grammatical 'subject', whereas the latter functions as an 'object'. Moreover, even when their grammatical functions are the same, different particles and suffixes can be added, depending on the context in which the word functions, including the phonological context. Therefore, a mere analysis of '정부' [government] does not reveal the whole picture of how 'government' is constructed in the corpus under examination.

One way of resolving this may be by replacing the particles and suffixes with a special symbol or character. Since the frequency of the occurrence of each collocate matters and the collocate contains all the different variations of the word in question in Korean, too many variants will be produced; hence, if '정부 (chŏngbu)*' is used as a search item,

Corpus-based critical discourse analysis in translation studies 107

the frequency list will return all possible variants, including '정부가 (chŏngbuga)', '정부는 (chŏngbunŭn)', and '정부를 (chŏngburŭl)'; this eventually leads WordSmith Tools to show numerous different relation scores of collocates, as shown in Figure 4.15, which shows the top twenty collocates of '북한 (pukhan)*' [NK*], which was acquired using the Dice-Coefficient technique, with an asterisk attached, listing items in order of collocation strength alongside the back translation of each item.

N	Word	Gloss	with	Gloss	Relation score
1	북한과	with North Korea	북한과	with North Korea	1.007
2	북한산	Bukhan [North Korea] mountain	북한산	Bukhan [North Korea] mountain	1.000
3	북한군은	North Korean army	북한군은	North Korean army	1.000
4	북한에서는	In North Korea	북한에서는	In North Korea	1.000
5	북한보다	Than North Korea	북한보다	Than North Korea	1.000
6	북한에선	In North Korea	북한에선	In North Korea	1.000
7	북한이나	North Korea or	북한이나	North Korea or	1.000
8	북한군이	North Korean army	북한군이	North Korean army	1.000
9	북한에서	In North Korea	북한에서	In North Korea	1.000
10	북한처럼	Like North Korea	북한처럼	Like North Korea	1.000
11	북한에게	To North Korea	북한에게	To North Korea	1.000
12	북한에도	Also in North Korea	북한에도	Also in North Korea	1.000
13	북한측의	North Korean side	북한측의	North Korean side	1.000
14	북한으로서는	For North Korea	북한으로서는	For North Korea	1.000
15	북한에서도	Also in North Korea	북한에서도	Also in North Korea	1.000
16	북한측에	To North Korean side	북한측에	To North Korean side	1.000
17	북한인들은	North Korean	북한인들은	North Korean	1.000
18	북한측	North Korean side	북한측	North Korean side	1.000
19	북한에서의	In North Korea	북한에서의	In North Korea	1.000
20	북한군의	North Korean army's	북한군의	North Korean army's	1.000

Figure 4.15 Collocates of North Korea, ordered by relation score.

Figure 4.15 shows a number of repeated items because various particles and suffixes are attached to the same word, as explained above, and because WordSmith Tools reads and calculates some Korean words that mean the same thing differently. Although those particles and suffixes do not affect the basic referential meaning of the words to which they are attached, the software program recognises each variant as a different word. For example, all three items appearing in the list below, '북한에서는' (line 4), '북한에선' (line 6) and '북한에서' (line 9), mean 'in/at North Korea'. However, because each form contains a different particle or suffix (as italicised), some tools, including WordSmith Tools, count each as a distinct item.

108 *Critical Discourse Analysis in Translation Studies*

One solution for addressing such issues, while ensuring that the software processes it reliably, is to use a specific marker after every instance of the node word to identify it clearly, irrespective of the various particles and suffixes that might be attached to it. For example, a small square box can be used to substitute a particle or a suffix. For example, '북한은' [NK, subject] can be changed to '북한□'. The particle or suffix itself is deleted, with the square box indicating a missing particle but not which particle. The alternative would have been to retain an unmanageable number of forms ending in different particles and being counted separately by the software. As long as the study is not about particles and the particles have no impact on the meaning of the keyword (node), this seems to be an acceptable measure.

Alternatively, the collocate output can be further corrected and refined by using the 'lemmatising' function. This enables several entries that appear in groups on a list of collocates to be treated as a set and for their total frequency to be calculated. The software processes it automatically, but it requires a plain text (.txt) file.

4.2.4 Analysing concordance lines

Although a collocate list provides a good starting point of analysis by showing the overall patterns across a corpus, it is insufficient to build a strong argument or to explain how a collocate is used in a specific context. For example, in the corpus of the U.S. media about North Korea mentioned above, Kim Jong Il, the late leader of the latter, appears to have 'Dear/Great leader' as one of its strong collocates. However, examining longer stretches of texts that feature these collocates revealed that 'Great Leader' is often enclosed in quotation marks and capitalised, signalling that it is used as a title or a designation, such as 'Mr' and 'Dr'. Therefore, to compensate for the limitation of collocational analysis, concordance lines can be examined.

A *concordance* is a list of every example of a word(s) or expression in question in a stretch of texts held in a machine-readable form. However, regarding a corpus-based research study, a concordance line generally refers to a stretch of text with a search word in context: one line on the screen that displays a search word and a few words on either side of the search item. A concordance can be sorted, or processed further, to refine the result, depending on the aim of the research. The usefulness of concordance lines is that they enable researchers to easily identify recurrent patterns in text (see Figure 4.16).

For example, searching for concordance lines using the search word 'tea' in the English corpus in Sketch Engine reveals a strong pattern for the 'cup of tea'. This is unsurprising, but this function can also return something unexpected (see Figures 4.17). Figure 4.17 shows the list of concordance lines associated with 'NK' (North Korea) identified in the corpus as 'North American news reports about North Korea'. Using the search word 'North Korea' returned a number of concordance lines, and it is evident from the list that 'rogue states like NK' is a discursive pattern found in the US media under examination. A similar method was used by Kim and Choi (2021), who have examined South Korean news media reports – both centre-right and centre-left – about Muslim refugees in Korea. Using 난민 (nanmin)[refugee] as a search word, the authors identified a discursive pattern: Concordances associated with the search word returned a strong pattern of 가짜난민 (katchananmin) [fake refugee], which reflects Korean media institutions' labelling of refugees.

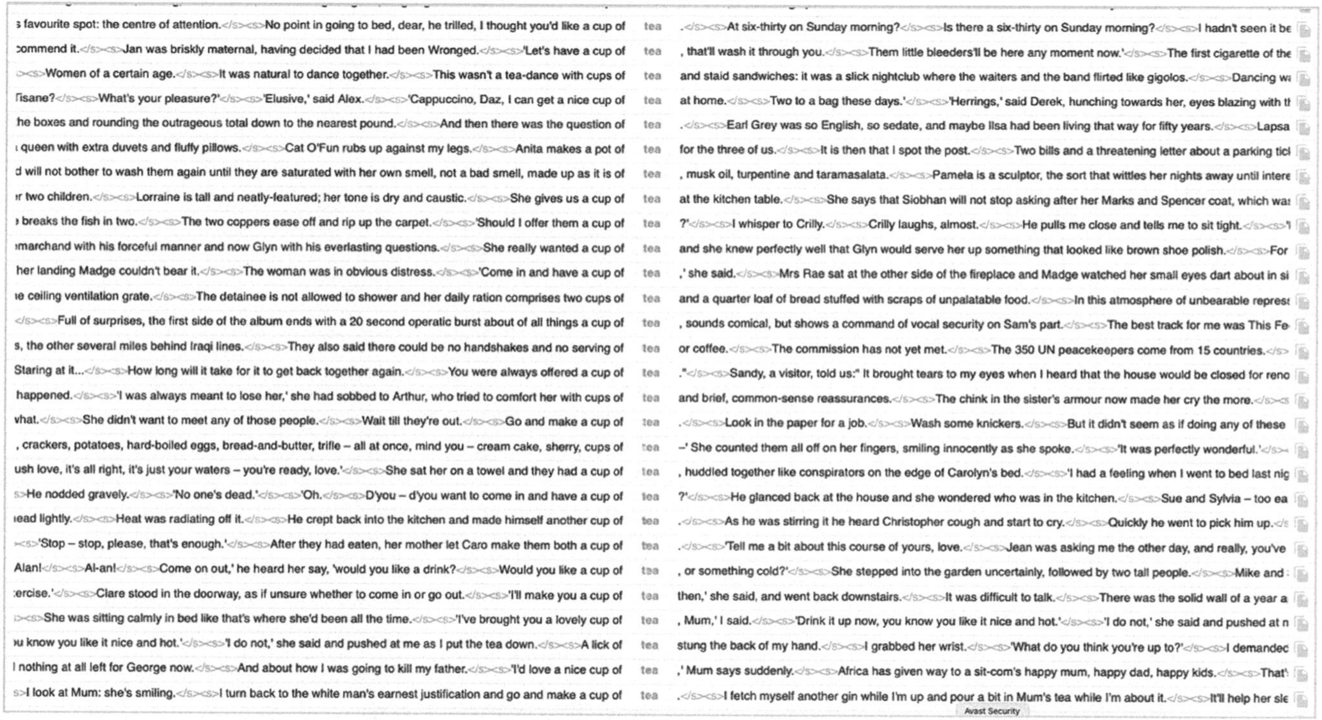

s favourite spot: the centre of attention.</s><s>No point in going to bed, dear, he trilled, I thought you'd like a cup of	tea	.</s><s>At six-thirty on Sunday morning?</s><s>Is there a six-thirty on Sunday morning?</s><s>I hadn't seen it be
commend it.</s><s>Jan was briskly maternal, having decided that I had been Wronged.</s><s>'Let's have a cup of	tea	, that'll wash it through you.</s><s>Them little bleeders'll be here any moment now.'</s><s>The first cigarette of the
<s>Women of a certain age.</s><s>It was natural to dance together.</s><s>This wasn't a tea-dance with cups of	tea	and staid sandwiches: it was a slick nightclub where the waiters and the band flirted like gigolos.</s><s>Dancing wa
Tisane?</s><s>What's your pleasure?'</s><s>'Elusive,' said Alex.</s><s>'Cappuccino, Daz, I can get a nice cup of	tea	at home.</s><s>Two to a bag these days.'</s><s>'Herrings,' said Derek, hunching towards her, eyes blazing with th
he boxes and rounding the outrageous total down to the nearest pound.</s><s>And then there was the question of	tea	.</s><s>Earl Grey was so English, so sedate, and maybe Ilsa had been living that way for fifty years.</s><s>Lapsa
queen with extra duvets and fluffy pillows.</s><s>Cat O'Fun rubs up against my legs.</s><s>Anita makes a pot of	tea	for the three of us.</s><s>It is then that I spot the post.</s><s>Two bills and a threatening letter about a parking tick
d will not bother to wash them again until they are saturated with her own smell, not a bad smell, made up as it is of	tea	, musk oil, turpentine and taramasalata.</s><s>Pamela is a sculptor, the sort that wittles her nights away until intere
r two children.</s><s>Lorraine is tall and neatly-featured; her tone is dry and caustic.</s><s>She gives us a cup of	tea	at the kitchen table.</s><s>She says that Siobhan will not stop asking after her Marks and Spencer coat, which was
breaks the fish in two.</s><s>The two coppers ease off and rip up the carpet.</s><s>'Should I offer them a cup of	tea	?'</s><s>I whisper to Crilly.</s><s>Crilly laughs, almost.</s><s>He pulls me close and tells me to sit tight.</s><s>'I
marchand with his forceful manner and now Glyn with his everlasting questions.</s><s>She really wanted a cup of	tea	and she knew perfectly well that Glyn would serve her up something that looked like brown shoe polish.</s><s>For
her landing Madge couldn't bear it.</s><s>The woman was in obvious distress.</s><s>'Come in and have a cup of	tea	,' she said.</s><s>Mrs Rae sat at the other side of the fireplace and Madge watched her small eyes dart about in si
e ceiling ventilation grate.</s><s>The detainee is not allowed to shower and her daily ration comprises two cups of	tea	and a quarter loaf of bread stuffed with scraps of unpalatable food.</s><s>In this atmosphere of unbearable repres
</s><s>Full of surprises, the first side of the album ends with a 20 second operatic burst about of all things a cup of	tea	, sounds comical, but shows a command of vocal security on Sam's part.</s><s>The best track for me was This Fe
s, the other several miles behind Iraqi lines.</s><s>They also said there could be no handshakes and no serving of	tea	or coffee.</s><s>The commission has not yet met.</s><s>The 350 UN peacekeepers come from 15 countries.</s>
Staring at it...</s><s>How long will it take for it to get back together again.</s><s>You were always offered a cup of	tea	."</s><s>Sandy, a visitor, told us:" It brought tears to my eyes when I heard that the house would be closed for reno
happened.</s><s>'I was always meant to lose her,' she had sobbed to Arthur, who tried to comfort her with cups of	tea	and brief, common-sense reassurances.</s><s>The chink in the sister's armour now made her cry the more.</s><s
what.</s><s>She didn't want to meet any of those people.</s><s>Wait till they're out.</s><s>Go and make a cup of	tea	.</s><s>Look in the paper for a job.</s><s>Wash some knickers.</s><s>But it didn't seem as if doing any of these
, crackers, potatoes, hard-boiled eggs, bread-and-butter, trifle – all at once, mind you – cream cake, sherry, cups of	tea	–' She counted them all off on her fingers, smiling innocently as she spoke.</s><s>'It was perfectly wonderful.'</s>
ush love, it's all right, it's just your waters – you're ready, love.'</s><s>She sat her on a towel and they had a cup of	tea	, huddled together like conspirators on the edge of Carolyn's bed.</s><s>'I had a feeling when I went to bed last nig
s>He nodded gravely.</s><s>'No one's dead.'</s><s>'Oh.</s><s>D'you – d'you want to come in and have a cup of	tea	?'</s><s>He glanced back at the house and she wondered who was in the kitchen.</s><s>Sue and Sylvia – too ea
ead lightly.</s><s>Heat was radiating off it.</s><s>He crept back into the kitchen and made himself another cup of	tea	.</s><s>As he was stirring it he heard Christopher cough and start to cry.</s><s>Quickly he went to pick him up.</s
<s>'Stop – stop, please, that's enough.'</s><s>After they had eaten, her mother let Caro make them both a cup of	tea	.</s><s>'Tell me a bit about this course of yours, love.</s><s>Jean was asking me the other day, and really, you've
Alan!</s><s>Al-an!</s><s>Come on out,' he heard her say, 'would you like a drink?</s><s>Would you like a cup of	tea	, or something cold?'</s><s>She stepped into the garden uncertainly, followed by two tall people.</s><s>Mike and
ercise.'</s><s>Clare stood in the doorway, as if unsure whether to come in or go out.</s><s>'I'll make you a cup of	tea	then,' she said, and went back downstairs.</s><s>It was difficult to talk.</s><s>There was the solid wall of a year a
<s>She was sitting calmly in bed like that's where she'd been all the time.</s><s>'I've brought you a lovely cup of	tea	, Mum,' I said.</s><s>'Drink it up now, you know you like it nice and hot.'</s><s>'I do not,' she said and pushed at m
u know you like it nice and hot.'</s><s>'I do not,' she said and pushed at me as I put the tea down.</s><s>A lick of	tea	stung the back of my hand.</s><s>I grabbed her wrist.</s><s>'What do you think you're up to?'</s><s>I demanded
I nothing at all left for George now.</s><s>And about how I was going to kill my father.</s><s>'I'd love a nice cup of	tea	,' Mum says suddenly.</s><s>Africa has given way to a sit-com's happy mum, happy dad, happy kids.</s><s>That'
s>I look at Mum: she's smiling.</s><s>I turn back to the white man's earnest justification and go and make a cup of	tea	.</s><s>I fetch myself another gin while I'm up and pour a bit in Mum's tea while I'm about it.</s><s>It'll help her sle

Figure 4.16 An example of recurrent concordance lines, associated with 'tea' in Sketch Engine.

110 *Critical Discourse Analysis in Translation Studies*

N	Concordance	File
1	If it works, it could intercept a limited attack from a state like NK. Mr. Bush's decision marked a major turn	NYT_33.txt
2	op a missile defense system primarily to defend against states like NK. They have said China is not an intende	NYT_23.txt
3	elop missile defense system primarily to defend against states like NK, and that China is not intended target	NYT_23.txt
4	sile shield built to protect the USA from any attack by states like NK and Iran. It's set for launch sometime	CNNEE_66.txt
5	ssile shield built to protect the USA from an attack by states like NK and Iran. And it's set for launch time,	CNNEE_66.txt
6	ir view is that when dealing with a heavily armed crazy state like NK -- which will probably never give up som	NYT_32.txt
7	, it argued that the USA should never allow a desperate state like NK to crank up a plutonium production line	NYT_36.txt
8	his switch is intended to thwart perceived threats from states like NK or Iraq, or groups that acquire the abi	NYT_22.txt
9	est, could protect the USA and Europe from threats from states like NK, dispensing with the need for the admin	NYT_14.txt
10	t the threat of a limited ballistic missile attack from states like NK, Iran and Iraq. It was not immediately	NYT_18.txt
11	ystem, if it works, could intercept limited attack from state like NK, Congress must still approve $1.5 billio	NYT_33.txt
12	nded to counter threats posed by smaller, missile-armed states like NK. Mr. Putin then stops in Blagoveshchens	NYT_14.txt
13	e found this year because of concern over rogue nuclear states like NK; holds that events of past two years--p	NYT_59.txt
14	e found this year because of concern over rogue nuclear states like NK. Fears of a new nuclear arms race had k	NYT_59.txt
15	he defended Russia's continuing involvement with rogue states like NK, Iraq and Iran in distinctly lukewarm t	NWE_15.txt
16	nded by Under Secretary of State John Bolton that rogue states like NK should take Saddam's lesson to heart, o	NYT_41.txt
17	tary of State John R. Bolton, said this week that rogue states like NK should take a lesson from the events in	NYT_41.txt
18	defense system, because everyone recognized that rogue states like NK and Iran posed a threat to Europe, to R	CNNEE_57.txt
19	world today is not from Moscow but from so-called rogue states like NK, Iran and Iraq which are not party to t	CNNEE_3.txt
20	defense network with the notion that a so-called rogue state like NK could one day lob a nuclear weapon towar	NYT_21.txt
21	s intended only to counter threats from small ''rogue'' states like NK, said the official, Sha Zukang, in an i	NYT_12.txt
22	s. While Mr. Bush has tended to focus narrowly on rogue states like NK and Iran, Mr. Kerry wisely favors a mor	NYT_55.txt
23	e intended to protect against the missiles of ''rogue'' states like NK. The Europeans question the depth of th	NYT_12.txt
24	ncerned about a potential new missile threat from rogue states like NK, Libya, Iraq and Iran--which, according	NWE_16.txt
25	he possibility of a ballistic missile attack from rogue states like NK, Iran or Iraq no longer a distant threa	NYT_5.txt
26	threat of a small number of missiles launched by rogue states like NK, Iraq and Iran, all of whom have shown	NYT_12.txt
27	se it of being nuclear scofflaw whose actions aid rogue states like NK and Iran; Brazil has resisted allowing	CNNEE_28.txt
28	rts of being a nuclear scofflaw whose actions aid rogue states like NK and Iran? Ever since it began observing	NYT_56.txt
29	se, which proponents say would defend against ''rogue'' states like NK and Iran, has called the treaty into qu	NYT_12.txt
30	s to deploy against ballistic missile attack by a rogue state like NK. The radar's job, figure out which is th	CNNEE_28.txt
31	o deploy against a ballistic missile attack buy a rogue state like NK. The radars job is to figure out which 1	CNNEE_28.txt
32	's possible that bin Laden may have gone to a terrorist state like NK or Cuba. But he says that sort of thinki	CNNEE_5.txt
33	t week that the threat of a missile strike from a rogue state like NK, Iraq or Iran justified building a limit	NYT_5.txt
34	proliferation, and should not be sold arms, and a rogue state like NK... BIDINGER: Like Israel? (CROSSTALK) GO	CNNEE_13.txt
35	ystem. In the long run, if some of the most threatening states like NK or Pakistan actually did begin to open	NWE_1.txt
36	ns to terrorist groups and anti-American, unpredictable states like NK. Mr. Bolton praised Libya in particular	NYT_52.txt

Figure 4.17 An example of recurrent concordance lines.

Of course, discourse analysis cannot be solely based on discovered discursive patterns. For instance, a pattern should be discussed in terms of percentages since the primary reason for using a corpus-based method is to obtain objective, quantifiable information. In addition, a long stretch of text should be analysed in the way in which the whole is constructed because the exercise is a discourse analysis and not an investigation of isolated lexical items. Nevertheless, concordance is a useful starting point of analysis.

4.3 Linguistic analysis: semantic prosody and semantic preferences

As mentioned in the introduction to this chapter, some scholars have pointed out the methodological limitation of the traditional CDA approach. For example, Stubbs[9] argued that CDA scholars find "what they expect to find, whether absences or presences" (1997, 102) because their lack of attention to methodology issues has demonstrated how an analysis of 'care', using large diachronic and contemporary corpora, reveals that the lexeme had "undergone a change from predominantly personal uses (to take care of someone) to very frequent institutional uses (child care)" (1997, 112). Additionally, in another case study carried out in 1995, where Stubbs examined different uses and collocational patterns of four adjectives – 'little', 'small', 'big', and 'large' – found that 'little' occurs predominantly with girl(s) and 'small' with boy(s), thereby imbuing 'little' with strong connotative meanings of 'cute and cuddly'. "The combination 'little man'", on the other hand, "is almost always pejorative, as is 'ridiculous little man'" (1997, 113). As seen from Stubbs' work, the kind of issues that concern CDA scholars can be addressed more systematically through corpora.

Stubbs' findings can be largely understood in relation to the notion of 'semantic prosody', although he does not use this term in the studies referred to here. Both this, and the related notion of 'semantic preference' have proved to be very productive in corpus-based studies (Louw 1993; Sinclair 1987b, 1991). However, although Zethsen (2006, 284) argues that "within the very broad area of CDA [...] semantic profile of a given word could be used as the basis for investigating our perception/the status of objects or concepts in a social or political context, either generally speaking or within specific discourses", these notions have not yet been applied in CDA studies. However, they are useful in explaining the way in which positive or negative discourses are generated.

The concept of semantic prosody can be traced back to 1948, when Firth first mentioned it in his paper 'Sounds and Prosodies'. However, his use of the term was limited to its definition: "phonological colouring which spreads beyond semantic boundaries" (Zhang 2010, 190). The first serious discussion and analyses of semantic prosody emerged in 1987 when Sinclair first discussed a phenomenon that later became known as 'semantic prosody', although he did not specifically coin the term. Sinclair noted that "many uses of words and phrases show a tendency to occur in a certain semantic environment" (1991, 112). However, it was not until 1993 that the term 'semantic prosody' was coined by Louw (1993, 159), who defined it as a "constant aura of meaning with which a form is imbued by its collocates". Since then, several studies on semantic prosody have appeared; they include Partington (1998, 2004), who refers to it as "the spreading of connotational colouring beyond single word boundaries" (1998, 68). Although 'semantic prosody' and 'connotation' are considered by Partington to be partly interchangeable, semantic prosody is different from connotation because it is "more strongly collocational than the schematic aspects of connotation" (Louw 2000, 50), whereas 'connotation' is limited to a single word or item. Xiao and McEnery (2006), Louw and Chateau (2010), and Stewart (2010) have all discussed this subject.

The primary function of semantic prosody is to express speaker/writer attitudes or evaluations (Louw 2000, 58), which may be negative, positive or neutral. Different scholars use various terms to describe the particular aura of meaning, or attitudinal load, it possesses; however, 'negative/unfavourable/unpleasant' or 'positive/favourable/pleasant' and 'neutral' are the principal labels attached to it in the literature. It may also contribute to communicating irony, in that a speaker or writer may "violate a semantic prosody condition to achieve some effect in the hearer" (Xiao and McEnery 2006, 106); this is achieved when there is "sufficient distance between the expected collocation and the combination of words proposed by the author" (Louw and Chateau 2010, 757).

Although semantic prosody has attracted the attention of a growing number of linguists,[10] an overwhelming majority of studies are monolingual and focus on Indo-European languages; hence, cross-linguistic studies of semantic prosody are rare. One of the few studies examining an Asian language was conducted by Xiao and McEnery (2006), who carried out a cross-linguistic analysis of English and Chinese. In terms of genre, literary texts have been widely used to examine semantic prosody, but other genres, such as courtroom transcripts (Cotterill 2001) and news (Gabrielatos and Baker 2008), have also been examined from the perspective of semantic prosody.

However, semantic prosody can also be used in the analysis of translation to identify a dominating textual discourse. For example, one of the most common patterns identified in Korean translations about North Korea that had been published in *Newsweek Hangukpan* [Newsweek Korea], which includes Korean translations of the English *Newsweek,* and *CNN Hangeul News* [CNN Korea], which provides the Korean translations of the selected materials from the *CNN* between 1998 and 2010 and from 2008 to 2010, respectively, was 독재자 김정일 (tokchaeja kimjŏngil) [dictator Kim Jong Il]. A negative semantic prosody was evident and reinforced by lexical items, such as: 땅딸막한 (ttangttalmakhan) [pudgy/stumpy], 괴짜 (koetcha) [oddball], 파악하기 힘든 (p'aakhagi himdŭn) [slippery], 위험한 (wihŏmhan) [dangerous], 무자비한 (mujabihan) [cruel], 잔인한 (chaninhan) [merciless], 악행 (akhaeng) [evil], 흐트러진 머리 (hŭt'ŭrŏjin mŏri) [fuzzy-haired], and 미치광이 (mich'igwangi) [wacky].' Although a further in-depth analysis of more extended stretches of text and collocate lists is required, it can be argued, in a most simple term, that a negative semantic prosody can be identified in examples from the concordance lines.

Semantic preference concerns a similar form of patterning, where a set of semantically related collocates of a given lexical item (or 'node') are identified and provide insight into the lexical environment and, ultimately, the semantic prosody characteristic of the use of the relevant item. Oster and van Lawick (2008, 335) used semantic preference to refer to "the semantic field a word's collocates predominantly belongs to" and to define semantic prosody as a "more general characterisation of these collocates", whether positive or negative.

Partington (2004, 151) also states that the role of semantic preference is restricted to relating the node to a lexical item from *a particular semantic set* (my emphasis), whereas prosody can affect wider stretches of text. Xiao and McEnery (2006, 107) also argue that semantic prosody covers "affective meanings of a given node with its typical collocates", whereas semantic preference is a semantic set of collocates. Therefore, semantic preference is a feature of the semantic patterning of a lexical item, which can be captured by identifying a specific set of collocates that share some semantic property. For example, 'happen' (Sinclair 1987a), 'utterly' (Louw 1993) and 'cause' (Stubbs 1995) can be characterised by negative semantic prosody because they each regularly occur in the environment of a set of collocates that may not belong to a semantic set but are unpleasant or negative: for example, 'utterly pointless' and 'utterly unacceptable' reflect the same negative prosody, but the adjectives 'pointless' and 'unacceptable' belong to different semantic sets. On the other hand, 'dollar', 'pound', 'won' and 'money' belong to the same semantic set, as do 'desk', 'chair', 'bed' and 'table', and are therefore examples of semantic preference.

Mautner (2007) demonstrated that corpora offer considerable potential for discourse and semantic preferences analysis. She investigated the word 'elderly' in a 57 million-word online spinoff from the more than 500 million-word *Bank of English* corpus with the goal of identifying evidence of stereotypical constructions of age and ageing. Mautner's findings suggest that the dominant semantic preferences of 'elderly' include 'care', 'illness', 'disability', 'vulnerability' and 'crime' and that semantic prosody is often strongly negative, with 'elderly' "emerging less as a marker of chronological age than of perceived social consequences" (ibid., 51). Here, 'age' is used as "the basis for a whole chain of stereotypical assumptions about individuals' attributes, needs, and life chances", which means that "someone who is old and fit, old and wealthy, or old and powerful, or a combination of all these, is much less likely to be referred to as *elderly* than are those who are old and disabled, old and poor, or old and dependent (or, as is quite likely, a combination of all these)" (ibid., 51, 63–64).

While expressing some reservations about applying a corpus methodology within the framework of CDA, including the issue of neglecting accompanying visuals, Mautner (2007, 66) defends the use of corpora in CDA. Mautner said "there is no miracle cure for the perennial tension between macro and micro levels of analysis, and between quantitative and qualitative procedures, but enriching projects in sociolinguistics and discourse analysis with corpus methodology can go some way toward turning this tension into fruitful dialogue". For example, some interesting patterns of semantic preference were found in the analysis of the North Korea corpus mentioned earlier (i.e., the manually built corpus consisting of texts about North Korea and published in American news media outlets – *Newsweek, New York Times,* and *CNN* from 1998 to 2010), which can be understood in terms of the political and social landscape. Semantic preferences found in the English corpus were reflected in the semantic groups that featured ways of controlling North Korean nuclear production sites and programme and revealed the imbalance of power between North Korea and the USA. (Phrasal) verbs such as 'condemn', 'constrain', 'control', 'dismantle', 'deter', 'halt', 'rein in', 'shut down' and 'tolerate' form a coherent semantic group that has something to do with ways of dealing with North Korean issues. Interestingly, concordance lines of 'North Korea's' revealed that the actors involved in dealing with North Korean issues (i.e., the parties who 'deter', 'dismantle', 'shut down', and 'tolerate') are predominantly South Korea and the USA. The entities that 'condemn', 'shut down' and 'dismantle' include the United Nations (UN), KEDO (Korean peninsula Energy Development Organisation), South Korea, China, Russia, the US and the Group of 8 (G8). The USA is involved in all three organisations mentioned above – UN, KEDO[11] and G8[12]. The countries that have the most powerful hold on North Korea, then, are the current 'world powers', most notably the USA. Another important pattern of semantic preference features North Korea being construed as a defendant and the USA as jury. Items such as 'affirm', 'data', 'defend', 'evidence', 'experts', 'investigate', 'investigation', 'reports', 'speculation is rampant', and 'fact' appear in the vicinity of the node word (i.e., North Korea). They can be grouped semantically to reveal a tendency to set the reporting within a judicial or semi-judicial context in which North Korea has to be investigated and the facts regarding its 'illegal' activities established.

Semantic prosody and semantic preference interact with each other: "semantic preference contributes powerfully to building semantic prosody", whereas semantic prosody "dictates the general environment which constrains the preferential choices of the node item" (Partington 2004, 151). Patterns associated with semantic prosody and semantic preference in translations can be examined. For example, the same translational corpus mentioned above, i.e., the corpus consisting of English ST news articles and their corresponding Korean translations from *Newsweek Hangukpan* [Newsweek Korea] and *CNN Hangeul News* [CNN Korea] between 1998 and 2010 and from 2008 to 2010, has shown that negative semantic prosodies were attested in the environment of Kim Jong Il, in relation, for example, to his appearance, hair style, and relatively short height, both of which are caricatured in the media, both in the English ST corpus and the Korean TT corpus. In contrast, a positive semantic prosody was identified in the concordance lines of the late South Korean President Kim Dae Jung, which feature collocates such as 'engagement', 'rapprochement', 'peace' and 'warm', specifically with reference to his 'sunshine policy' – the foreign policy that aimed at achieving peace on the Korean peninsula through reconciliation and cooperation by easing North-South tensions.

A similar method for examining semantic prosodies and preferences can be applied to the study of translations especially when identifying any shifts in discourses in translation. In the corpus discussed above, for example, the same pattern was found in the English ST corpus, which comprises English texts chosen for translation by Korean media institutions. The analysis of the semantic prosodies and preferences and concordance lines of North Korea revealed that North Korea was projected as a voiceless party subjected to a judicial process in which the USA acts as a judge and pronounces North Korea's 'suspicious' acts. However, in the Korean translation, by contrast, North Korea appears to exert some control in a process of 'negotiation' with the USA, further supporting the idea that the purpose of news translation is "to adapt texts to the needs of different publics, which requires not only reorganizing and contextualizing information but also an exercise of *subtle rewriting* in order to *heighten the effectiveness of the original text in the new context*" (Bielsa and Bassnett 2009, 104, my emphasis).

As demonstrated above, semantic prosodies and preferences enable scholars to identify existing, or any dominant, discourse in ST and TT, respectively, and any patterns of shifts in semantic prosodies and preferences in translation can then be interpreted in relation to changes in discourse, which can then be discussed in terms of the socio-political contexts in which both ST and TT are produced.

4.4 Analytical data: corpus-based CDA that reveals ideological orientations

Corpus-based CDA analysis has been extensively employed by scholars in linguistics because both concordance lines and collocates, as shown earlier, provide scholars with the opportunity to pinpoint dominant patterns that contribute to the construction of certain discourses and to explain them in relevant socio-political and cultural settings. The corpus-based CDA approach has been used to query texts of various genres, such as British media discourse characterised by sexism (Pérez-González 2000), government and academic publications on lifelong learning (Piper 2000), and legislative discourse (Graham 2001). However, of the studies carried out to date, most have looked at press and newspaper articles. This is unsurprising given the nature of CDA, which essentially reveals the relationship between discourse and hidden power and the linguistic devices used to construct a particular discourse. Henry and Tator (2002, 72) also acknowledged this point by stating that CDA is "a tool for deconstructing the ideologies of the mass media and other elite groups and for identifying and defining social, economic and historical power relations between dominant and subordinate groups".

For instance, Baker et al. (2008)[13] examined a corpus of 140 million words consisting of articles from twelve national and three regional newspapers published between 1996 and 2005, relating to refugees, asylum seekers, immigrants and migrants (collectively referred to as RASIM). Their CDA analysis, which focused on a small number of articles, revealed that what appeared to be positive topoi in a small number of articles (assumed through corpus analysis to take a less negative attitude toward RASIM) were not positive after all (ibid., 296). The study thus challenged the view of broadsheets as "consistently neutral or only positive toward RASIM" (ibid., 290). In 2020, Baker and McGlashan conducted a similar corpus-based CDA study to examine how typically linguistically Romanians are represented in news reports and reader comments from the British right-leaning tabloid the *Daily Express* in the period up to Brexit, which reported that "Brexit was blamed on the German chancellor Angel Merkel's 'open-door approach' to immigration" (Baker and McGlashan 2020, 223). They categorised collocates of Romanians into several groups, such as a movement group that included arriving, settle, gain, and arrive, and a law-and-order group that included words like visa, loophole, gang, curbs, and controls. Alongside the collocates, metaphors in headlines such as a 'tide of immigrants', 'swarms of migrants' present immigration presented as problems, "figuratively constructing migrants as a kind of flying pest or insect" (Baker and McGlashan 2020, 235). However, what is distinctive in this study is that the patterns in comments and reports were compared. For example, several personal pronouns (e.g., they, we, our, them, us, and so on) were found to be more frequent in comments. However, the investigation of verb collocates of us and them in comments revealed that unwanted action has been carried out on us and that a sense of being attacked is constructed through verbs such as imposing, imposed, forcing, bleed, rob, threaten, betrayed and invade, whereas negative discourse prosodies are found through verbs such as smuggle, shove, deporting, and shoving, although the latter was not specifically to Romanians but more generally to immigrants coming to the UK (Baker and McGlashan 2020, 232–234). They argue, on the basis of a detailed qualitative analysis of an article and comments, that articles and comments work in tandem; thus, both should be considered to understand how "the newspaper like *The Express* and its commentators played in the decision of the British people to leave the EU" (Baker and McGlashan 2020, 228). These studies confirm that examination of news corpora can reveal the underlying attitudes and ideologies of media outlets, whether positive or negative, towards a particular object of study.

Qian (2010) conducted a similar corpus-based CDA study of 'terrorism', using the *People's Daily*, the Chinese newspaper, and *The Sun*, the British newspaper, before and after the 9/11 2001 terrorist attacks on the World Trade Centre in Manhattan, looking at ways in which discourses on terrorism changed in the Chinese and UK press between 2000 and 2002. Although this study was a comparative analysis of original English texts, not translation, studies such as this can still offer new findings because, although Qian maintains that the *People's Daily*, the Chinese broadsheet, and *The Sun*, the UK tabloid, are similar in that they are both daily newspapers, they have different attitudes (one being tabloids and the other broadsheets) and the different political systems of the two countries, whereby "[the] UK does not have government-controlled newspapers, while all newspapers in China are subject to state censorship to some degree" (ibid., 47).

A corpus-based approach was also used by Mouka, Saridakis, and Fotopoulous (2015) when they explored register shifts in the English STs and Spanish and Greek translations of racism-oriented discourses in films. They examined the contemporary feature films produced between 1989 and 2006, whose narratives revolve around racism and interracial relations. The authors adopted appraisal theory, particularly the concept of attitudes, to investigate the negative expressions of racism. In addition to cases where racial slurs are mitigated or omitted by a translator, the shift identified in their study showed other instances where racist attitudes were over-toned (i.e., interpersonal meaning was intensified). Similarly, Li and Pan (2021) probed a corpus consisting of work reports by the National Congress of the Communist Party of China, work reports and white papers issued by the Central Chinese Government, and their translations. The analysis highlighted shifts in the English translation of Chinese political discourse. Some individual translators who do not share the ideological translation principles of Chinese political discourse or who adopt a target reader-oriented approach intervene in the translation, even when the equivalent strategy is a canonical guideline issued to translators who subscribe to the government subservience to source authorship.

4.5 Corpus-based CDA approach to translation research

This combined methodology is beneficial for translation research. House (2015, 126) also recognised the benefit of using a corpus method in translation quality assessment by arguing that "corpus studies provide the assessor with information about whether and how far characteristics of a single translation are in line with the norms and conventions of the Genre in the target culture". Corpus-based CDA has helped scholars in translation studies uncover translation shifts – the "small linguistic changes that occur in translation of ST to TT" (Munday 2001, 55) and interpret these shifts in the context of a source culture and a target culture.

Although some linguistically oriented studies may examine "obligatory shifts" (i.e., shifts due to differences in linguistic systems), most corpus-based CDA investigations pay more attention to "optional shifts" that are "opted for by the translator for stylistic, ideological or cultural reasons" (Bakker, Koster, and van Leuven-Zwart 1998, 228). The analysis may involve taking the following steps. First, recurrent patterns in both a ST corpus and a translation corpus are identified. Second, the identified patterns are compared. Third, the different patterns are subjected to closer scrutiny, whereby longer stretches of text are explored in more detail. Finally, any shift or deviation is examined and discussed in terms of the historical, political, and societal contexts in which both STs and TTs are embedded. Here, the frameworks discussed in Chapter 2 can be employed.

A translational corpus can comprise more than two sub-corpora from different media outlets, thereby advancing comprehensive analysis. For example, a corpus can consist of an English ST corpus and a Thai TT corpus (i.e., parallel corpora, in Mona Baker's terms (1995)), covering the same period and outlet. The patterns identified in the analysis of the STs can then be compared against the patterns identified in the TTs. A corpus can consist of the English ST corpus, which includes texts originally produced in English from, say, 2000 to 2020 in *Cosmopolitan* and *Vogue*, and the Thai TT corpus, which contains their corresponding Thai translations (translations published in *Cosmopolitan Thailand* and *Vogue Thailand*), as shown in Figure 4.18.

118 *Critical Discourse Analysis in Translation Studies*

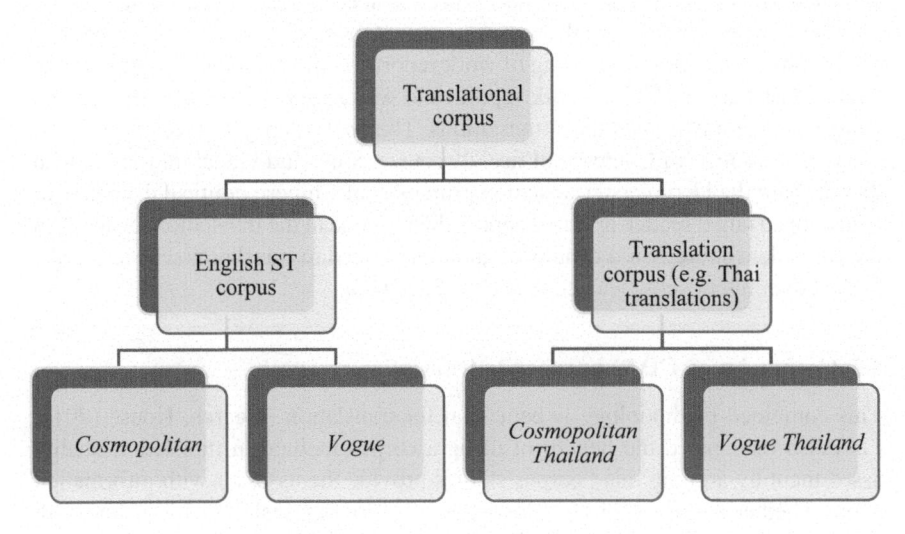

Figure 4.18 An example of a composition of a translational corpus for a corpus-based CDA analysis.

Such corpus construction can facilitate an examination of (1) a general pattern in the English ST and Korean TT, (2) a recurrent pattern specific to a given media outlet and (3) a shift in patterns between the English ST and Korean TT. The findings pertaining to item (3) can then be discussed, again, in terms of the sociopolitical and historical contexts in which the texts are embedded.

Figures 4.19 and 4.20 present examples of different patterns identified in the corpus that I built for the purpose of my work, which can be discussed using a CDA framework. My English ST corpus consisted of articles about North Korea published in *Newsweek* and *CNN* from 1998 to 2010 after North Korea opened its borders to South Korea in 1998. As a first step in the analysis, I examined the English ST corpus, using a software program. This step revealed a recurrent pattern in relation to Kim Jong Il, with the 'leader' most discursively used to refer to the former leader. The same process undertaken at the second step for the Korean TT corpus revealed that a proper designation, such as 'Chairman/Chairman of the National Defence Commission',[14] was disproportionately used to refer to Kim Jong Il in the Korean translations.

Item	Number of concordance lines	% of total concordance lines	Kim Jong Il/ Kim Jong-Il/ Kimg Jung Il
leader	79	19%	
dictator	28	7%	
regime	28	7%	
strongman	14	3%	

Figure 4.19 Patterns associated with 'Kim Jong Il' identified in the English ST corpus.

Item	Gloss	Number of concordance lines	% of total concordance lines	Kim Jong Il/ Kim Jong-Il/ Kim Jung Il
wiwŏnjang/ kukpangwiwŏnjang	Chairman/Chairman of the National Defence Commission (CNDC)	339 (209/130)	39%	
chŏnggwŏn	Political power/ Regime	115	13%	
chidoja	leader	80	9%	
tokchaeja	dictator	19	2%	

Figure 4.20 Patterns associated with Kim Jong Il identified in the Korean TT corpus.

Examples 1 and 2 show instances where the word 'dictator' is replaced by 'Chairman' or 'Chairman of the National Defence Commission' in the Korean translation.

Example 1

ST (Newsweek, 27 October 2002)[15]
Just ask Japanese Prime Minister Junichiro Koizumi, who is under the gun to explain certain lines in a joint declaration, he signed with *NKn dictator Kim Jong Il* at a summit meeting in Pyongyang on Sept. 17.

TT
chinan 9wŏl 17il p'yŏngyangesŏ yŏllin puk, il chŏngsanghoedamesŏ koijŭmi chunich'iro ilbonch'ongniwa *kimjŏngil kukpangwiwŏnjang* [CNDC kim jong Il]i sŏmyŏnghan kongdongsŏnŏnmun chung ilbu naeyongi kŭ chohŭn yeda.

Gloss
A good example is part of a joint declaration on which Japanese Prime Minister Junichiro Koizumi and *CNDC Kim Jong Il* signed.

Example 2

ST (Newsweek, 11 August 2007)[16]
Since *NKn dictator Kim Jong Il* began a programme of pseudoreforms in July 2002, outside investment has increased from places as diverse as Britain, Germany, SK and China.

> **TT**
> 2002nyŏn 7wŏl *kimjŏngil pukhanjidoja [the north korean leader kim jong Il]*ka kŏnmoyangppunin kaehyŏk p'ŭrogŭraemŭl sijakhan irae yŏngguk, togil, han'guk, chungguk tŭng tayanghan chiyŏgŭrobut'ŏ oegugin t'ujaga nŭrŏtta.
>
> **Gloss**
> Since *North Korean leader Kim Jong Il* began a programme of pseudoreforms in July 2002, various outside investments have increased from places such as the UK, Germany, South Korea and China.

These shifts may be partly the result of adopting general Korean journalistic norms, or they may be part of a process of recontextualisation, whereby a text is rewritten in subtle ways to promote a particular view of the world. Kang (2010), who examined an interview article in *Newsweek* and its corresponding Korean version in *Newsweek Hangukpan*, discovered a shift in the image of President Roh between the ST and the TT, where, according to her, *Newsweek Hangukpan* adapted a problematic news article for a different cultural audience. Therefore, conventions issued by the media outlet under examination alongside cultural contexts need to be considered before establishing an argument. Indeed, as Bielsa and Bassnett (2009, 70) argues, agency style manuals are "useful codes specifying and regulating the most important operations for the production of news", and they contain "full style guides addressing potentially problematic words".

The Joong Ang Ilbo in 1997 for Newsweek Hangukpan Korean translators published in Korea (The JoongAng Ilbo 1997) clearly states that historical figures and household names can be referred to without their occupational designation, e.g., 'Churchill', rather than 'Churchill, the then prime minister of the UK'. The guidelines also explain that 'Bill Clinton, the president of the US' can be simplified to 'President Clinton' or 'Clinton'. If this is so, then some leeway was allowed for reference to Kim Jong Il by his first name without mentioning his official title (i.e., 'Kim Jong Il' instead of 'CNDC Kim Jong Il'), at least in some instances. 'Chairman' was clearly the default term for referring to Kim Jong Il in the Korean translations, even when the collocate 'leader' was among the most frequently occurring in the English corpus under examination. This choice shows a translator's agency and intervention. It may also reflect the political climate at the time the news reports were produced, which might have influenced the translators' choices because "news translation can entail the thorough-going transformation of the source text and the production of a new one designed to suit specific audiences according to the journalistic norms of the region" (Bielsa and Bassnett 2009, 84). On the basis of these data, and after consulting the journalistic conventions and guidelines in the cultural context in which the translations were produced, a tentative argument can be made that the effect of, or the reason for, such relatively minor cumulative shifts is that North Korea was, at least at the time of translation, perceived by a South Korean audience as a neighbouring country rather than as an 'enemy regime who consistently carries out a series of provocative acts against their country'.

Such a corpus-based CDA-informed approach can also be used to reveal interesting linguistic patterns in ideological news reporting where positive or negative prosodies associated with a particular body may be identified. By using a CDA framework – van Dijk's framework, for example – the reason for such shifts in news translation and the extent to which they influence how people interpret the world can be explained.

A traditional CDA-informed approach, which typically involves exploring a limited number of texts, or part of a text, might not have returned the same result as that derived through a quantitative, corpus-based approach. It would have failed to justify the selection of a particular text as well. As demonstrated above, however, not only does a corpus-based method provide objective figures based on which an argument can be established, it also attaches further weight to the argument made in relation to the ideological orientations of news outlets.

Thus, a growing number of studies have employed the corpus-based CDA approach, whereby (optional) translation shifts in translation and interpreting are identified and discussed in terms of the historical and socio-political contexts where each ST and TT are embedded. Some studies in Chapter 3 have used a corpus-based method. For example, Li and Zhang (2021) manually built a corpus consisting of interpreting transcriptions of Chinese foreign minister Wang Yi's annual press conferences during the National People's Congress and the National Committee of the Chinese People's Political Consultative Conference sessions held between 2016 and 2018. The authors wanted to investigate the gatekeeping roles played by government press conference interpreters in China in answering journalists' questions. They used the CDA framework to explain interpreters' linguistic choices – particularly the translation shifts and identified discursive patterns – in terms of ideology and power relations. Shifts in interpersonal metafunction realised in mood, speech function, and appraisal were the focus of the study. They argue that a press conference interpreter "significantly controls and filters the original messages in the interpreting process by withholding, modifying and supplementing the interpersonal meanings in the ST" (Li and Zhang 2021, 123), and this type of gatekeeping practice is motivated by ideological and institutional alignment with the Chinese government because Chinese press conference interpreters are government employees. Thus, more modifications of interpersonal meanings occur primarily in the interpreted utterances of foreign journals, as they tend to raise more sensitive or face-threatening questions than Chinese journalists do.

A corpus-based, CDA-informed translation analysis is one of the main research domains pursued by Tao Li, who uses corpus tools to capture significant patterns and uses mainly van Dijk's ideological square model (see Chapters 2 and 3) to explain linguistic patterns and translation shifts (Li and Zhu 2020; Li and Pan 2021). A corpus-based method is used to examine news discourses, as demonstrated in Ping's (2021), who used a corpus consisting of translated English and Chinese media coverage of the 2014 Hong Kong protests from *Reference News* (mainland

China), *EJ Insight* (Hong Kong), *BBC Chinese* (the UK), and *NYT Chinese* (the US) between 28 September and 15 December 2014 and Sketch Engine as a corpus analysis tool. To determine discourses about the 2014 Hong Kong protest (also known as the Occupy Central or Umbrella Movement) and discourse shifts in translation, Ping focused on high-frequency words and semantic prosodies. Ping argues that significant differences between the translated discourses are revealed, where the *BBC* and *NYT* Chinese often relate protests with democracy, but "the democratic associations are significantly less prominent in *RN* [Reference News] discourses and are mixed with less favourable connotations" (Ping 2021, 167). Other corpus-based CDA-informed translation studies with other language pairs include Baumgarten's studies (2007, 2009), which examined the eleven English translations of Hitler's *Mein Kampf* (discussed in Chapter 3), and Daghigh, Sanatifar and Awang's work (2018). In addition to another work in 2018 discussed in Chapter 3 (section 3.1.3), the authors built a custom-made corpus comprising 31 opinion articles in English and their corresponding Persian translations discussing the Iranian nuclear programme to examine political discourse translation. The highlight of their study is that they proposed a typology of "manipulative operations" (2018, 213) in journalistic and political translation – (1) blocking undesired representations of a ST in a TT; (2) demoting undesired representations of a ST in a TT; (3) promoting desired representations of a ST in a TT; and (4) preserving the desired representation of a ST in a TT – and what they call 'manipulation techniques', such as omission, euphemism, changes in modality, addition, and lexicalisation. Like other studies of political discourse translation, their analysis demonstrated that conscious and unconscious translation shifts by mediators, including translators, conform to the socio-political expectations of the target media and community. Gu has worked extensively on interpreting using a corpus-based CDA as the main research method and framework. He used a corpus to establish a discursive pattern found in interpreting transcripts to identify the mediating role – more specifically, the ideological involvement – of interpreters (Gu 2018) and shed light on the agency of Chinese press conference interpreters (Gu 2019b, 2021).

Practice essay questions

1 Build your own translational corpus. Provide your rationale for the choice of genre and texts and explain the text selection criteria.
2 Formulate an argument for, or against, the use of corpora in translation analysis using authentic examples.
3 Al-Hejin (2007) examined 23 articles (totalling 14,148 words) on the Muslim veil authored by BBC journalists and correspondents in the French and British contexts. The textual analysis revealed a number of important trends. First, prejudice against the veil was not always questioned. Second, the veil often collocates with words such as 'extremism', 'fundamentalism', 'radicalism', and 'backwardness' and is hence constructed as a 'threat and

a problem'. A similar analysis of 'veil' in the British National Corpus also reveals that in 59% of all occurrences, the adjectival form ('veiled') tends to collocate with negative words such as 'threats', 'hostility' and 'racism'. Al-Hejin argues that subtle linguistic devices contribute to "negative and inaccurate representations of the veil", which include "reluctance to specify the form of veil being discussed; referring to the veil as a symbol, a tradition or cultural practice" (ibid., 29). This situation, according to Al-Hejin, can be interpreted in relation to the change in political climate after the 2005 terrorist bombings in London. These events led to a discoursal shift in the position of New Labour away from 'multiculturalism', the slogan that the then-government had associated with Britain since 1997, and towards 'integration'. This often meant that "Muslims should conform to the British way of life", thus making the veil a problem. At the same time, the government framed the events in question as evidence that multiculturalism did not work (ibid., 27–30). The BBC reports ultimately reflect the shift involved in promoting the discourse of 'integration'.

Discuss these findings in terms of language and society, focusing on the extent to which the linguistic patterns, features and tendencies revealed in the analysis of news items reflect prevailing political attitudes towards a certain issue. You can argue for or against the contentions that linguistic usage encodes representations of the world and that the language used in news reports is not neutral, random or intuitive but rather chosen selectively.

Notes

1 Corpus Linguistics is a branch of linguistics which relies on "the large scale analysis of a very large body of authentic running text to capture regularities in language use" where the texts are held in machine readable form (Baker 2000, 6). Software programs are used to identify recurring linguistic patterns. Corpus linguistics pay more attention to linguistic description and to the development of quantitative, as well as qualitative, models of language based on empirical data than linguistic competence.
2 Due to the phonological ambiguity of transcription, the Korean character 'Jong' may be romanised as 'Jung' or 'Jeong'. Although this book follows the Korean romanisation whereby 'Jong' may be transcribed as 'Jeong' or 'Jung', only 'Kim Jong Il', not 'Kim Jeong Il', will be used throughout the chapter, because; (1) the latter is more widely used in the media – indeed, no concordance line of 'Kim Jeong Il' was found; (2) due to lack of space, and because this research does not involve an analysis of Kim Jung(-)Il/Kim Jong(-)Il/Kim Jeong (-)Il'. However, this research will also investigate concordance lines of other cases, thus, 'Kim Jong Il' will also refer to Kim Jong Il/Kim Jong-Il/Kim Jeong Il/Kim Jeong-Il/Kim Jung Il/Kim Jung-Il. The same rule applies to Kim Jong Un (/Kim Jong-Un/Kim Jeong Un/Kim Jeong-Un/Kim Jung Un/Kim Jung-Un), Kim Jong Nam (/Kim Jong-Nam/Kim Jeong Nam/Kim Jeong-Nam/Kim Jung Nam/Kim Jung-Nam) and Kim Dae Jung (/Kim Dae-Jung/Kim Dae Joong/Kim Dae-Joong).

3 https://genealogiesofknowledge.net (last accessed 15 September 2024).
4 What Sinclair (2004, 28) calls "frequent co-occurrence of words". See below Section 4.2.2 for more discussions about collocates.
5 For more information about the way in which WordSmith tests statistical significance, see Scott (2022).
6 The case-sensitive option was not activated when obtaining the frequency list used for processing relation scores, for the following reasons: (1) the collocate list is computed case-insensitively and there is no option to allow the researcher to change this setting; (2) if the case-sensitive option is activated, the program generates a word list that distinguishes between a word appearing in upper case and one appearing in lower case, which means that many words, like 'Nuclear' and 'nuclear', would be counted separately, resulting in an even less manageable list; (3) where relevant, different forms of a word or compound are manually simplified, for instance, the 'US', 'U.S' and 'US' are replaced by 'USA', which means they are readily distinguished from lower case forms that might confuse the issue – in this case, the pronoun 'us'.
7 Baker (2009) favours log-log and argues that it returns fewer low-frequency words than the MI score; however, log-log is not included among the statistical packages currently available from WordSmith.
8 A Korean word is largely comparable to an English word, because both writing systems are syllabic. Korean uses spaces to separate words, as is the case in English, although the basic unit in Korean is '*eojeol*', for which there is no equivalent in English. There are three ways to explain the concept of '*eojoeol*': *Bunseoksik Chegye, Jeolchungsik Chegye* and *Jonghapsik Chegye*, all of which are based on different understandings of what constitutes the basic unit of analysis. The present study adopts the *Jonghapsik Chegye* system, which does not consider Korean particles, verb-endings and suffixes (called '*josa*' and '*eomi*', e.g. *-eun, -neun, -ga* and *-ida*) – that cannot be used independently and that do not have meanings as such – as a separate unit of analysis. Rather, according to *Jonghapsik Chegye*, each element separated by spaces in a sentence is a single '*eojeol*', irrespective of whether it contains particles and suffixes; this contrasts with other systems that count particles and/or suffixes as separate '*eojeols*'. In this sense, the concept of '*eojeol*' in Korean is largely equivalent to an English orthographic word in the *Jonghapsik Chegye* system. Accordingly, the current study treats every Korean element separated by spaces as a single unit of analysis; hence, 'word' and '*eojeol*' are used interchangeably.
9 It should be noted that Stubbs does not consider himself a CDA scholar and has in fact been one of the vocal critics of CDA (see Stubbs 1997).
10 See Xiao and McEnery (2006, 106), where earlier studies on semantic prosody are summarised in tabular form.
11 KEDO is an organisation founded by the US, South Korea and Japan in order to deal with North Korea's nuclear power plant development and its construction of a light-water reactor nuclear power plant. KEDO now also includes Australia and the countries of the European Union, which joined the organisation after its foundation in 1995. Membership of the council of KEDO, however, continues to be restricted to the US, Japan and South Korea.
12 G8 consists of eight countries: Germany, Russia, the US, the UK, Italy, Japan, Canada and France, which is a forum of governments that exercise a powerful hold on the world's economy
13 Similar studies can be found in Baker and McEnery (2005), Baker et al. (2007) and Gabrielatos and Baker (2006 and 2008).

14 'Chairman' was, and still is, one of the official titles of Kim Jong Il. The Korean Central News Agency in North Korea (KCNA) claimed in 2012 that there were more than 1200 titles for Kim Jong Il (Noh 2012), including 'the sun of life', 'the sun of socialism', 'the great master of diplomatic resource', and 'the leader of versatile talents'. Even after his death, he is still referred to as a chairman, and, more specifically, as 'kukpangwiwŏnjang' [Chairman of the National Defence Commission (hereafter CNDC)]: CNDC is defined as 'the supreme commander of the armed forces of North Korea' (The Academy of Korean Studies 2012). The default reference to Kim Jong Il is therefore as 'chairman'.
15 www.newsweek.com/asian-security-losing-face-over-nukes-146359 (last accessed 14 August 2024)
16 www.newsweek.com/investing-north-korea-99279 (last accessed 14 August 2024)

Suggestions for further reading

Baker, Mona. 1993. "Corpus Linguistics and Translation Studies: Implications and Applications." In *Text and Technology: In Honour of John Sinclair*, edited by Mona Baker, Gill Francis and Elena Tognini-Bonelli, 233–250. Amsterdam & Philadelphia: John Benjamins.
Baker, Mona. 1996. "Corpus-Based Translation Studies: The Challenges That Lie Ahead." In *Terminology, LSP and Translation*, edited by Harold Somers, 175–186. Amsterdam & Philadelphia: John Benjamins.
Baker, Paul. 2009. *Using Corpora in Discourse Analysis*. London and New York: Continuum.
Baker, Paul, Costas Gabrielatos, Majid Khosravinik, Michal Krzyzanowski, Tony McEnery, and Ruth Wodak. 2008. "A Useful Methodological Synergy? Combining Critical Discourse Analysis and Corpus Linguistics to Examine Discourses of Refugees and Asylum Seekers in the UK Press." *Discourse & Society* 19 (3): 273–306.
Baker, Paul, Costas Gabrielatos, Majid Khosravinik, Michal Krzyzanowski, Tony McEnery, and Ruth Wodak. 2009. *Translating Hitler's "Mein Kampf": A Corpus-aided Discourse-analytical Study*. Saarbrücken: VDM Verlag Dr Müller.
Hu, Kaibao, and Lingzi Meng. 2018. "Gender Differences in Chinese-English Press Conference Interpreting." *Perspectivese* 26 (1): 117–134.
Li, Tao, and Feng Pan. 2021. "Reshaping China's Image: A Corpus-Based Analysis of the English Translation of Chinese Political Discourse." *Perspectives*. doi:10.1080/0907676X.2020.1727540.

References

Al-Hejin, Bandar. 2007. *Representations of the Muslim Veil in the BBC News Website: A Critical Discourse Analysis*, MRes (New Route PhD Programme) Dissertation. Lancaster, Applied Linguistics: Lancaster University.
Baker, Mona. 1993. "Corpus Linguistics and Translation Studies: Implications and Applications." In *Text and Technology: In Honour of John Sinclair*, edited by Mona Baker, Gill Francis and Elena Tognini-Bonelli, 233–50. Amsterdam & Philadelphia: John Benjamins.
Baker, Mona. 1995. "Corpora in Translation Studies: An Overview and Some Suggestions for Future Research." *Target* 7 (2): 223–43.
Baker, Mona. 1996. "Corpus-Based Translation Studies: The Challenges That Lie Ahead." In *Terminology, LSP and Translation*, edited by Harold Somers, 175–186. Amsterdam & Philadelphia: John Benjamins.

Baker, Mona. 2000. "Towards a Methodology for Investigating the Style of a Literary Translator." *Target* 12 (2): 241–66. doi:10.1075/target.12.2.04bak.

Baker, Paul. 2009. *Using Corpora in Discourse Analysis*. London and New York: Continuum.

Baker, Paul, Costas Gabrielatos, Majid Khosravinik, Michal Krzyzanowski, Tony McEnery, and Ruth Wodak. 2008. "A Useful Methodological Synergy? Combining Critical Discourse Analysis and Corpus Linguistics to Examine Discourses of Refugees and Asylum Seekers in the UK Press." *Discourse & Society* 19 (3): 273–306.

Baker, Paul, Costas Gabrielatos, and Tony McEnery. 2013. "Sketching Muslims: A Corpus Driven Analysis of Representations around the Word 'Muslim' in the British Press 1998–2009." *Applied Linguistics* 34 (3): 255–78. doi:10.1093/applin/ams048.

Baker, Paul, and Mark McGlashan. 2020. "Critical discourse analysis". In *The Routledge Handbook of English Language and Digital Humanities*, edited by Svenja Adolphs and Dawn Knight, 220–241. London: Routledge.

Bakker, Matthijs, Cees Koster, and Kitty van Leuven-Zwart. 1998. "Shifts of Translation." In *Routledge Encyclopedia of Translation Studies*, edited by Mona Baker and Gabriela Saldanha, 1st edition, 226–231. London & New York: Routledge.

Baumgarten, Stefan. 2007. *Translation as an Ideological Interface: English Translations of Hitler's Mein Kampf*. PhD Thesis. Birmingham: Aston University.

Baumgarten, Stefan. 2009. *Translating Hitler's "Mein Kampf": A Corpus-aided Discourse-Analytical Study*. Saarbrücken: VDM Verlag Dr Müller.

Bielsa, Esperança, and Susan Bassnett. 2009. *Translation in Global News*. London and New York: Routledge.

Buts, Jan. 2020a. "Community and Authority in ROAR Magazine." *Palgrave Communications* 6. doi:10.1057/s41599-020-0392-9.

Buts, Jan. 2020b. "Translation and Prefiguration: Consolidating a Conceptual Encounter." *Perspectives: Studies in Translatology* 28 (2): 224–37. doi:10.1080/0907676X.2019.1682626.

Chen, Juiching Wallace. 2006. "Explicitation through the Use of Connectives in Translated Chinese: A Corpus-Based Study." The University of Manchester.

Choi, Jinsil. 2020. "Lost in Translation: A Parallel Corpus-Based Study of South Korean Government Translation." *InTRAlinea* 22. www.intralinea.org/current/article/lost_in_translation_south_korean_government_translation.

Clear, Jeremy. 1993. "From Firth Principles – Computational Tools for the Study of Collocation." In *Text and Technology: In Honour of John Sinclair*, edited by Mona Baker, Gill Francis and Elena Tognini-Bonelli, 271–92. Philadelphia and Amsterdam: John Benjamins.

Cotterill, Janet. 2001. "Domestic Discord, Rocky Relationships: Semantic Prosodies in Representations of Marital Violence in the O. J. Simpson Trial." *Discourse & Society* 12 (3): 291–312.

Daghigh, Ali Jalalian, Mohammad Saleh Sanatifar, and Rokiah Awang. 2018. "Modeling van Dijk's Ideological Square in Translation Studies: Investigating Manipulation in Political Discourse Translation." *InTRAlinea* 20. www.intralinea.org/archive/article/modeling_van_dijks_ideological_square_in_translation_studies.

Daghigh, Ali Jalalian, Mohammad Saleh Sanatifar, and Rokiah Awang. 2018. "A taxonomy of manipulative operations in political discourse translation". *FORUM* 16 (2): 197–220.

Fairclough, Norman. 1992. *Discourse and Social Change*. Cambridge: Polity.

Fairclough, Norman. 2000. *New Labour, New Language?* London: Routledge.

Fattah, Ashraf Abdul. 2010. "*A corpus-based study of conjunctive explication in Arabic translated and nontranslated texts written by the same transaltors/authors.*" University of Manchester.
Firth, John. R. (1948) "Sounds and prosodies." *Transactions of the Philogical Society* 47 (1): 127–152.
Gabrielatos, Costas, and Paul Baker. 2008. "Fleeing, Sneaking, Flooding: A Corpus Analysis of Discursive Constructions of Refugees and Asylum Seekers in the UK Press, 1996–2005." *Journal of English Linguistics* 36 (1): 5–38.
Gallego, Silvia Soler. 2018. "Audio Descriptive Guides in Art Museums: A Corpus-Based Semantic Analysis." *Translation and Interpreting Studies* 13 (2): 230–249. doi:https://doi.org/10.1075/tis.00013.sol.
Graham, Philip. 2001. "Space: Irrealis Objects in Technology Policy and Their Role in a New Political Economy." *Discourse & Society* 12 (6): 761–788.
Gu, Chonglong. 2018. "Forging a Glorious Past via the 'Present Perfect': A Corpus-Based CDA Analysis of China's Past Accomplishments Discourse Mediat(Is)Ed at China's Interpreted Political Press Conferences." *Discourse, Context & Media* 24: 137–49.
Gu, Chonglong. 2019a. "Interpreters Caught up in an Ideological Tug-of-War? A CDA and Bakhtinian Analysis of Interpreters' Ideological Positioning and Alignment at Government Press Conferences." *Translation and Interpreting Studies* 14 (1): 1–20.
Gu, Chonglong. 2019b. "Mediating 'Face' in Triadic Political Communication: A CDA Analysis of Press Conference Interpreters' Discursive (Re)Construction of Chinese Government's Image (1998–2017)." *Critical Discourse Studies* 16 (2): 201–21.
Gu, Chonglong. 2021. "'The Main Problems in China-Japan Relations Lie in the FACT That Some Leaders in Japan Keep on Visiting the Yasukuni Shrine': A Corpus-Based CDA on Government Interpreters' Metadiscursive (Re)Construction of Truth, Fact and Reality." In *Advances in Discourse Analysis of Translation and Interpreting: Linking Linguistic Approaches with Socio-Cultural Interpretation*, edited by Binhua Wang and Jeremy Munday, 40–63. London and New York: Routledge.
Hardt-Mautner, Gerlinde. 1995. "Only Connect. Critical Discourse Analysis and Corpus Linguistics." In *UCREL Technical Paper 6*. Lancaster: Lancaster University. http://ucrel.lancs.ac.uk/ papers/techpaper/vol6.pdf.
Henry, Frances, and Carol Tator. 2002. *Discourses of Domination: Racial Bias in the Canadian English-Language Press*. Toronto, Buffalo and London: University of Toronto Press.
House, Juliane. 2015. *Translation Quality Assessment: Past and Present*. London: Routledge.
Hu, Kaibao. 2016. *Introducing Corpus-Based Translation Studies*. Berlin: Springer.
Hu, Kaibao, and Xiaoqian Li. 2016. "语料库翻译学与翻译认知研究:共性与融合 [Corpus-Based Translation Studies and Translation Cognition Research]." *Shandong Journal of Social Sciences* 10: 39–44.
Hu, Kaibao, and Lingzi Meng. 2018. "Gender Differences in Chinese-English Press Conference Interpreting." *Perspectivese* 26 (1): 117–34.
Hu, Kaibao, and Qing Tao. 2013. "The Chinese-English Conference Interpreting Corpus: Uses and Limitations." *Meta: Translators' Journal* 58 (3): 626–42.
Hunston, Susan. 2002. *Corpora in Applied Linguistics*. Cambridge: Cambridge University Press.
Ji, Meng. 2010. *Phraseology in Corpus-Based Translation Studies*. Oxford: Peter Lang.
Johnstone, Barbara. 1994. "Repetition in Discourse: A Dialogue." In *Repetition in Discourse: Interdisciplinary Perspectives*, edited by Barbara Johnstone, 1–20. Norwood, NJ: Ablex.

Jones, Henry. 2020. "Jowett's Thucydides: A Corpus-Based Analysis of Translation as Political Intervention." *Translation Studies* 13 (3): 333–51.

Kang, Ji-Hae. 2010. "Positioning and Fact Construction in Translation." In *Text and Context: Essays on Translation and Interpreting in Honour of Ian Mason*, edited by Mona Baker, Maeve Olohan and Maria Calzada Perez, 157–187. Manchester: St. Jerome.

Kim, Kyung Hye. 2013. "Mediating American and South Korean News Discourses about North Korea through Translation: A Corpus-Based Critical Discourse Analysis." Unpublished PhD thesis. The University of Manchester.

Kim, Kyung Hye. 2014. "Examining US News Media Discourses about North Korea: A Corpus-Based Critical Discourse Analysis." *Discourse and Society* 25 (2): 221–244. doi:10.1177/0957926513516043.

Li, Tao, and Feng Pan. 2021. "Reshaping China's Image: A Corpus-Based Analysis of the English Translation of Chinese Political Discourse." *Perspectives* 29 (3): 354–370.

Li, Tao, and Yifan Zhu. 2020. "How Does China Appraise Self and Others? A Corpus-Based Analysis of Chinese Political Discourse." *Discourse & Society* 31 (2): 153–171.

Li, Xin. 2018. "Mediation through Modality Shifts in Chinese-English Government Press Conference Interpreting." *Babel* 64 (2): 269–293. doi:https://doi.org/10.1075/babel.00036.li|.

Li, Xin, and Ranran Zhang. 2021. "Interpreting as Institutional Gatekeeping: A Critical Discourse Analysis of Interpreted Questions at the Chinese Foreign Minister's Press Conferences." In *Advances in Discourse Analysis of Translation and Interpreting*, edited by Binhua Wang and Jeremy Munday, 106–27. London: Routledge.

Louw, Bill. 1993. "Irony in the Text or Insincerity in the Writer?" In *Text and Technology: In Honour of John Sinclair*, edited by Mona Baker, Gill Francis and Elena Tognini- Bonelli, 157–176. Philadelphia, PA/Amsterdam: John Benjamins.

Louw, Bill. 2000. "Contextual Prosodic Theory: Bringing Semantic Prosodies to Life." In *Words in Context: A Tribute to John Sinclair on His Retirement*, edited by Chris Heffer and Helen Sauntson, 48–94. Birmingham: University of Birmingham.

Louw, Bill, and Carmela Chateau. 2010. "Semantic Prosody for the 21st Century: Are Prosodies Smoothed in Academic Contexts." In *JADT 2010: 10th International Conference on Statistical Analysis of Textual Data*. Rome: Sapienza University of Rome.

Mautner, Gerlinde. 2007. "Mining Large Corpora for Social Information: The Case of Elderly." *Language in Society* 36 (1): 52–72.

McEnery, Tony, and Andrew Wilson. 2001. *Corpus Linguistics: An Introduction*. Edinburgh: Edinburgh University Press.

Milani, Tommaso M. 2013. "Are 'queers' really 'queer'? Language, identity and same-sex desire in a South African online community". *Discourse & Society*, 24 (5): 615–633. https://doi.org/10.1177/0957926513486168

Ministry of Foreign Affairs and Trade: www.mofat.go.kr/main/index.jsp [last accessed 31 May 2012].

Mouka, Effie, Ioannis E. Saridakis, and Angeliki Fotopoulou. 2015. "Racism Goes to the Movies: A Corpus-Driven Study of Cross-Linguistic Racist Discourse Annotation and Translation Analysis." In *New Directions in Corpus-Based Translation Studies*, edited by Claudio Fantinuoli and Federico Zanettin, 35–69. Berlin: Language Science Press.

Munday, Jeremy. 2001. *Introducing Translation Studies*. London and New York: Routledge.

Noh, Jaehyeon. 2012. "北 kimjŏngil hoch'ing charang … 'konggaedoen kŏnman 1ch'ŏn200kae'" [North Korea showing off the titles of Kim Jong Il … over "1,200 official titles"], *Yonhapnews*, 12 January, http://media.daum.net/politics/north/newsview?newsid=20120112171710411 [last accessed 14 January 2013].

Oster, Ulrike, and Heike van Lawick. 2008. "Semantic Preference and Semantic Prosody." *Translation and Meaning* 8: 333–44.

Pan, Feng. 2020. "Norms and Norm-Taking in Interpreting for Chinese Government Press Conferences: A Case Study of Hedges." In *Corpus-Based Translation and Interpreting Studies in Chinese Contexts: Present and Future*, edited by Kaibao Hu and Kyung Hye Kim, 89–111. Cham: Palgrave Macmillan.

Pan, Feng, and Binghan Zheng. 2017. "Gender Difference of Hedging in Interpreting for Chinese Government Press Conferences: A Corpus-Based Study." *Across Languages and Cultures* 18 (2): 171–93.

Pan, Yun. 2021. "A Corpus-Based Analysis of Trainee Translators' Performance in Medical Translation." *Asia Pacific Translation and Intercultural Studies* 8 (3): 267–85.

Partington, Alan. 1998. *Patterns and Meanings: Using Corpora for English Language Research and Teaching*. Amherst: John Benjamins.

Partington, Alan. 2004. "Utterly Content in Each Other's Company: Semantic Prosody and Semantic Preference." *International Journal of Corpus Linguistics* 9 (1): 131–56.

Pérez-González, Luis. 2000. "Women in the Era of Post-Feminism: A Corpus-Based Appraisal of Equality in the News." In *Lengua, Discurso, Texto*, edited by José Jesús de Bustos Tovar, Patrick Charaudeau, José Luis Girón Alconchel, Silvia Iglesias Recuero y Covadonga López Alonso, 2105–2119. Madrid: Editorial Visor.

Ping, Yuan. 2021. "Representations of the 2014 Hong Kong protests in news translation: A corpus-based critical discourse analysis" In *Advances in Discourse Analysis of Translation and Interpreting*, edited by Binhua Wang and Jeremy Munday, 150–69. London: Routledge.

Piper, Alison. 2000. "Some have credit cards and others have Giro Cheques: 'Individuals' and 'People' as Lifelong Learners in Late Modernity." *Discourse & Society* 11 (4): 515–542.

Qian, Yufang. 2010. *Discursive Construction around Terrorism in the People's Daily (China) and the Sun (UK) before and after 9.11: A Corpus-Based Contrastive Critical Discourse Analysis*. Oxford: Peter Lang.

Scott, Mike. 2022. "Collocation." *WordSmith Tools 8.0 Help*. https://lexically.net/downloads/version8/HTML/collocation_basics.html.

Sinclair, John. 1987a. "Collocation: A Progress Report." In *Language Topics: Essays in Honour of Michael Halliday*, edited by Ross Steele and Terry Threadgold, 319–32. Amsterdam, Philadelphia: Benjamins.

Sinclair, John. 1987b. *Looking Up*. London and Glasgow: Collins.

Sinclair, John. 1991. *Corpus, Concordance, Collocation*. Oxford: Oxford University Press.

Sinclair, John. 2004. "The Search for Units of Meaning." In *Trust the Text: Language, Corpus and Discourse*, edited by John Sinclair and Ronald Carter, 24–48. London & New York: Routledge.

Stewart, Dominic. 2010. *Semantic Prosody: A Critical Evaluation*. New York and Oxon: Routledge.

Stubbs, Michael. 1995. "Collocations and Semantic Profiles: On the Cause of the Trouble with Quantitative Studies." *Functions of Language* 2 (1): 23–55.

Stubbs, Michael. 1996. *Text and Corpus Analysis: Computer-Assisted Studies of Language and Culture*. Oxford: Blackwell.

Stubbs, Michael. 1997. "Whorf's Children: Critical Comments on Critical Discourse Analysis (CDA)." In *Evolving Models of Language*, edited by Ann Ryan and Alison Wray, 100–116. Clevedon: Multilingual Matters.

Subtirelu, Nicholas Clos, and Paul Baker. 2017. "Corpus-based approaches." In *Routledge Handbook of Critical Discourse Studies*, edited by John Flowerdew and John E. Richardson, 106–119. Oxon and New York: Routledge.

The Academy of Korean Studies. 2012. *Encyclopaedia of Korean Culture*. http://encykorea.aks.ac.kr/ [last accessed 14 November 2012].

The Joong Ang Ilbo. 1997. *Newsweek han'gukp'an sŭt'ailbuk [Newsweek Hangukpan Stylebook]*. Seoul: The Joong Ang Ilbo.

van Dijk, Teun A. 1988. *News Analysis: Case Studies of International and National News in the Press*. Hillsdale, NJ: Erlbaum.

Wang, Binhua, and Dezheng Feng. 2018. "A Corpus-Based Study of Stance-Taking as Seen from Critical Points in Interpreted Political Discourse." *Perspectives* 26 (2): 246–60.

Wodak, Ruth and Michael Meyer. 2009. "Critical Discourse Analysis: History, Agenda, Theory, and Methodology." In *Methods for Critical Discourse Analysis*, edited by Michael Meyer and Ruth Wodak, second revised edition, 1–33. London: Sage.

Xiao, Richard, and Tony McEnery. 2006. "Collocation, Semantic Prosody, and Near Synonymy: A Cross-Linguistic Perspective." *Applied Linguistics* 27 (1): 103–29.

Zanettin, Federico, Gabriela Saldanha, and Sue-Ann Harding. 2015. "Sketching Landscapes in Translation Studies: A Bibliographic Study." *Perspectives* 23 (2): 161–182. doi:10.1080/0907676X.2015.1010551.

Zethsen, Karen Korning. 2006. "Semantic Prosody: Creating Awareness about a Versatile Tool." *Tidsskrift for Sprogforskning* 4 (1): 275–94.

Zhang, Changhu. 2010. "An Overview of Corpus-Based Studies of Semantic Prosody." *Asian Social Science* 6 (6): 190–94.

5 CDA-informed translation and interpreting research in a healthcare setting and the digital era

Key points of learning

- The abundant resources are available for discourse analysis on social media, especially for investigating the power of discourse circulated through social media, ultimately leading to societal changes.
- Discourse studies has engaged with theories and empirical work on social media to explore the realisation of cross-cultural social relations in a rapidly evolving communicative environment.
- CDA analyses of medical texts have focused on how cultural and institutional ideologies concerning power influence the languages we use in relation to health behaviours and knowledge.
- Some CDA studies examine social media texts to reveal their role in constructing, disseminating, and challenging discourses, whereas others investigate the empowerment and democratising roles that social media plays in challenging current, established, or institutionalised social systems and power.
- CDA-informed research on translation and health can focus on how translation is used to provide alternative views and discourses on health, gender, and the body.
- Scholars in medicine have increasingly recognised the vital role that language and communication play, bringing scholars in the distant fields of medicine and linguistics together.

The discussions in previous chapters (especially those in Chapters 3 and 4) were primarily based on written texts. However, the changes wrought in this digital era have prompted scholars of discourse and translation studies to consider new types of texts – from social media to online, alternative journalism – because news platforms have been opened up for participatory journalism and civic engagements. Consequently, one of these rapid developments has been the establishment of a new discipline, digital humanities.

DOI: 10.4324/9781003029083-6

Although, as discussed in the previous chapter (Chapter 4), corpus tools can address some of the shortcomings of CDA, which concerns inherent subjective individual interpretation, corpus-based CDA is still not immune to criticism. One of the notable criticisms of CDA remains greater, if not exclusive, and focuses on texts and linguistic analysis, as alluded to in previous chapters (especially Chapter 3 and 4). These criticisms have shifted the focus towards studying language in combination with other modes of communication, such as images, gestures, music, and even silence (Kress and van Leeuwen 2001, 2006; O'Halloran 2004). This has resulted in the emergence of a novel theoretical paradigm known as multimodal discourse analysis (O'Halloran 2011; Kress 2012; Winston and Roy 2015), which involves various modes – from visual to gestural, spatial, and auditory. Later, multimodal CDA was developed inspired by Halliday's SFL, which considers the social use of language, and early works on multimodality, such as Kress and van Leeuwen's *Reading Images* (1996/2006). Catalano and Waugh (2013) exemplify the CDA-spired multimodality research. They draw on CDA, multimodal analysis and cognitive linguistic frameworks to examine visual metaphorical patterns alongside texts concerning immigrants in US media discourse. In this study, van Dijk's 'negative representation of other and positive representation of us' pattern was also found in both verbal and visual elements: their analysis revealed "the negative portrayal of Latinos in crime reports has been used as a rationale for unjust immigration laws and policies", and positive portrayal of Wall Street CEOs has helped to permit them to continue (Catalano and Waugh 2013, 422). Similarly, a multimodal CDA study conducted by Ledin and Machin (2017) demonstrated how semiotic resources employed in the management and construction of discourse can be examined. In addition, CDA is employed not only to analyse a film genre, as Bateman (2018) stated but also to analyse new digital media text genres, such as social media; hence, the framework has proved to be useful for analysing micro-blogging platforms, particularly those such as Twitter (now changed to 'X')[1] and Weibo. Addressing the concerns raised over losing non-verbal elements of texts, such as images (Koller and Mautner 2004), and making a move to use CDA to analyse different modes is certainly encouraging.

Scholars recognised the potential of the web as a subject of CDA enquiry as early as 2000. In 2005, Mautner noted the lack of interest in CDA and emphasised the importance of the web as a "vast storehouse" (2005, 821) that offered an abundance of textual data for analysis while still highlighting the analysis of non-web-based text, which remains a worthwhile pursuit. Almost twenty years later, digital media is strongly associated with daily life. Especially when COVID-19 has significantly restricted mobility (see Section 5.3 below), the virtual engagement of lives and the establishment of connections and communication online have become increasingly common. Consequently, many texts are produced daily via social media and the Internet. Social media, such as Twitter/X and Facebook/Meta, have become powerful tools for connecting with others beyond straightforward enjoyment. For example, individuals used these tools to demonstrate their solidarity to change society, as was the case during the 2011 Egyptian Revolution. The

Occupy movement in New York in 2011, which addressed economic and social inequality following the financial crisis in 2007 and the Great Recession in 2011, used the '#OccupyWallStreet' hashtag on Twitter to inspire protests and expand the movement, which eventually gained traction. As Gwen Bouvier (2015) has argued, such an evolving online environment where media discourses are closely related to social practices means that discourse studies can no longer isolate online activities from discourse analyses.

However, as alluded to by various scholars, online texts pose several challenges for CDA studies. Interaction and communications online may differ from offline face-to-face encounters, in addition to a few elements mentioned by Mautner (2005, 815–16) as "authorship (e.g. institutional versus individual, gender, expert or lay status), time of publication […] geographic, cultural, and national origin (bearing in mind, however, that on the web the latter is difficult to identify)". Online users may act more politically or socially or craft a different persona that is likely to attract attention. Additionally, other modes, such as images and music, rather than written texts, are easily employed online to construct particular discourses or identities effectively. For example, Thompson's (2012) multimodal CDA analysis of the design of a mental health community website demonstrates that mental health discourses shifted from 'biomedical' to 'social-therapeutic' and that this shift was reflected in the shift in visuals.

This chapter also discusses CDA studies that examine translation and interpretation activities in healthcare settings. Since the global coronavirus disease 2019 (COVID-19) pandemic in December 2020, a number of conflicting discourses regarding vaccine reliability have been produced, and several CDA studies of vaccine equity have been conducted, as it has affected racial and ethnic minority groups. This resulted in the circulation of various new discourses about power and safety regarding vaccines, including 'who has the power to monitor, evaluate, and monitor its safety?', 'who is in a position to allocate and distribute limited vaccines?' and 'what is the co-relation between low vaccination rates and fair and equitable access to vaccines?'. The power dynamics between patients and health professionals, and among patients, health professionals and interpreters, have also been subject to discourse analysis. This period has resulted in a body of CDA literature on health, and a notable effort to analyse health discourses has been made using digital technologies by the Sustainability and Health Corpus.

Therefore, this chapter discusses the application of CDA beyond translation studies. It explores the engagement of discourse studies with theories and empirical work on social media to examine the realisation of cross-cultural social relations in a dynamically evolving communicative environment. Novel types of translational corpus tools, which are developed to encourage research into concepts and conceptualisations, will also be introduced. More attention will be given to discourse studies of crowd-sourcing and other digitally based translational activities, which demonstrate how discourses are produced, promoted, or challenged in a digital sphere. It will also posit that digital spaces are rich data sources and that CDA offers translation studies scholars a robust framework for pursuing such under-explored avenues in future research.

First, we discuss recent discourse scholarship on social media and then introduce certain research that examines the role of translation in constructing discourses on social media.

Activity 1

Ask yourself:

1   What social media platform do you frequently use?
2   What are the recent hashtag(s) you have used?
3   What kind of discourses do you think are associated with the hashtags you recently used?
4   If there are any countering discourses, what kind of hashtags did the opposing groups use?
5   To what extent are those countering comments (or tweets) identical to each other in terms of argumentation?
6   How do you determine if the post is influential? Is it by the viewing count, the sharing count, or the person who tweeted or shared it?

5.1 Digital and new media era: discourse construction in social media

CDA has been employed to analyse new types of texts, with social media being the most representative example. As Bouvier and Way (2021) argue, every content – overtly politically charged or mundane and banal – is both ideological and political to a certain degree. Even social media feeds becoming fit can be argued to be either ideological or political because "they present ideas and values about how people should act and behave, laying out what priorities we should have, and how we should evaluate others"; this also results in queries concerning what is highlighted, what is missing, and how ideologies are negotiated (Bouvier and Way 2021, 346–47).

The abundant resources available for discourse analysis on social media and its power to cause societal changes have been recognised by numerous CDA scholars (e.g. Bouvier 2020, 2022; Bouvier and Machin 2018). Gwen Bouvier is among those scholars who have extensively conducted CDA studies using social media texts to reveal their role in constructing, disseminating, and challenging discourses. She has undertaken (critical) discourse analyses of #MeToo Twitter feeds (Bouvier 2022), a social justice hashtag campaign on Twitter (Bouvier 2020), and journalistic practices in choosing discourses carried by Twitter feeds as news sources, where she has also analysed the accompanying images (Bouvier 2019). Bouvier contends that discourse studies must engage with theories and empirical work on social media to examine how cross-cultural social relations are realised in this new communicative environment's rapidly evolving landscape (2015, 2016). Similarly, McEnery, McGlashan, and Love (2015) conducted a study that explored the role of social media in constructing discourses and their relationships with the press and demonstrated that social media data analysis can enhance the understanding of various aspects of the discourse production and reception processes. In this study, they indicated that social media and the press are intertwined, with a focus on the contrast between how the UK press and social media reacted to the Lee Rigby case and the murder of an off-duty soldier in London in 2013. They discovered that the press exerts a notable influence through social media but does not always lead the latter (McEnery, McGlashan, and Love 2015, 237). The authors further propose that retweeting can be theorised as a crucial social practice through which a user's ideological stance is repeated (McEnery, McGlashan, and Love 2015, 243).

This analytical method can address one of the criticisms that have levelled at CDA: "reader response or audience reception is often naively assumed on the basis of the researcher's interpretation of the text" (Breeze 2011, 520). McEnery, McGlashan, and Love (2015) explain that Twitter data can counter criticisms that corpus-based CDA "focuses too often on the text itself, looking less at processes of production and reception [...since...] retweeting can be important in showing how oppositional discourses on Twitter are perceived and either promoted or ignored by users" (McEnery, McGlashan, and Love 2015, 256). This may explain why 'new media' is among the notable themes of clusters in Xiao and Li's (2021, 494–95) bibliometric analysis of CDA studies. Indeed, a growing body of CDA research on social media has emerged, with KhosraviNik (2017b) labelling it social media-critical discourse studies.

In such social media CDA, the focus of the analysis still primarily concentrates on topics such as power, ideology, institutions, and context, particularly how a particular discourse is constructed, promoted, and diluted. Some CDA-informed analyses of social media texts have examined the empowerment and democratising roles that social media plays, which "creat[e] spaces for non-mainstream views", whereby "new possibilities for alternative points of view or for challenging social systems and power" are witnessed (Bouvier and Machin 2018, 180). However, on the basis of some journalism studies, the authors also state that most citizen-generated content is "simply absorbed into the typical kinds of news values and frames used by mainstream outlets"; thus, the citizen voice "does not challenge the top-down elite discourses, but is used as a resource to further legitimise them" (Bouvier and Machin 2018, 180–81).

Although social media data provide discourse analysts with opportunities to expand their analytical views, this new data type poses various challenges to analysts. This is mainly because social media texts significantly differ from the usual written texts that have been subject to intellectual enquiry in CDA studies, mainly in three aspects. First, they feature many non-textual elements that convey meaning (i.e., multimodal). Emojis, videos, images, and hashtags are not texts in a traditional sense; for example, hashtags are fragmented words. Although they are not 'text', they contribute to meaning-making processes and are often used as discourse markers, and messages can also be hidden behind them (Bouvier 2019; Cohn, Engelen, and Schilperoord 2019; Grosz et al. 2023). For this reason, the frequent use of emojis on social media platforms has been the subject of discourse analysis research, as shown in the studies by Zappavigna and Logi (2021) and Grosz et al. (2023). Furthermore, the meaning these non-textual elements convey may differ from one culture to another, thus posing further challenges for translators. For example, a happy smiley face emoji typically indicates that the user (who sends the message) is happy. However, Chinese native speakers use the same emoji on the Chinese messenger application WeChat to imply that the speaker feels OK despite not being happy with the situation/person/object.

Second, online communities and cultures are often vastly different from those offline. The ability to communicate instantly and freely with anyone anonymously has resulted in a significant amount of communication being left online as a vast number of textual fragments. Twitter has only allowed up to 280 English characters, which means that the fragmented small units of text rather than a long, constructed piece became subject to analysis. In addition, texts are immensely dynamic and are constantly shared and revised. A well-known example is Wikipedia, a free online encyclopaedia that has collectively and collaboratively contributed to and shaped volunteers worldwide. Fragmented monolingual as well as translated texts are constantly contributed, added, removed, revised, and edited, which is vastly different from how written text is produced offline (see Henry Jones' work 2017, 2018a, 2018b, 2019).

Online interactions pose such challenges for scholars, but this does not mean that CDA offers little to study online communities and cultures. In particular, 'hashtag activism' has become a common place to show solidarity and support and a valuable resource for CDA research (Jackson, Bailey, and Welles 2020). The nature of Twitter, which enables easy and prompt dissemination of information, has enabled discourse analysts, who are interested in discursive and repetitive linguistic patterns that contribute to the (de)construction of power, to capture them by studying retweets. Moreover, CDA helps researchers examine how online users who, behind their pseudo identities, often engage in both challenging discourses and their activities can influence power relations in society. A well-known example, perhaps, is the 'ice bucket challenge' that went viral. It involves pouring a bucket of ice water over a person's head to promote awareness of amyotrophic lateral sclerosis (Lou Gehrig's disease). A typical post would include a short video of someone pouring ice water over the head and hashtags, such as #icebucketchallenge. In this case, the whole video and the fragmented text (hashtag) deliver a message, and the number of times the post is shared relays meaning to users, demonstrating solidarity with disenfranchised and marginalised populations to those people and organisations involved with social issues. Another example occurred during the campaign against the compulsory hijab-wearing law in Iran. In this case, photos were projected on the social media of citizens holding white headscarves or fragments of white clothing, accompanied by the hashtag #whitewednesdays (Hatam 2017). Other examples include #MeToo and #BlackLivesMatter. All of these and similar messages can be subject to discourse analysis. Translation also plays a significant role in this context, where partial or a full text is translated for wider dissemination of the discourse beyond geographical boundaries.

While the power of the Internet has led to the spreading of dissident discourses, scholars such as Frost (2020) have cast doubts concerning social media's "transformative" potential (Tufekci 2017), dismissing it as merely tokenistic. However, using a case study of the Egyptian uprising of 2011, Lim (2012) explored the role of social media as a force for social change. In this study, she illustrates that online activism and offline protests are inextricably linked and infused, whereby online activism on social media is transformed into offline protests. This suggests that it is an oversimplification to frame the Egyptian revolution exclusively as either a "Facebook revolution" or a "people's revolution" (Lim 2012, 232). Cottle (2011, 658), indicating the integral but multifaceted role of the media and communications network in building and mobilising support, expands the discussion further by drawing attention to its "transnationalising" nature. In addition, Bouvier and Way (2021) and Bouvier (2022), through their CDA analyses, caution against taking social media feeds at face value because much more complex negotiation processes and countervailing values and ideologies also occur on social media. For example, regarding Chinese Weibo feeds about fitness and lifestyle, Bouvier and Way (2021, 357) explain that "women fitness gurus position themselves against hegemonic notions of femininity, but at the same time communicate through a go-getting enterprising self, presenting themselves through the appropriate codes for middle class taste and modernity".

Some scholars have argued that social media has enabled CDA scholars to focus not only on discourse and power by elites and institutions but also on how it has democratised "bottom-up discourse" formations (KhosraviNik 2017b). However, other scholars such as Bouvier and Way (2021) and Bouvier (2022) warn that dominant discourses will harness bottom-up discourses. They explain that social media feeds are rarely composed of clear and coherent discussions but tend to limit "rational and careful discussion of issues" (Bouvier and Way 2021, 349).

Some recent studies that examine social media texts – mostly Twitter/X – have sought to understand how CDA can be applied to the analysis of social media texts. Aljarallah (2017) has investigated the hashtags used on Twitter/X concerning Saudi women's right to drive to reveal how opposing campaigns construct social beliefs. Aljarallah identified the extent to which views regarding women driving are distinctive, with reference to the different genders holding them. Using hashtags concerning women's driving movements in Saudi Arabia, such as '#Women_car_driving', '#I_will_drive_my_car_June15' (used by those who supported the movement), and '#I_will_enter_my_kitchen_June15' (used by those who were against the movement), and drawing on Fairclough's three-dimensional framework (see Chapter 2), Aljarallah focused on referential and nominative strategies. It revealed that #Women_car_driving was considered less threatening to anti-driving advocates and to current social beliefs and norms; therefore, there was less of supporters participating in the '#Women_car_driving' hashtag (Aljarallah 2017, 75). The findings suggested that negative naming and referential terms were used to construct negative discourses about opponents and supporters. Through this study, we can observe that the simple number of retweets does not necessarily equal the level of domination, where one hashtag is not preferred because it was deemed less threatening to the established system and social norms. Moreover, the analysis of social media texts should be more nuanced and multifaceted.

However, surprisingly, the discussion of the role of translation is lacking in these studies discussed thus far, even when dissemination and circulation of discourses beyond the geographical boundaries for wider reach is simply not possible without the help of translation. Translation can also be used as a tool to support, strengthen, or challenge discourses. Various social media texts are translated to introduce the idea that potentially threatens the existing mainstream discourse, and part or a fragmented part of a news report is translated and shared to provide users with competing discourses that are not available within a community.

While the previously mentioned study focuses more on how different groups construct discourse on social media, the study by Gonsalves, McGannon, and Pegoraro (2021) focuses on how cultural and institutional ideologies concerning power influence the languages used in relation to health behaviours and knowledge. Drawing on CDA as a framework, they identify various discourses concerning cardiovascular disease by analysing the #MoreMoments cardiovascular disease awareness campaign that the Heart and Stroke Foundation of Canada (HSFC) initiated. Additionally, they investigate the implications of "subject positions for risk reduction and health promotion" (2021, 1472) by analysing texts accompanying a #MoreMoments hashtag, whereby tweeted texts, videos, and GIFs glorify the medical and research industries. The analysis revealed two primary discourses – tragedy and loss and life and health, similar to the studies of the metaphor of illness (e.g., Hommerberg, Gustafsson, and Sandgren 2020; Semino et al. 2015) and two identity/subject positions: visionary leaders and successful survivors. Interestingly, it also reveals "partnerships between health organizations and for-profit organizations in promoting public health through corporate social responsibility" (Gonsalves, McGannon, and Pegoraro 2021, 1474) and that the demographic of the consumers of this particular hashtag is affluent, heteronormative, and white; and they consume "#MoreMoments on Twitter by promoting corporate goals of the HSFC" (Gonsalves, McGannon, and Pegoraro 2021, 1479). However, this CDA study raises enquiries regarding the discourse type and identities that are mediated, as well as the types of hashtags used for cardiovascular disease in health messages on social media by communities other than the affluent, heteronormative, and white.

Activity 2

Visit Twitter ("X") and search for a hashtag that has received significant attention in your culture. For example, it can be #OscarsSoWhite (Long, 2023).

Examine the data and ask the following questions:

1 What other lexical items are used as other hash tags in the Twitter comments under examination?
2 What kinds of discourses are constructed and by whom? Does it involve any translation?
3 Are there any differences in the discourses constructed by the individual users and institutions?
4 Are there any competing discourses surrounding the hashtag? If so, to what extent can van Dijk's ideological square model explain the discourse patterns of each opposing group?

Then, drawing on Fairclough's three-level analytical model (1992), examine the data more carefully while focusing on the following:

1 Text analysis: who is setting the agenda? how are identities constructed? what about voice (active or passive)? transitivity? modality?
2 Interpretation: how is the hashtag produced, circulated and consumed? How does each tweet intertwine with the texts (i.e., intertextuality)?
3 Explanation: establish the relationship between the discursive practices identified in (2) and their social contexts.

Activity 3

Bouvier and Machin (2018, 181) argue that "[s]ince the 1990s, news delivery became much more focused on niche market groups, which were of high value to advertisers. Individual journalists began to be trained in how to write in ways that addressed such niche markets, marking a shift away from audiences being addressed as citizens to being addressed as consumers".

Read some news reports on social media associated with the above hashtag you found in Activity 2. Then, identify and read some news reports that have been published in newspapers on the same topic. To what extent are they similar, or different, in terms of their style, implied target audience, and how were the discourses constructed? Are the news reports shared on social media accompanied by translations? If so, who shared the translation(s)? How many translations can you establish? Who translated it? Who circulated the translations? Is it a full translation or is it a partial translation (i.e., a trans-edited version)?

> **Activity 4**
>
> Social media may limit users to a particular frame (KhosraviNik 2017a), which can mean that social media tends to "lock us into viewpoints that we like, thereby creating nodes of discourse or discursive 'echo chambers'" (Bouvier and Machin 2018, 182). Bouvier and Machin (2018, 184–185) further argue that text is no longer a point of analysis but we may have to position texts on the basis of "what users do with them" because "ideologies are disseminated across such bundles of activity".
>
> Now, think about a hashtag associated with activism, e.g., #BlackLivesMatter. To what extent did the online movement in the form of a text transfer to an offline one? What types of social practices are related? What are the allowed views, and what kinds of discourses and practices are excluded? To what extent has such a movement transformed the dominant discourse in society? To what extent is the discourse constructed by liberal media outlets different from that constructed by conservative outlets?

The significance of digital spaces as a data source is increasingly acknowledged in translation studies as well, as evidenced by the growing interest in collaborative translation, crowdsourced translation and fansubbing (e.g., McDonough Dolmaya 2012; 2015; Jiménez-Crespo 2017; Cho and Cho 2021), and translation activities on social media (e.g., Desjardins 2019), such as YouTube (e.g., Suh and Cho 2019). Some CDA-informed analyses of translations of/and social media texts exist as well. While not strictly within the field of translation studies, Albawardi (2018) examines the use of Arabic by young Saudi women on WhatsApp, exploring how they manage social interactions and establish cultural identities. Code mixing, or trans-languaging, between English and Arabic and Arabicised English – writing English using Arabic characters – was found to be a frequent linguistic behaviour of young Saudi women in this social media form; in this way, they "create new forms of cultural identity", moment-by-moment, which adds to their Arabic/Saudi identities (Albawardi 2018, 75). Tweets and their translations have been the subject of research in translation studies, as in studies by Hernández Guerrero (2020) and Sadler (2022); although, they are not CDA-based analyses. Considering the ever-growing digitally based translation activities, further research should examine how discourse is produced, translated, promoted, and challenged in social media. Such a study could investigate what kind of tweets are translated and shared in a particular culture regarding a social issue, which may lead to the construction of a discourse regarding the issue. For example, concerning Japan's discharge of radioactive water from the Fukushima Daiichi Nuclear Power Plan into the sea, we can address research questions for a CDA analysis, e.g., what 'scientific evidence' regarding safety or danger was selected, quoted, translated, and shared on Twitter/X? How is the radioactive water named in Japanese, Korean, and Chinese (the languages of neighbouring countries), and how is the "evidence" translated and shared on social media, and by whom?

5.2 CDA and health

The disciplines of medicine and pharmacy may appear disconnected from translation studies or linguistics. However, language use and language services in hospitals have been extensively studied in translation studies. Scholars such as Angelelli (2004) and Pöchhacker (2006) have specifically examined interpreting activities and the dynamic interactions and power structure among patients, doctors, and interpreters. Similarly, scholars in medicine have increasingly recognised the pivotal role that language plays, which has brought scholars in the distant fields of medicine and linguistics together. For example, the Sustainability and Health Corpus (to be discussed later) has made one such attempt to examine texts about health and healthcare published in numerous different sectors of society, from international organisations, such as UNAIDS and WHO, to grassroots initiatives. Moreover, CDA scholars appear to have been aware of the numerous ways of addressing health issues from a CDA perspective. Nevertheless, as Eriksson and Machin (2020, 6) explain, it is not always easy:

> In Critical Discourse Analysis one challenge for the analyst is to show how social practices, such as being healthy or saving the planet, become recontextualized to serve specific interests. This means looking for what aspects of such social practices become deleted, replaced, abstracted, foregrounded or backgrounded.

However, as I draft this book, novel coronavirus 2019 (hereafter COVID-19) has affected almost every corner of the world, and this period enabled scholars to more clearly see various conflicting discourses about health emerged and how social practices become recontexualised to serve specific interests in different cultures. It is highly contagious and is transmitted rapidly indoors when it is near via airborne droplets. Confusingly, symptoms vary, ranging from fever and cough to loss of taste and smell to pneumonia. Since its first identification in Wuhan, China, in December 2019, it has rapidly spread across the globe. According to the World Health Organization (WHO), as of the 4th of May 2023, 765,222,932 people have been confirmed to be COVID-19 positive, and 6,921,612 have died since December 2019.[2]

21st-century international mobility has contributed to the accelerated spread of the virus from China across Europe and the USA, resulting in cases skyrocketing daily. Various measures have been taken to prevent its transmission, from closing borders and imposing travel restrictions to making mask wearing and social distancing mandatory. Certain countries, such as Korea and China, introduced a quick response (QR)-coded electronic entry log system to track, trace, and contain the virus and respond quickly to new cases. Multinational pharmaceutical and biotechnology companies, such as AstraZeneca, Pfizer, and Moderna, have made significant efforts to develop vaccines.

The event sparked massive debate from which a number of different and conflicting discourses emerged (and are still developing), all of which can be subject to CDA research, and much of them involved the issue of translation, e.g. anti- and pro-mandatory use of masks discourses, and discourse about the environmental impact of the disposable face masks; whether only 'authorised' face masks (KF94 and N95s) would effectively stop transmission vs. any form of face-covering would succeed; and discourses about translation and interpreting services in a medical setting especially for minority language groups in multilingual societies. Other discourses related to the degree to which a state can take the administration of life and population as its subject and exert its power on the population's freedom and liberty during the pandemic.

Particularly regarding the COVID-19 outbreak, the WHO declared a Public Health Emergency of International Concern on 30 January 2020. Nevertheless, on 11 March 2020, the WHO characterised the novel virus as a pandemic. Here, we can raise a question through the CDA lens, such as who has the power to determine when to declare a pandemic. An even greater controversy is raging regarding vaccines, from their effectiveness and reliability to the inequality of their distribution. With respect to inequalities in vaccine uptake, some discourses about global inequality can be identified. For instance, low-income countries face more severe rationing than wealthier nations do. Even within some of these nations, there are disparities among different groups, including young healthcare workers and other vulnerable groups, such as some people over 60 years old and those with disabilities, and marginalised groups with limited healthcare access in the countries to which they have migrated. These situations prompt competing discourses regarding inequality and power relations.

Competition among discourses frequently occurs when sources are translated from other languages, and it becomes obvious that they have been selectively appropriated to support an intended outcome. Since COVID-19 was declared a pandemic, each country's response and strategy have been of interest to other countries; thus, they have constantly commented on social media, often around the clock. Citizens living in countries other than these countries share their experiences and the different restrictions imposed on them, which (either full or text fragments) are then translated and presented to people of different nations. For example, anti-vaccine discourses in the UK and the USA, including stories by both citizens and health professionals, are translated into Korean and shared among parents, such as those who are concerned about the reliability of vaccines (which would be given to their children) and who then compete against pro- or anti-vaccine discourses in that country.

Against this backdrop, it is not surprising that COVID-19 accelerated scholarly discussions on health, not only in science and medicine but also in discourse studies. In critical discourse studies, discussions could centre around the issue of who has the power to circulate discourses concerning health and medicine, who are left outside the discussions of health, medicine, and health rights, and how media constructs and, often, manipulates them. Some health-related corpora have been expressly developed to analyse health discourses linguistically. Thus, I will introduce CDA studies on health discourses in this section, some of which will be exemplified and comprehensively discussed, hoping that they will offer readers novel perspectives on their study. Studies of health discourses are discussed from the perspective of translation studies, and the Sustainability and Health Corpus, comprising medical texts, is introduced as a resource for medical discourse analysis.

Even before COVID-19 spread, discourse on health was an ongoing subject of CDA research. Examples of such discourses include Zambian adolescents' lack of agency in fertility control decision-making and their restricted access to sexual and reproductive health information services (Munakampe, Michelo, and Zulu 2021) and debates about policies related to the use of nurse practitioners in the Australian healthcare system (Smith 2007). However, certain studies, which do not necessarily explicitly state that they are CDA-informed, present a result that the CDA framework can explain. For example, Hommerberg, Gustafsson, and Sandgren (2020) built a 2.6-million-word corpus of texts from Swedish blogs about approximately 27 individuals diagnosed with advanced cancer. Their analysis revealed the illness discourses of 'battle', a 'journey', 'imprisonment', and a 'burden', which make the patients and families "feel guilty" if they do not recover. This finding was confirmed in other studies. For example, Hendricks et al. (2018) discovered that 'battle' and 'journey' were the two metaphors that are most commonly used regarding cancer by patients, family carers, and healthcare professionals in conversations about their illness. However, the authors argue that the 'battle' discourse, in association with cancer, is likely to make patients feel *guilty* should they not recover, whereas the 'journey' metaphor infers that they may feel more *positively* regarding their end, thereby making peace with themselves in the interim.

Other scholars who have conducted diachronic corpus-based studies have identified ways in which changes in the power structure of society may be reflected in medical language. For instance, Budgell, Kwong, and Millar (2013) examined the changes in the language of chiropractic treatment in 1950 and between 2005 and 2008. Their analysis revealed that language changes also reflected societal changes, such as increased attention in medicine given to evidence-based treatments and patient-centred care and a shift from predominantly masculine use of pronouns to more feminine or gender-neutral references (e.g., patients, subjects) in contemporary texts (Budgell, Kwong, and Millar 2013, 52).

Activity 5

Some scholars adopt a CDA approach to investigate how a particular illness is discussed in the media and the power structure within which patients interact with medical research. Bailey, Dening, and Harvey (2021) conducted diachronic research on how dementia was discussed in the British press between 2012 and 2017. See below for excerpts and discuss what the findings suggest and how CDA can be used to interpret the findings.

> the dementia brain is likened to a failing machine: there is a circuit board ('wiring'), an engine ('misfire') and a 'failing computer'. The metaphor of 'body as a machine' is prevalent in the language of disease pathology and physiology...
> (368p)
>
> * Their findings suggest a certain dehumanisation of individuals/patients where dementia is presented in biomedical terms. Frequent keywords are related to medical practice, where patients' experiences are limited. On the basis of these findings, they argue that in the media, authority and power are granted to scientists, medicine, institutions, and pharmaceutical research rather than individuals with dementia.

Scholars in translation studies have already worked on this topic in medical and healthcare contexts (Angelelli 2004; Pöchhacker 2006). Angelelli (2003, 2003, 2004, 2006, 2008, 2011, 2012, 2014, 2018, 2019), in particular, has pursued extensive research in this area. However, like other studies conducted in this field, Angelelli's studies do not always necessarily or explicitly draw on CDA. Earlier studies, such as Pöchhacker and Shlesinger's (2007) and Álvaro Aranda and Lázaro Gutiérrez's (2022), mention discourse and employ discourse analytical frameworks to analyse mediated interactions in healthcare settings. However, their use of discourse is more general and does not strictly adhere to Fairclough's or van Dijk's CDA framework, which specifically explores the power struggle featured in language use.

Like in discourse studies, COVID-19, an unheralded and unpredictable major pandemic of the 21st century, encouraged translation studies scholars to explore further translation and interpreting activities in medical and healthcare settings. The most recent studies on translation and interpreting, discourse, and health include *The Routledge Handbook of Translation and Health*, edited by Susam-Saraeva and Spišiaková (2021). The studies included in the handbook do not specifically draw on Fairclough's, van Dijk's, or Wodak's CDA; rather, most mention medical 'discourse' and examine how medical communication functions in various discourse settings. These studies investigate the role of translation and interpreting in constructing or contesting various discourses concerning health, illness, and the body: disability discourse (i.e., the language of disability); medicalised concepts of transsexuality; discourses around health and the body; discourses on pregnancy, childbirth, and women's bodies; and discourses on the nutritional value of food and its ingredients.

The handbook presents certain interesting case studies that focus on the translation and interpreting activities in healthcare and medical settings from multiple perspectives. For example, remote (telephonic) interpreting became more common in some cultures during the COVID-19 pandemic, thus entailing several issues that require attention, from difficulties in coordinating discourse due to a lack of visual context to interpreters being subject to heavy pressure with respect to their digital literacy and unlimited working hours, resulting in emotional stress. Interpreters operating in mental healthcare, the extent to which the environment they are in allows them to follow their Codes of Conduct, and the emotional stress that leads to these are matters that have rarely been discussed.

From the patient's perspective, long days of COVID-19 lockdown were challenging. Unsurprisingly, being confined to small spaces and not being allowed to see friends and family was even more difficult for people with mental illness. These situations resulted in more demands for interpreters. Bot (2021) explains that 'faithful rendition' is not completely applicable to dialogue interpreting for psychotic patients whose utterances can "sometimes diverge from regular speech patterns or grammatical norms", which can be full of repetitions, pauses, and the use of words that do not exist. Although she does not necessarily discuss interpreters in mental healthcare during the pandemic, Bot also discusses dialogue interpreters' supportive interference in the medical healthcare setting. While discussing dialogue interpreting in mental healthcare, which focuses on such supportive interference, Bot provides an interesting example from her previous study (2005), which shows that "[d]ivergence does not necessarily lead to misunderstandings". Bot (2021, 373) adds that:

> the interpreter systematically changes religious references (if God permits/ gives; God forbid) into secular terms, making the patient secular and also changing the perspective from a patient relying on help and rules from god into a self-conscious acting person.

The translation of sexual health, especially queer and transfeminism – "a form of feminism that is informed by transgender politics" (Baldo 2021, 316) and women's health are highly relevant to discourse studies. As Baldo's work shows, translations are used to provide "visibility to an alternative imaginary, one based not on gender binarism, but on the importance of legitimising fluid embodiments of masculinity and femininity" (2021, 319). Thus, CDA-informed research on translation and health can focus on how translation provides alternative views and discourses on health, gender, and the body. Studies can also consider volunteer, nonprofessional, and activist translators, who consciously select and translate texts on abortion and reproductive health, for example, focusing on which texts are chosen and the extent to which these translations are circulated and to challenge a dominant discourse concerning abortion and reproductive health in society. Studies are needed to examine machine translations used in the healthcare sector, similar to the study conducted by Haddow, Birch, and Heafield (2021), which discusses how various models of MT fit into the translation workflow in healthcare settings by showcasing the various projects in which the authors were involved. Finally, with respect to Chen et al. (2020)'s work, the role of translation in challenging or consolidating social media discourse about vaccines can also be investigated.

5.2.1 Corpus-based CDA analysis of health and the sustainability and health corpus

As shown in the previous chapter, a corpus-based method that presents objective results has attracted the attention of scholars of both discourse and translation studies. Similarly, CDA has inspired corpus linguists and translation studies by enabling analyses that go beyond linguistic boundaries. Most corpora developed for discourse and translation analysis are custom-built and thus remain unshared due to copyright issues, whereas some are purposefully built to be sold. Nevertheless, some corpora are publicly available online for research purposes. Sketch Engine, a corpus management and text analysis software, allows corpora to be shared within the platform; consequently, researchers can use what is built explicitly for linguistic enquiries. This approach is useful and will prompt much interesting research. However, some corpora built and available within Sketch Engine provide limited information regarding the criteria by which it was built, often making it challenging for researchers to explain the patterns they may have identified. That is, information such as the publication date and publisher, source, and translator profiles is indispensable for particularly news discourse analyses where the sociopolitical orientation of the news outlet is crucial in identifying and critically examining discourses constructed and languages used in a particular news article.

Researchers in disciplines other than linguistics, such as medicine, have acknowledged the power of a corpus (discussed in Chapter 4) in identifying repeated and subtle linguistic patterns that contribute to constructing specific discourses. The corpus-based method may not be the main approach widely used in such fields. However, it has occasionally been used, for example, to study the predominant topics shared in electronic messaging and anonymously submitted to an online healthcare consultation platform (Harvey et al. 2007; Gray et al. 2008) to gain insight into how a particular illness is discussed in the media and to reveal the power structure within which patients interact with medical research. Other studies have used corpora to identify metaphors that patients, families, and healthcare professionals use to overcome adversity.

A corpus-based method also helps trainers rethink their teaching material and focus. For example, Atkins and Harvey (2010) examined 62,794 health advice-seeking emails from a UK-based adolescent health advice website. One of the findings was that adolescents tended to use the verb 'catch' in relation to AIDS, which UNESCO has continually warned against its use, and this "implies specific notions of agency on the part of subjects in the sense that it is within their power to prevent infection" (Atkins and Harvey 2010, 613). Thus, the findings can help trainers and teachers alert students against the use of this specific verb.

One of the most notable attempts to build a large electronic corpus of medical texts – not at an individual level but at the university/research centre-level – could be the Sustainability and Health Corpus (SHE), which was initiated by the Centre for Sustainable Healthcare Education at the University of Oslo, Norway. The corpus consists of various medical-related texts, including reports by international health organisations, such as the WHO and UNAIDS; policy documents published by the Centre for Disease Control and Prevention in the USA; and the European Centre for Disease Prevention and Control. It also includes online magazines and scientific journals from *The Lancet* and the *Wellcome Trust* and collectives, such as Doctors in Unite. This corpus is distinguished from other medical corpora because it includes publications from nongovernmental organisations, such as Health Poverty Action, Amnesty International, Medical Justice, and even individuals' (such as a journalist) personal blogs (copyright granted). The texts are annotated and saved in the corpus, encouraging corpus-based medical text analyses.

Such a vast range of sources, from established government-led organisations to civil society and community groupings down to individual contributors, help scholars examine conflicting discourses and the evolution of (medical) concepts and investigate how those concepts, and even specific terms, are appropriated. For example, the term 'abortion rights' is used and interpreted in US government-led institutional texts, such as those produced by the Centre for Disease Control and Prevention, as well as initiatives and movements such as Medact and Medical Justice. It will be interesting to examine how the concept of 'abortion rights' evolved through history, how it has been redefined by powerful agents and players in society, what discourses are constructed in association with the term, how the same term is differently defined and interpreted by distinct groups and communities in various cultures, and how they are reinterpreted, redefined, and appropriated in translation.

Some research questions can be addressed using the SHE corpus, especially in 2023, when the USA Supreme Court overturned Roe v. Wade, the landmark decision by which the USA Constitution used to protect a pregnant woman's liberty to either continue or end her pregnancy.[3] This abortion policy indicates that a woman's reproductive rights now fall at the behest of each separate state, several of which have opposed that right. Unsurprisingly, such a Supreme Court decision has produced several conflicting discourses. Consequently, it is intriguing to examine how reproductive and health rights are currently defined, discussed, and translated both by abortion policymakers and women's rights groups and what linguistic devices are being used to rationalise, legitimise, de-legitimise, or otherwise challenge the status quo.

Other CDA-informed questions can also be answered by using the SHE corpus. For example:

1 Who has the power to declare the end of a pandemic?
2 How has a pandemic been defined at different points in history?
3 How is a target group defined in the context of the HIV/AIDS epidemic?
4 Who decides and defines the target group in terms of infectious diseases in the context of epidemic?
5 Who may be missing out from any such 'target group' definition?'
6 What discourses are there regarding 'key populations of AIDS/HIV'?
7 Which groups may have been overlooked from the definition of 'key populations'?

Unlike other medical corpora that are available and freely accessible, the list of the corpus, together with the selection criteria, appears explicitly on SHE's website,[4] which helps researchers interpret (1) a pattern and (2) the use of a word or an expression in its context in relation to the text's title and other metadata, such as an author's name, publication date, and the particular organisation. At the time of

148 *Critical Discourse Analysis in Translation Studies*

writing, the SHE's size was over 10 million (English) words, and it is still growing. Moreover, it has a significant advantage over other corpora in that it addresses the limitations of the corpus-based method's inability to annotate images and tables. Thus, SHE enables scholars who are interested in visual patterns – or 'visual grammar' in Kress and Van Leewen's terms (Kress and van Leeuwen 2006) – to be included in the corpus because, in medicine, numbers and figures are a considerable part of reports and policy documents.

The corpus can also be used for various CDA-informed translation analyses and is being expanded to include health-related texts written in other languages; currently, it includes several Spanish texts. Therefore, once the SHE corpus includes more texts written in languages other than English or the corresponding translations of the English texts already existing in the SHE corpus, some translation-related research questions can also be addressed.

Activity 6

Visit the Sustainability and Healthcare Corpus website (www.shecorpus.net) and open the SHE corpus web interface, which allows access to the corpus. Once you load the software programme, put 'bring about' in the search box and hit 'enter'. Once you have all the instances that feature 'bring about', examine the concordance lines if you can identify a particular pattern(s) across the cases. Subsequently, obtain all the instances featuring 'cause'. Next, using 'cause' as a search word, establish a particular pattern. Can you find a distinctive pattern in the way 'cause' and 'bring about' are used in the context of medical texts? If you can, what types of discourses are constructed in each case? To what extent are the discourses distinctive?

Activity 7

Load the SHE corpus software program and identify discourses on 'rights' in texts by an institution (e.g., the WHO) and an NGO (e.g., Medact). Establish and compare discourses constructed by each institution concerning 'rights'.

Activity 8

Visit the UNAIDS webpage (https://unaids.org/en) to find annual reports. First, observe how those living with HIV have been referred to from

1996, when it was founded, to 2023, by focusing on cohesive devices and collocations. Can you find any changes throughout the period?

1 Compare the pattern against how people living with HIV are referred to in a language other than English.
2 Compare the English language annual reports with their translations, which you will find on the UNAIDS webpage.

Notes

1 The usual word limit for Twitter/X is 280. However, Twitter/X massively expanded the tweet character limit to 4,000 characters for the subscribers (www.forbes.com/sites/nicholasreimann/2023/02/08/twitter-boosts-character-limit-to-4000-for-twitter-blue-subscribers/?sh=4e734ca65ab8). Twitter Blue subscribers (on payment) can post up to 4,0000 characters (www.bbc.com/news/technology-64577731, last accessed 15 September 2024)
2 https://covid19.who.int (last accessed 4 May 2023)
3 As of June 2022, most abortions are banned in fourteen states in the USA, according to *The New York Times* (www.nytimes.com/interactive/2022/us/abortion-laws-roe-v-wade.html) (last accessed 10 May 2023)
4 www.shecorpus.net (last accessed 8 May 2023)

Suggestions for further reading and video resources

Angelelli, Claudia V. 2011. "Can You Ask Her about Chronic Illnesses, Diabetes and All That?" In *Methods and Strategies of Process Research: Integrative Approaches in Translation Studies*, edited by Cecilia Alvstad, Adelina Hild and Elisabet Tiselius, 231–246. Amsterdam: John Benjamins.
Bouvier, Gwen. 2015. "What Is a Discourse Approach to Twitter, Facebook, YouTube and Other Social Media: Connecting with Other Academic Fields?" *Journal of Multicultural Discourses* 10 (2): 149–62.
Bouvier, Gwen, ed. 2016. *Discourse and Social Media*. London: Routledge.
Bouvier, Gwen, and David Machin. 2018. "Critical Discourse Analysis and the Challenges and Opportunities of Social Media." *Review of Communication* 18 (3): 178–92. https://doi.org/10.1080/15358593.2018.1479881.

Visit the following YouTube links by Centre for Sustainable Healthcare Education at the University of Olso for more information about how SHE can be used for discourse analyses:

How to use Sustainability and Healthcare Corpus – part 1: www.youtube.com/watch?v=nunkF11w6SM
How to use Sustainability and Healthcare Corpus – part 2: www.youtube.com/watch?v=pAT4ENp7gdk
Corpus Analysis: www.youtube.com/watch?v=m1mlQJOBOo0
Outlining a case: www.youtube.com/watch?v=kIVS8r63RI8
Concepts and Clusters: www.youtube.com/watch?v=DmfYLCmj9BY

References

Albawardi, Areej. 2018. "The Translingual Digital Practices of Saudi Females on WhatsApp." *Discourse, Context & Media* 25: 68–77.

Aljarallah, Rayya. 2017. "A Critical Discourse Analysis of Twitter Posts on The Perspectives of Women Driving in Saudi Arabia." Unpublished MA dissertation. Arizona State University.

Álvaro Aranda, Cristina, and Raquel Lázaro Gutiérrez. 2022. "Functions of Small Talk in Healthcare Interpreting: An Exploratory Study in Medical Encounters Facilitated by Healthcare Interpreters." *Language and Intercultural Communication* 22 (1): 21–34.

Angelelli, Claudia. 2019. *Healthcare Interpreting Explained*. 1st edition. Oxon and New York: Routledge.

Angelelli, Claudia V. 2003. "The Visible Collaborator: Interpreter Intervention in Doctor/Patient Encounters." In *From Topic Boundaries to Omission: New Research on Interpretation*, edited by Melanie Metzger, Steven Collins, Valerie Dively and Risa Shaw, 3–25. Washington: Gallaudet University Press.

Angelelli, Claudia V. 2004. *Medical Interpreting and Cross-Cultural Communication*. Cambridge: Cambridge University Press.

Angelelli, Claudia V. 2006. "Validating Professional Standards and Codes: Challenges and Opportunities." *Interpreting* 8 (2): 175–93.

Angelelli, Claudia V. 2008. "The Role of the Interpreter in the Healthcare Setting: A Plea for a Dialogue between Research and Practice." In *Building Bridges: The Controversial Role of the Community Interpreter*, edited by Carmen Valero Garcés and Anne Martin, 139–52. Amsterdam: John Benjamins Publishing Company.

Angelelli, Claudia V. 2011. "Can You Ask Her about Chronic Illnesses, Diabetes and All That?" In *Methods and Strategies of Process Research: Integrative Approaches in Translation Studies*, edited by Cecilia Alvstad, Adelina Hild and Elisabet Tiselius, 231–246. Amsterdam: John Benjamins.

Angelelli, Claudia V. 2012. "Health-Care, Medical, and Mental Health Interpreting." In *The Encyclopedia of Applied Linguistics*, edited by Carol Chapelle. London: Wiley-Blackwell.

Angelelli, Claudia V. 2014. "Interpreting in the Healthcare Setting: Access in Cross-Linguistic Communication." In *The Routledge Handbook of Language and Health Communication*, edited by Heidi Hamilton and Silvia Chou, 573–85. London and New York: Routledge.

Angelelli, Claudia V. 2018. "Cross-Border Healthcare for All EU Residents? Linguistic Access in the European Union." *Journal of Applied Linguistics and Professional Practice* 11 (2): 113–34.

Atkins, Sarah, and Kevin Harvey. 2010. "How to Use Corpus Linguistics in the Study of Health Communication." In *The Routledge Handbook of Corpus Linguistics*, edited by Anne O'Keeffe and Michael J. McCarthy, 1st edition, 605–19. Oxon and New York: Routledge.

Bailey, Annika, Tom Dening, and Kevin Harvey. 2021. "Battles and Breakthroughs: Representations of Dementia in the British Press." *Ageing & Society* 41: 362–76.

Baldo, Michela. 2021. "Queer Feminisms and the Translation of Sexual Health." In *The Routledge Handbook of Translation and Health*, edited by Şebnem Susam-Saraeva and Eva Spišiaková, 314–30. London and New York: Routledge.

Bateman, John A. 2018. "John A. Bateman." In *The Routledge Handbook of Critical Discourse Studies*, edited by John Flowerdew and John E. Richardson, 612–25. London: Routledge.

Bot, Hanneke. 2005. *Dialogue Interpreting in Mental Health*. Leiden: Brill.

Bot, Hanneke. 2021. "Dialogue Interpreting in Mental Healthcare: Supportive Interference." In *The Routledge Handbook of Translation and Health*, edited by Şebnem Susam-Saraeva and Eva Spišiaková, 369–84. London and New York: Routledge.
Bouvier, Gwen. 2015. "What Is a Discourse Approach to Twitter, Facebook, YouTube and Other Social Media: Connecting with Other Academic Fields?" *Journal of Multicultural Discourses* 10 (2): 149–62.
Bouvier, Gwen, ed. 2016. *Discourse and Social Media*. London: Routledge.
Bouvier, Gwen. 2019. "How Journalists Source Trending Social Media Feeds." *Journalism Studies* 20 (2): 212–31.
Bouvier, Gwen. 2020. "Racist Call-Outs and Cancel Culture on Twitter: The Limitations of the Platform's Ability to Define Issues of Social Justice." *Discourse, Context & Media* 38: 100431. https://doi.org/https://doi.org/10.1016/j.dcm.2020.100431.
Bouvier, Gwen. 2022. "From 'Echo Chambers' to 'Chaos Chambers': Discursive Coherence and Contradiction in the #MeToo Twitter Feed." *Critical Discourse Studies* 19 (2): 179–95.
Bouvier, Gwen, and David Machin. 2018. "Critical Discourse Analysis and the Challenges and Opportunities of Social Media." *Review of Communication* 18 (3): 178–92. https://doi.org/10.1080/15358593.2018.1479881.
Bouvier, Gwen, and Lyndon C. S. Way. 2021. "Revealing the Politics in 'Soft', Everyday Uses of Social Media: The Challenge for Critical Discourse Studies." *Social Semiotics* 31 (3): 345–64. https://doi.org/https://doi.org/10.1080/10350330.2021.1930855.
Breeze, Ruth. 2011. "Critical Discourse Analysis and its Critics". *Pragmatics* 21 (4): 493–525.
Budgell, Brian S., Alice Kwong, and Neil Millar. 2013. "A Diachronic Study of the Language of Chiropractic." *The Journal of the Canadian Chiropractic Association* 57 (1): 49–55.
Catalano, Theresa and Linda R. Waugh. 2013. "The ideologies behind newspaper crime reports of Latinos and Wall Street/CEOs: a critical analysis of metonymy in text and image." *Critical Discourse Studies* 10 (4): 406–426.
Chen, Li, Qi Ling, Tingjia Cao, and Ke Han. 2020. "Mislabeled, Fragmented, and Conspiracy-Driven: A Content Analysis of the Social Media Discourse about the HPV Vaccine in China." *Asian Journal of Communication* 30 (6): 450–69. https://doi.org/10.1080/01292986.2020.1817113.
Cho, Sung-Eun, and Won-Seok Cho. 2021. "Pangt'ansonyŏndan p'aendŏm 'ami(ARMY)' wa p'aenbŏnyŏk [BTS Army Fandom and Fan Translation]." *Pŏnyŏkhagyŏn'gu [Journal of Translation Studies]* 22 (1): 247–78.
Cohn, Neil, Jan Engelen, and Joost Schilperoord. 2019. "The Grammar of Emoji? Constraints on Communicative Pictorial Sequencing." *Cognitive Research: Principles and Implications* 4: 33. https://doi.org/https://doi.org/10.1186/s41235-019-0177-0.
Cottle, Simon. 2011. "Media and the Arab Uprisings of 2011: Research Notes." *Journalism* 12 (5): 647–659.
Desjardins, Renée. 2019. "A Preliminary Theoretical Investigation into [Online] Socialself-Translation: The Real, the Illusory, and the Hyperreal." *Translation Studies* 12 (2): 156–176.
Eriksson, Göran, and David Machin. 2020. "Discourses of 'Good Food': The Commercialization of Healthy and Ethical Eating." *Discourse, Context & Media* 33: 100365.
Fairclough, Norman. 1992. *Discourse and Social Change*. Cambridge: Polity.
Frost, Amber A'Lee. 2020. "The Poisoned Chalice of Hashtag Activism." *Catalyst* 4 (2). https://catalyst-journal.com/2020/09/the-poisoned-chalice-of-hashtag-activism

Gonsalves, Christine A, Kerry R McGannon, and Ann Pegoraro. 2021. "A Critical Discourse Analysis of Gendered Cardiovascular Disease Meanings of the #MoreMoments Campaign on Twitter." *Journal of Health Psychology* 26 (10): 1471–81.

Gray, Nicola Jane, Kevin Harvey, Aidan Macfarlane, and Ann McPherson. 2008. "Help! Adolescent Health Language in Email Messages." *Journal of Adolescent Health* 42 (2): S5–6.

Grosz, Patrick Georg, Gabriel Greenberg, Christian De Leon, and Elsi Kaiser. 2023. "A Semantics of Face Emoji in Discourse." *Linguistics and Philosophy*. https://doi.org/ https://doi.org/10.1007/s10988-022-09369-8.

Haddow, Barry, Alexandra Birch, and Kenneth Heafield. 2021. "Machine Translation in Healthcare." In *The Routledge Handbook of Translation and Health*, edited by Şebnem Susam-Saraeva and Eva Spišiaková, 108–29. London and New York: Routledge.

Harvey, Kevin James, Brian Brown, Paul Crawford, Aidan Macfarlane, and Ann McPherson. 2007. "'Am I Normal?' Teenagers, Sexual Health and the Internet." *Social Science & Medicine* 65: 771–81.

Hatam, Nassim. 2017. "Why Iranian women are wearing white on Wednesdays." *BBC*. 14 June. www.bbc.com/news/world-middle-east-40218711

Hendricks, Rose K., Zsófia Demjén, Elena Semino, and Lera Boroditsky. 2018. "Emotional Implications of Metaphor: Consequences of Metaphor Framing for Mindset about Cancer." *Metaphor and Symbol* 33 (4): 267–79.

Hernández Guerrero, María José. 2020. "The Translation of Tweets in Spanish Digital Newspapers." *Perspectives* 28 (3): 376–92.

Hommerberg, Charlotte, Anna W. Gustafsson, and Anna Sandgren. 2020. "Battle, Journey, Imprisonment and Burden: Patterns of Metaphor Use in Blogs about Living with Advanced Cancer." *BMC Palliative Care* 19 (59): 1–10.

Jackson, Sarah J., Moya Bailey, and Brooke Foucault Welles. 2020. *#HashtagActivism: Networks of Race and Gender Justice*. Cambridge, Massachusetts, London: The MIT Press.

Jiménez-Crespo, Miguel A. 2017. *Crowdsourcing and Online Collaborative Translations*. Amsterdam and Philadelphia: John Benjamins Publishing.

Jones, Henry. 2017. "*Multilingual Knowledge Production and Dissemination in Wikipedia: A Spatial Narrative Analysis of the Collaborative Construction of City-Related Articles within the User-Generated Encyclopaedia*." PhD Thesis, University of Manchester.

Jones, Henry. 2018a. "Wikipedia as a Disruptive Translation Environment: An Analysis of the Istanbul/İstanbul Controversy." *Revista Tradumàtica. Tecnologies de La Traducció* 16: 104–13.

Jones, Henry. 2018b. "Wikipedia, Translation and the Collaborative Production of Spatial Knowledge(s): A Socio-Narrative Analysis." *Alif: Journal of Comparative Poetics* 38: 264–97.

Jones, Henry. 2019. "Wikipedia as a Translation Zone: A Heterotopic Analysis of the Online Encyclopedia and Its Collaborative Volunteer Translator Community." *Target* 31 (1): 77–97.

KhosraviNik, Majid. 2017a. "Right Wing Populism in the West: Social Media Discourse and Echo Chambers." *Insight Turkey* 19 (3): 53–68.

KhosraviNik, Majid. 2017b. "Social Media Critical Discourse Studies (SM-CDS)." In *The Routledge Handbook of Critical Discourse Studies*, edited by John Flowerdew and John E. Richardson, 582–596. London & New York: Routledge.

Koller, Veronika, and Gerlinde Mautner. 2004. "Computer Applications in Critical Discourse Analysis." In *Applying English Grammar: Corpus and Functional Approaches*, edited by C. Coffin, A. Hewings, and K. O'Halloran, 216–28. London: Arnold.

Kress, Gunther. 2012. "Multimodal Discourse Analysis." In *The Routledge Handbook of Discourse Analysis*, edited by James Paul Gee and Michael Handford, 35–50. London & New York: Routledge.
Kress, Gunther, and Theo van Leeuwen. 1996. *Reading Images: The Grammar of Visual Design*. 1st edition. London: Routledge.
Kress, Gunther, and Theo van Leeuwen. 2001. *Multimodal Discourse: The Modes and Media of Contemporary Communication*. London: Edward Arnold.
Kress, Gunther, and Theo van Leeuwen. 2006. *Reading Images-The Grammar of Visual Design*. 2nd edition. London: Routledge.
Ledin, Per, and David Machin. 2017. "Multi-modal Critical Discourse Analysis". In *Routledge Handbook of Critical Discourse Studies*, edited by John Flowerdew and John E. Richardson, 60–76. Oxon and New York: Routledge.
Lim, Merlyna. 2012. "Clicks, Cabs, and Coffee Houses: Social Media and Oppositional Movements in Egypt, 2004–2011." *Journal of Communication* 62: 231–248.
Long, Sophie. 2023. "How #OscarsSoWhite changed the Academy Awards." *BBC*. 9 March. www.bbc.com/news/world-us-canada-64883399
Mautner, Gerlinde. 2005. "Time to Get Wired: Using Web-Based Corpora in Critical Discourse Analysis." *Discourse & Society* 16 (6): 809–28.
McDonough Dolmaya, Julie. 2012. "Analyzing the Crowdsourcing Model and Its Impact on Public Perceptions of Translation." *The Translator* 18 (2): 167–91. https://doi.org/10.1080/13556509.2012.10799507.
McDonough Dolmaya, Julie. 2015. "Revision History: Translation Trends in Wikipedia." *Translation Studies* 8 (1): 16–34.
McEnery, Tony., Mark McGlashan, and Robbie Love. 2015. "Press and Social Media Reaction to Ideologically Inspired Murder: The Case of Lee Rigby." *Discourse & Communication* 9 (2): 237–59. https://doi.org/10.1177/1750481314568545.
Munakampe, Margarate N., Charles Michelo, and Joseph M. Zulu. 2021. "A Critical Discourse Analysis of Adolescent Fertility in Zambia: A Postcolonial Perspective." *Reproductive Health* 18 (75): 1–12.
O'Halloran, Kay L., ed. 2004. *Multimodal Discourse Analysis: Systemic Functional Perspectives*. London: Continuum.
O'Halloran, Kay L. 2011. "Multimodal Discourse Analysis." In *Continuum Companion to Discourse Analysis*, edited by Ken Hyland and Brian Paltridge, 120–37. London and New York: Bloomsbury Academic.
Pöchhacker, Franz. 2006. "Research and Methodology in Healthcare Interpreting." *Linguistica Antverpiensia* 5: 135–59.
Pöchhacker, Franz, and Miriam Shlesinger, eds. 2007. *Healthcare Interpreting: Discourse and Interaction*. Amsterdam/Philadelphia: John Benjamins.
Sadler, Neil. 2022. *Fragmented Narrative: Telling and Interpreting Stories in the Twitter Age*. Oxon: Routledge.
Semino, Elena, Zsófia Demjén, Jane Demmen, Veronika Koller, Sheila Payne, Andrew Hardie, and Paul Rayson. 2015. "The Online Use of Violence and Journey Metaphors of Patients with Cancer, as Compared with Health Professionals: A Mixed Methods Study." *BMJ Supportive & Palliative Care* 7 (1): 60–66.
Smith, Jennifer L. 2007. "Critical Discourse Analysis for Nursing Research." *Nursing Inquiry* 14 (1): 60–70.
Suh, Jungye, and Sungeun Cho. 2019. "Yut'yubŭ k-pyut'i k'ont'ench'ŭ chamak pŏnyŏk yŏn'gu [Translation of YouTube K-Beauty Contents]." *Pŏnyŏkhagyŏn'gu [Journal of Translation Studies]* 20 (1): 127–55.

Susam-Saraeva, Şebnem, and Eva Spišiaková, eds. 2021. *The Routledge Handbook of Translation and Health*. Oxon and New York: Routledge.

Thompson, Riki. 2012. "Looking Healthy: Visualizing Mental Health and Illness Online." *Visual Communication* 11 (4): 395–420.

Tufekci, Zeynep. 2017. *Twitter and Tear Gas: The Power and Fragility of Networked Protest*. New Haven and London: Yale University Press.

Winston, Elizabeth A., and Cynthia Roy. 2015. "Discourse Analysis and Sign Languages." In *Sociolinguistics and Deaf Communities*, edited by Adam C. Schembri and Cecil Lucas, 95–119. Cambridge: Cambridge University Press.

Xiao, Han, and Lei Li. 2021. "A Bibliometric Analysis of Critical Discourse Analysis and Its Implications." *Discourse & Society* 32 (4): 482–502.

Zappavigna, Michele, and Lorenzo Logi. 2021. "Emoji in Social Media Discourse about Working from Home." *Discourse, Context & Media* 44: 100543.

Index

actor 10, 17, 24, 37, 39, 41, 43, 71–72, 76, 100, 114
agency 37, 48, 53, 57, 59, 63, 73, 74, 75, 120, 122, 125, 143, 146
appraisal 1–4, 23–24, 27–30, 43, 48–49, 54–55, 58, 61–62, 63, 73–74, 76, 116, 121
appraisal system 30, 54–55, 58, 63
appraisal theory 1–4, 23–24, 27–28, 43, 48–49, 54, 61–62, 73–74, 76, 116; attitude 28–29, 48, 54; engagement 28–29, 54; graduation 28–30, 54–55
Arabic 53, 67–68, 140
assessment 29, 50–51, 117
authentic 1, 3, 7, 11, 13–15, 86, 122–123
authorship 59, 117, 133

belief 4, 31, 33, 39–40, 58–59, 73, 137
bibliometric 11, 35, 63, 135

CDA 1–5, 7, 9, 11–12, 15–19, 23–24, 30–38, 43, 48–51, 53, 55–65, 67, 68, 70–77, 85–88, 90, 93–95, 97, 103, 111, 113, 115–118, 121–122, 124, 131–148
CDA-informed 16–19, 24, 48, 56–57, 62–63, 75, 77, 87–88, 97, 121–122, 131, 135, 140, 143, 145, 147–148
CDA-inspired 2, 11
Chinese 2, 12, 17, 20, 29, 53–55, 57–59, 62–63, 67, 71, 73–76, 93, 99–100, 102, 105–106, 112, 116–117, 121, 122, 136–137, 140
collocate 85, 90, 93–108, 112–116, 120, 122–124
collocate list 93–103, 105–106, 108, 112, 124
collocation 87, 94–95, 97, 104, 107, 112
collocational patterns 95, 111

conflict 7–8, 13, 59, 61–63, 73–74, 95, 99, 133, 141–142, 147
context 2–5, 7–14, 16, 18–19, 23–27, 32, 34, 37, 38, 40, 48–51, 53–57, 61–64, 73–76, 85, 87, 95, 103, 106, 108, 111, 114–115, 117–118, 120–122, 135–136, 139, 144, 147–148
context of culture 25–26, 50
context of situation 24–26
contextual/contextualized 9, 10, 14, 18, 26, 34, 49, 55, 63, 72, 76, 115, 120, 141
control 9–10, 13, 17, 23, 34–35, 38–41, 58, 62, 77, 114–116, 121, 143, 146–147
corpus 1, 4, 35–36, 51–53, 63, 75–77, 85–91, 93–95, 97–104, 106, 108, 109, 111, 113–123, 132–133, 135, 141, 143, 145–149; corpora 86–87, 90, 95, 98, 111, 113, 116, 117, 122, 142, 146–147
corpus-based 1, 4, 35–36, 51, 53, 63, 75, 77, 85–91, 93–95, 97, 103, 111, 115–118, 121–122, 132, 135, 143, 145–148
corpus-based CDA 1, 4, 51, 87–88, 90, 93, 95, 97, 103, 115–118, 121–122, 132, 135, 145
corpus linguistics 53, 86, 123
communicative 4, 8, 11–12, 20, 23, 27, 31, 33, 37, 51, 58, 77, 131, 133–134
community 9–11, 17, 27, 37, 40, 59, 94–95, 122, 133, 138, 147
concordance 85, 89–90, 99, 103, 108–112, 114–115, 118–119, 123, 148
construct 2, 4, 7, 8, 10, 11, 13, 16–18, 20, 23, 25, 27, 31, 33, 35, 37, 39–40, 42, 48, 49, 53, 58–59, 64, 72, 74–76, 85, 95, 97, 100–100, 106, 111, 113, 115–116, 118, 122, 124, 131–140, 142, 144, 146–148; deconstruct 64, 100, 115; reconstruct 48, 74, 100

156   Index

critical discourse analysis 7, 24, 30, 48, 50, 85, 141
critical linguistics 30
cross-cultural 4, 131, 133–134

diachronic 35, 60, 111, 143
dialectical-relational 3, 24, 37; three-dimensional 10, 23, 30–32, 34, 55–56, 61–62, 73, 137
dialogue interpreting 145
digital media 132
discourse 1–24, 26–27, 29–43, 48–51, 53–59, 61–64, 69, 70–77, 85–86, 90–91, 93–94, 97, 100–101, 103, 111–117, 121–123, 131–148
discourse-historical 24
discourse practice 32
discourse studies 2–4, 7, 15–19, 36–38, 40, 56, 64, 74, 131, 133–135, 142, 144–145
discourse theory 3, 7, 15–19
discursive pattern 88, 91, 108, 111, 121, 122
discursive practice 17, 24, 30–32, 36, 56
dominance 7, 23, 35, 38

Egypt 67–71, 132, 137
empowerment 131, 135
evaluative 23, 27, 54–55, 59, 75

Fairclough, Norman 3–4, 7–8, 10, 12–13, 20, 23–24, 30–37, 48–49, 55–56, 61–62, 73–74, 77, 86, 95, 103, 137, 139, 144
fragment 35, 87, 103, 135–136, 138, 142
frequency list 90–91, 93–94, 102, 104, 107, 124

gender 10, 13, 33, 35, 131, 133, 137, 143, 145
gatekeeping 17, 73, 76, 121

Halliday, M. A. K 1, 3, 14, 23–26, 31, 33, 43, 48–49, 51, 53–54, 132
Hallidayan 1, 3, 23–24, 33, 48–49, 53–54
hashtag 133–140
health 2, 43, 73, 77, 131, 133, 138, 141–149
healthcare 77, 131, 133, 141–146, 148–149
headlines 42, 54–55, 116

ideational 26, 50, 54
identity 4, 8, 35–36, 39, 58, 138, 140
ideological square model 1, 3–4, 10, 23, 29, 40, 42, 58–60, 63, 73, 89, 121, 139; Us-Them binary 40–41

ideology 8, 10–11, 33, 36, 38–40, 48, 53, 55, 58–60, 63, 93, 121, 135; ideologies 3, 31, 37–41
immigrant 38–39, 115–116, 132
immigration 10, 38, 62, 116, 132
inequality 7, 17, 23, 35, 38, 40, 63, 66, 133, 142
in-group 40
institution 1, 8–9, 12, 17–18, 23, 32, 35, 38, 40, 54, 57, 62–63, 65, 70–73, 89, 97, 100–102, 109, 114, 131, 135, 137, 139, 144, 148
institutional 2, 29, 32, 35, 38, 49, 57, 59, 62, 64, 71–72, 76, 111, 121, 131, 133, 138, 147
institutional discourse 2, 10, 62, 64, 71–72
institutionalized 38, 59, 131
interactional 23, 31, 75
interpreting studies 48, 62, 74–76
interpersonal 26–28, 30, 50–51, 53–54, 117, 121
interpreter 2, 4, 17, 20, 48, 70, 74–77, 121–122, 133, 141, 144–145
interpreter-mediated 69, 75
intertextuality 11, 20, 51, 139
intervention 33–34, 48, 54, 58, 65, 74–75, 120
invisibility 48, 50

Japanese 2, 57, 99, 100, 102, 105, 119, 140
journalism 63, 131, 135
journalistic 89, 120, 122, 134

Korean 2, 17, 41, 43, 53, 57, 66, 89, 97–103, 105–108, 109, 112, 114–115, 118–121, 123–125, 140, 142

label 65, 75, 112; labeling 76, 111, 137
legitimise/ligitimising/legitimization 20, 38, 40, 76, 135, 145, 147

mainstream 17, 41–42, 75, 89, 135, 138
manipulation 31, 60, 63, 122
marginalized 12, 136, 142
meaning-making 20, 24, 49–51, 135
media 2–4, 9–10, 14, 17–20, 23, 26, 34–40, 42, 48–49, 54, 57–59, 61–64, 71–76, 89–90, 97, 99–101, 103, 106, 108, 113–117, 120–123, 133–146
media outlet 76, 89, 113, 116–117, 120
mediating agents 48, 57, 64
mediation 23, 37, 48, 54–55, 71, 73–75
mediator 58–59, 63, 122
medical 71, 77, 131, 138, 142–148

mental health 133, 145
mental model 12, 75
metafunction 26–27, 50–51, 54, 121
metaphor 31, 40, 54–55, 64, 116, 138, 143–144, 146; metaphorical 132
minorities 38–40, 133, 142
modality 19, 26, 53–54, 122, 132, 139
multimodal 132–133, 135
multimodality 19, 132
multilingual 57, 65, 68, 75, 142

naming 26, 137
news media 17–18, 39–40, 54, 62, 73, 89, 97, 108, 113
newspaper 11, 40–42, 73, 90, 95, 106, 115–116, 139
non-critical 30
non-textual 135–136
non-verbal 7, 9, 11–12, 132
norms 29, 31, 33, 35, 37, 42, 59, 72, 117, 120, 137–138, 145

oppression 9, 62
out-group 40

pattern 8, 10, 14, 16, 18, 38, 40, 42, 53, 63, 85–91, 93, 95, 97, 99, 101, 105, 108, 109, 111–119, 121–123, 132, 136, 139, 145–149; patterning 112–113
political discourse 2, 10, 27, 48, 54–55, 57–59, 62–64, 70, 74, 117, 122
political speech 62, 64
poststructuralist/poststructuralism 3, 16, 24
power 1, 3, 7–10, 16–18, 23–24, 30–31, 33–35, 38–39, 41, 58, 62–65, 67, 71–72, 76–77, 85, 114–115, 119, 121, 124, 131, 133–138, 140–144, 146–147
power abuse 7, 38
pragmatic 8–9, 14, 16, 25, 48, 50–51, 75
prejudice 36, 38, 122
press conference 17, 60, 72, 74–76, 93, 121–123

qualitative 53, 85–88, 113, 116, 123
quality assessment 51, 117
quantitative 35–36, 53, 75, 77, 86–88, 94, 113, 121, 123

racism 10, 23, 35–36, 38–40, 42, 62, 116, 123
rationale 14, 54, 122, 132
recontextualization 55, 63, 120, 122
refugee 38, 42, 108, 115
reposition 19
reproduction 12, 33, 38

resistance 2, 9, 23, 35, 38–39, 55, 58, 137
Russian 72–73

semantic preference 111–114
semantic prosody 87, 111–115, 122, 124
shift 18–20, 33, 39, 42, 48–49, 53–56, 58–61, 63, 65, 73–76, 85, 97, 100, 115–118, 120–123, 132–133, 139, 143; obligatory shifts 117; optional shifts 117
simultaneous interpreting 75–76
Sketch Engine 90, 95, 96, 108–109, 122, 146
social actors 10, 24, 37, 39, 43
social change 31, 137
social cognition 23, 36–38
social interaction 8, 10, 36, 140
socially constitutive 10, 12, 23, 32; socially conditioned 12, 23, 32; socially constituted 10
social media 4, 63, 131–142, 145
socio-cognitive model 3, 23–24, 37
socio-cultural 24, 31, 32, 33, 37, 40, 56–58, 64, 72
sociology-oriented 1, 3
socio-political 3, 11, 19, 34, 36–37, 40, 42, 56, 61, 64, 85, 115, 121, 122
Spanish 55, 67, 116, 148
subjectivity 3, 16–18, 30, 43
subtitling 60
sustainability 33, 133, 141, 143, 145–146, 148–149
Sustainability and Health Corpus (SHE corpus) 133, 141, 143, 145, 146, 147–148
system 8, 26–31, 35, 38–40, 43, 49–51, 53–55, 58–59, 63, 116–117, 124, 130, 135, 138, 141, 143
systemic functional linguistic (SFL) 3, 23–24, 26–27, 31, 43, 48–51, 53–54, 61–62, 76, 132; field 26, 43; mode 26, 50–52; systemic functional analysis 75, 51–52, 54; systemic functional model 51; tenor 26, 51–52, 54

translation shift 39, 48, 54, 59, 60, 61, 63, 73–74, 85, 117, 121–122
Thai 65–67, 117–118

van Dijk, Teun A. 1, 3–4, 7, 10, 12–13, 23–24, 29–30, 34–40, 42–43, 48, 55, 58–61, 63, 73, 75–76, 86, 89, 121, 132, 139, 144
voice 18, 27, 29, 35, 42, 53, 59, 72, 76, 101, 115, 135, 139

WordSmith 90–92, 96–97, 103, 105, 107, 124

For Product Safety Concerns and Information please contact our EU representative GPSR@taylorandfrancis.com Taylor & Francis Verlag GmbH, Kaufingerstraße 24, 80331 München, Germany

Printed and bound by CPI Group (UK) Ltd, Croydon, CR0 4YY
15/07/2025
01916965-0011